P9-CKK-805

CARING FOR BIRDS & NATURE

100 Years of Seattle Audubon

Constance Sidles, Editor

Constance Sidles

*This special signed edition
is limited to 1200 numbered copies.*

This is copy 0293

SEATTLE AUDUBON
FOR BIRDS AND NATURE
CELEBRATING 100 YEARS

Caring for Birds & Nature: 100 Years of Seattle Audubon
edited by Constance Sidles, Constancy Press, LLC

First Edition

Note: All photographs and illustrations are used with permission of the
photographers and artists who created them and who retain their copy-
rights. The quoted material in the story titled "Multiples of One; Hazel
Wolf: Organizing Audubon" was excerpted from: **Starbuck, Susan. Hazel
Wolf: Fighting the Establishment © 2002.** Reprinted with permission of
the University of Washington Press.

This book is published and distributed by Seattle Audubon Society

Design, compilation, writing (where not otherwise noted),
copyediting, and production by Constancy Press, LLC

Printed in South Korea through Four Colour Print Group
September 2016

To obtain more copies of this book, write or call:
Seattle Audubon Society   (206)523-4483
8050 35th Avenue NE
Seattle WA 98115
www.seattleaudubon.org

ISBN 978-0-914516-17-0

DEDICATION

To the thousands of supporters, volunteers, and
staff who, for the past century, have devoted their time,
energy, substance, passion, and creativity to Seattle Audubon:
Many unnamed, none forgotten. You shall live in our hearts
for as long as the Society you built remains.
Here's to the next 100 years.

CONTENTS

INTRODUCTION

As a people, we Americans have always been more in love with the future than with the day-to-day life of the present. Perhaps it's because the future is filled with endless dreams of what might be, while the present is too stuck in what is. At heart, we are a nation of dreamers and innovators. We invent things both small and large. Most of all, we invent ourselves, and thus we shape our own future.

As for the past, it is gone, dead, unimportant. We may *say* the past should be remembered because otherwise we are doomed to repeat it. But we don't really believe that. The past never repeats itself, because *we* are never repeated. Each of us is an individual, unique in the world, unique in time. How can stories of a time long gone, of people long dead, tell us anything we need to know about today or tomorrow?

Worst of all, the past is set in stone. We can't change it or shape it, not like we can the future. So why bother with it at all? In particular, why bother to write a book about the history of Seattle Audubon? Yes, it's great that Audubon has lasted this long. Let's raise a glass, give a cheer, but then let's move on and tackle the things we *can* change.

Ah, but the past is one of the most important of those things we can change. For the past is mutable, malleable, marvelously amorphous. Not the facts of history, perhaps. Those really are set in stone, more or less.

But facts are not the heart of history. The past that really matters is made of stories that answer two questions:

Who are we, and why are we here?

Coming up with answers to those questions is what gives our lives meaning. And those answers change as we grow in understanding, as we learn more about how the world works, as we gain the confidence to tolerate others, as we become strong enough to love that which is different from us.

By reshaping the past, we reshape ourselves.

On the surface, this is a book about what Seattle Audubon members did in days gone by. But that is not the true story. The story that matters is the one we tell ourselves anew with every passing year, interpreting history in new ways that serve to inspire us to achieve our goals.

This book is filled with stories of people like ourselves, who faced challenges at least as daunting as ours. Sometimes they succeeded, sometimes they fell short, as we all do. But whatever the outcome, their lives illuminate ours.

The voices in this book ask that we take what they give us from the past and make of it something powerful and meaningful for the future. We are their heirs, and like them, we have an obligation to preserve the birds we love and all the natural wonders of the world for those who follow.

Listen to their stories. They have changed the world. And so can we.—C.S.

ACKNOWLEDGEMENTS

One of the best things about creating this book is the realization that the "Society" in our name really means something. From the time years ago when Jerry Joyce and the History Committee conceived this book and passionately promoted it until others (including me) caught fire, to the present when my lovely and sharp-eyed team of proofreaders lift me up with words of encouragement, I have experienced what participating in this community is all about. Dennis Paulson in his story on page 84 may have put it best: "We love each other and help each other."

Yes, we do. And so I have many people to thank for making this book possible, starting with Seattle Audubon's Board of Directors, who took the plunge to finance the effort, knowing we may never recover the cost. They echoed a similar commitment made nearly 50 years ago by another Board faced with a similar challenge. The debate was heated, but in the end, the past Board said (as the present one has), the expense of our project was essential "in order to help make the public more conservation-minded." Money matters. Of course it does. But the mission matters more.

One stellar group who believes this tenet is Seattle Audubon's staff, who unfailingly helped me to find the interviewees, tracked down needed facts, read the stories for accuracy, and answered all my questions. In particular, I am grateful to Russ Steele, Mary Bond, Claire Catania, Matt Mega, Christine Scheele, Toby Ross, John Brosnan, and Dan Bridge for their support. David Garcia, Cecania Alexander, and Cassandra Sandkam were always available to help in any way, and Leigh Hiura was magnificent in securing historic photographs.

Another star-studded group of people dedicated to Seattle Audubon's ideals are the volunteers, who gave their time and expertise to make this book accurate, timely, and inspirational. In particular, I want to thank Steve Geissler for his legal eye, his kindness, and steady support; Chris Peterson and Ellen Blackstone, who gave open-handedly of their deep and caring knowledge and wisdom; Richard Youel, who read every word I wrote and checked it all against his vast knowledge and love of Audubon; and Marina Skumanich, who is a walking encyclopedia of Audubon's past and who understands it all from the heart. I mentioned the original History Committee and proofreaders above, but I want to thank each one by name: Jerry Joyce and Marianne Moon (who, on top of everything else, created the basic design of this book), Eleanor Boba, Emory Bundy, John Lundin, Noel Angell, Sherry Rind, and Susan Barnes of the History Committee; and Alex MacKenzie, Nancy Kirkner, Nancy Jones, and Jen McKeirnan, my proofreaders beyond compare.

Perhaps the most important group I must thank are the interviewees themselves, the photographers and artists who helped illustrate their stories, and the writers who added so much history to our sidebars. I don't know if you can imagine this, but consider what it takes to put yourself into the public eye, revealing your life's work, your personality, your deepest feelings, perhaps even your foibles. We like to think we live in a tolerant world, and in many ways we do, but it is also a divided world, one in which people seem to think they can and should be harsh critics. It takes enormous courage to say to that world, "Here I am. This is what I believe. Here is my work for all to see. Take your best shot."

The people in this book went ahead anyway. They deserve our admiration and thanks, and so I name them individually: Tom Aversa, Paul Bannick, Neil Berg, Tim Boyer, Jan Bragg, Mita Brahma, Tom Campion, Stephanie Colony, Carolee Colter, Marvin Cooper, Herb Curl, Larry Engles, Fred Felleman, Girl Scouts of Greater Atlanta Archives (and Alicia Jordan), Nick Hatch, Hugo Henrikson, Dave Herr, Rebecca Hoff, Larry Hubbell, Gene Hunn, Chris Karrenberg, Mira Lamb, Jennifer Leach, Nukri Lekveishvili, Ed Lowe (and Lummi Island Heritage Trust), John Lundin, Alex MacKenzie, Diann MacRae, Ann Mehnke, Terry Mihashi, Loren Mooney, MOHAI, David Moss, Phyllis Moss, Linda Murray, Linda Murtfeldt, National Audubon Society, Ed Newbold, Doug Parrott, Kathy Paul, Dennis Paulson, Chris Peterson, Doug Plummer, Steve Ringman (and the *Seattle Times*), Toby Ross, Rick Rutz, Rob Sandelin, Tom Sanders, Kristi Sartnurak, Janet Sawyer, Doug Schurman, Adam Sedgley, Alex Sidles, Nathan Sidles, Marina Skumanich, Michael Stadler, Russ Steele, Jack Stephens, Laura Stone, Leland Sutton, Joe Sweeney, Diana Thayer, Daniella Théorêt, Paul Thomas (and the *Seattle Times*), Gregg Thompson, Emily Tompkins, University of Washington Libraries Special Collections (and their marvelous librarians), U.S. Fish and Wildlife Service (Pacific Southwest Region), Gerrit Vyn, Larry Ward, Izzy Wong, Frances Wood, Richard Youel, and Carleen and Neil Zimmerman.

I also want to thank the researchers who put in untold hours making sure this book is as accurate as possible. They helped me figure out legal and environmental issues that at times made me feel like my head was about to explode. They provided historical heft to this book and corrected the errors and misunderstandings that so easily creep in when one is on a learning curve as steep as the one I have tried to climb. Chief among these tireless and patient researchers are Todd True of Earthjustice and Alex Sidles, who lent me their legal and historical expertise—I do not know what I would have done without them. Also key were: Alex MacKenzie (for timelines, parks, and Audubon chapters); Hal Opperman and Herb Curl (for science); Bob Sieh, Charlie Kahle, Dick Butler, and John Lundin (for sanctuaries); Helen Engle (for Hazel Wolf and Nisqually); Lane Shtelen, Anderson Sandes, Virginia Bound, and Mary Childs (for feather art); Barbara Williams (for Zella Schultz); Carsten Lien's family (for Olympic National Park); Linda Sprague and Rachel Sidles (for Spanish translation); Noel Angell and Raelene Gold (for oral histories from the past); Sue Yates, Virginia Bound, Jen McKeirnan, Michael Hobbs, Roberta Robertson, Martin Miller, and Teri Martine (for Master Birders); and David Hutchinson (for publications).

If errors still exist, it is only because I failed to ask these wonderful people to check on something. The errors are mine alone, and I ask you, dear readers, to let me know what they are so I can correct them in future.

Finally, I want to thank my dear husband John for his unwavering support and patience over the past year. John has been the tech genius behind this project, happy to create 176 different styles in our layout software to suit every need. I counted. That's almost as many styles as there are pages in the book. It's crazy, but look at the result: a book as beautiful as it is informative. Engaging, funny, serious—and inspirational, I hope.

To all these people, and to the community we serve, thank you—*Constance Sidles, Editor*

Opposite page: Northern Spotted Owl. (Photograph © Doug Schurman)

CONSERVATION:
TAKING ACTION

FEATHER DIPLOMACY
José R. Alcaraz: Banning the Feather Trade from Mexico

When Europeans began to colonize America, the continent and its resources seemed infinite. Old growth deciduous forest covered the land so densely it was said a squirrel could travel from the Atlantic coast to the Mississippi River without touching the ground. In the Great Plains, bison herds numbered an estimated 60 million beasts. Overhead, Passenger Pigeons passed by in migratory flocks numbering in the billions. Cotton Mather noted in a letter written in 1712, "The flights have been so great that for four or five miles together, they have ... darkened the Horizon."[1]

By 1900, the deciduous forests were essentially gone, the bison herds had disappeared except for 300 animals, and the Passenger Pigeon was extinct in the wild. Food birds such as Eskimo Curlew were so decimated by commercial hunters they never recovered. Egrets and herons that had filled the young nation's marshes were fast disappearing, killed in the millions by hunters who took only their breeding plumes, leaving the carcasses to rot and the parents' babies to starve. People began to realize America's abundance was limited. If anything was to be saved, someone needed to do something.

In January 1896, Harriet Hemenway and her cousin Minna Hall decided they must act. They leafed through their copy of Boston's Social Register, which listed all the members of upper class society, and invited as many friends as possible to tea to discuss the formation of an organization that would stop the wanton killing of birds for their feathers. Out of this meeting was born the Massachusetts Audubon Society, the first in the nation.[2]

The idea spread rapidly to other states, which soon formed Audubon Societies of their own. By 1916, when Seattle Audubon was founded, laws had been passed giving wild birds at least partial protection. In particular, the Migratory Bird Treaty between Canada and the U.S. had been signed in 1916 and codified into law in 1918, creating federal protection for wild birds within the borders of our two countries. (See pp. 6–7 below.)

Seattle Auduboners believed the battle to ban the feather trade had been won, so the organization focused on other issues: getting the Seattle Parks Department to authorize Seward Park as a bird sanctuary; passing ordinances that would encourage pet owners to keep cats indoors so they wouldn't kill birds; and stopping poachers from taking old growth logs from city parks.

But in 1924, members got an unpleasant jolt when they learned that collages made from wild bird feathers and other bird parts were coming into the Port of Seattle from Mexico. Here is the correspondence from those days:[3]

Far left: November 1917 front cover of The Delineator, *a popular fashion magazine of the day, showing a model wearing a hat graced with flowing black aigrettes, plumes plucked from herons slain by commercial hunters and sold to milliners both here and abroad for mere pennies.*

The Correspondents

José R. Alcaraz, Director of Forestry and Hunting, Republic of Mexico
E. W. Camp, Director of Customs, U.S. Treasury
Frederick W. Cook, Corresponding Secretary, Seattle Audubon Society
T. Gilbert Pearson, President, National Audubon Society

Frederick W. Cook to T. Gilbert Pearson

Dear Mr. Pearson: *Seattle, March 24, 1924*

It has been brought to the attention of this Society, that importations of considerable value and extent are received from our Southern neighbor—MEXICO—of "Artificial Birds", made up of natural feathers, heads, legs, wings etc.,—all bird-structure—and offered for sale here and elsewhere in this Country.

While on the face of it, this is not as bad as the products of depredation by our Milliner's trade in the early '80s, considerable years of the '90s, and a little in the 1900s, still such traffic must be productive of much waste in wild-bird-life.

From a recent "squib" in a N.Y. Daily, we have it that Mexico is now sporting a full set of Game-Laws, though whether there is a section like our Migratory Bird Act, I have not learned. It has been considered by the Society, if an outline of this alleged situation was brought to your attention, your prompt and effective action, looking to an abatement of this International nuisance, would follow.

With assurances of our regard, very sincerely,
Fredk. W. Cook, Corresponding Secretary

T. Gilbert Pearson to Frederick W. Cook

Dear Mr. Cook: *New York, March 31, 1924*

Thank you for your favor of March 24. It appears to me that the law prohibiting the importation of feathers into the United States is being violated by this feather worked picture business coming in from Mexico, several references to which have come to my attention of late.

This work dates back to the days of the Aztecs and the Spanish Conquerors referring to them in their chronicles of that date. I have seen wonderful examples of this feather work in Mexico City. Evidently the traffic is now being pushed in many foreign countries. I recently received samples from London.

I have been thinking of writing to the Custom Authorities about the matter but rush of duties has prevented me from doing so to this date. Your letter, however, has stirred me up and I am writing today.

I am sailing Wednesday for Central America where at last an opening seems to have come to do something for bird protection. If we hear anything of importance from the Customs people my secretary will advise you.

I hope all is going well with you and your work.

Yours sincerely, T. Gilbert Pearson, President

E. W. Camp to T. Gilbert Pearson

Gentlemen:

Treasury Department
Washington, D.C., April 23, 1924

Receipt is acknowledged of your letter of March 31 inviting the Department's attention to the sale in the State of Washington of pictures made from feathers imported from Mexico.

The collector of customs at Seattle was called upon for a report and he has informed the Department that there is no record of such importations through his port.

If you are in a position to advise the Department the port through which the said pictures were introduced into the United States further investigation will be made of the matter.

Respectfully, E. W. Camp, Director of Customs

T. Gilbert Pearson to Frederick W. Cook

Dear Mr. Cook: *New York, May 12, 1924*

I inclose with this copy of a letter received from the Treasury Department regarding the importation of the Mexican feather work. Can you do anything further in the matter locally? I stand ready to help push this matter to the limit.

Yours cordially, T. Gilbert Pearson, President.

Frederick W. Cook to José R. Alcaraz

Dear Friend: *Seattle, March 25, 1924*

It has been brought to the attention of this Society, that importations of "Artificial Birds"—so called, are quite extensive here in the United States, also in evidence in the City of Seattle, the point of origin being your country—MEXICO.

These "Birds" are made of natural feathers, heads, wings, legs, feet etc., of wild-birds, and while your laws no doubt allow of this, such trade is very destructive of wild-bird-life.

If your Country had a law similar to the "Migratory Bird Act," which now applies to the Dominion of Canada, as well as the United States, the greater portion of the continent of North America would be under systematic protection for wild-birds.

Will you not kindly consider this the next time your game laws are up for revision or extension?

With assurances of our kind regard,

Sincerely, your Friends,
Seattle Audubon Society,
Frederick W. Cook, Corresponding Secretary

José Alcaraz to Seattle Audubon

Dirección Forestal y Caza

Al Señor Frederick W. Cook *México, 12 mayo 1924*

En respuesta a la atenta nota de usted de fecha 25 de marzo último relativa a las leyes para proteger a las aves migratorias manifiesto a usted que esta Dirección agradece mucho su advertencia y el interés que se toma en la conservación de las especies de nuestro país.

Precisamente dentro de muy pocos días se van a expedir unos Decretos Presidenciales prohibiendo la venta de plumas de todas clases y demás despojos de las aves, reglamentando la exportación de las aves canoras y de ornato y protegiendo las insectívoras. Además, esta Dirección tiene en estudio no solamente la celebración de un tratado semejante al "Migratory Bird Act" celebrado con el Dominio del Canada, sino que las leyes de Caza sean de aplicación internacional mediante convenios especiales, a efecto de que los cazadores furtivos que contravengan las leyes de México, por ejemplo, y se pasaran después a Estados Unidos con las presas adquiridas, bien sea como trofeos o bien para comerciar con ellas o sus productos y despojos, sean castigados allá como si la violación la hubieran cometido en los Estados Unidos mismos, y recíprocamente los que violen las leyes de Caza en los Estados Unidos y se pasaran a México serán castigados.

Reitero a usted mi muy atenta consideración.
SUFRAGIO EFECTIVO. NO REELECCION.[4]

J. Alcaraz
EL DIRECTOR.

Translation

Department of Forestry and Hunting

To Mr. Frederick W. Cook *Mexico City, May 12, 1924*

In reply to your recent note of last March 25th, relative to the laws for the protection of migratory Birds, I assure you that this office is very much pleased by the notice and the interest that is taken in the conservation of the birds of our country.

Inside of a very few days, some Presidential Decrees are going to be issued, prohibiting the selling of feathers of all kinds, and other destruction of birds regulating all exportation of birds both singing and ornamental, and protection for insectivorous birds. Besides, this office is now studying not only the issuance of a treatise similar to the "Migratory Bird Act" made with the Dominion of Canada, but also the hunting laws be of international application by special means, to the effect that the furtive hunters who go against the hunting laws of Mexico for example, and then go to the United States with the acquired booty, either as trophies or for commercial purposes with the products of the spoils, shall be punished here as if the violation had been committed in the United States and reciprocatingly those who violate the hunting laws in the United States and then come to Mexico shall be punished.

I reiterate to you my very attentive consideration.
EFFECTIVE SUFFRAGE, NO REELECTION.[4]

José R. Alcaraz,
Director

Note: Mexico signed the Migratory Bird Treaty in 1936, joining Canada and the United States.

LEGALIZING BIRD CONSERVATION
by Alex Sidles

In modern times, the U.S. Congress enjoys broad power to pass environmental legislation. This is thanks in part to a 1942 Supreme Court decision *(Wickard v. Filburn),*[5] which laid the foundation for our present-day understanding of the U.S. Constitution's Commerce Clause. It is this clause which jurists now believe allows the federal government to pass conservation laws such as the Endangered Species Act and the Marine Mammal Protection Act.

The Commerce Clause was not always seen as granting Congress such power. Prior to *Wickard*, the Commerce Clause allowed Congress to enact regulations affecting only actual interstate commerce. It did not allow Congress to protect wildlife. States had the power to regulate hunting, but the federal government did not.

Early state hunting regulations were inadequate. In the late 1800s and early 1900s, the bird populations of the United States were devastated by out-of-control market hunting and plume hunting. States had laws in place to control such hunting, but each state's laws were different. If a hunting season in one state was closed, hunters would move next door to another state whose hunting season was open. Hunters would also shoot birds illegally in one state and send the boxed-up carcasses to another state where shooting was legal, falsely claiming to have shot the birds in the legal state. State law does not apply beyond the borders of the state, so it was impossible for the state governments to keep up with the hunters.

To remedy this problem, Congress tried to use its limited Commerce Clause power to protect the birds. In 1900, it passed the Lacey Act,[6] which outlawed the interstate trade of birds killed in violation of state laws. The Lacey Act helped reduce bird hunting, and even today it remains an important tool in the fight against international poaching, but it wasn't enough. There were always just enough states with weak hunting

---

Left: Great Blue Heron. (Photograph © Doug Parrott) Right: Artwork made entirely of feathers by artist Nukri Lekveishvili, Tbilisi. Such works are legal in Georgia and show how truly alluring feather art can be in the hands of a master. (Courtesy of the artist and Virginia Bound)

laws that bird populations continued to decline, even with the Lacey Act restrictions on trade.

The Passenger Pigeon, once the most numerous bird in North America, was shot to extinction by 1914. The Carolina Parakeet, Heath Hen, Great Auk, and Labrador Duck all disappeared during this era, killed for their meat or their valuable feathers. Eskimo Curlews were dealt a blow from which they never recovered; they haven't been seen for decades. Cranes, herons, and egrets were also hard hit, because they were hunted for their breeding plumes. Even gulls and terns were affected by the plume hunters.

Alarmed by the states' ineffectiveness, the U.S. Congress passed a federal law to regulate bird hunting nationwide in 1913, the Weeks-Mc-Lean Act. This act went beyond the 1900 Lacey Act by establishing a unitary, nationwide closed season for hunting. Although the Weeks-McLean Act was more protective of birds than the Lacey Act, it was constitutionally weaker. The lower federal courts and the Supreme Courts of several states held that Congress had no power under the Constitution's Commerce Clause to pass a conservation law. The U.S. Supreme Court never ruled on the Weeks-McLean Act, but it was obvious to all observers that the high court would uphold the lower courts' holdings and throw out the law.

Aided by conservationists, the federal government got creative. In 1916, the United States signed a treaty with Great Britain—in those days acting on behalf of Canada—pledging both countries to regulate bird hunting within their borders. In 1918, Congress passed the Migratory Bird Treaty Act, a law that regulated bird hunting nationwide, in order to comply with the terms of the treaty it had just signed. The new act created a nationwide hunting season and allowed the government to require the use of hunting permits, which would be issued in limited numbers.[7]

State governments were angry at what they perceived as an end run around their power and a threat to their local hunting industries. Just as they had done in response to the 1913 Weeks-McLean Act, the states claimed that the 1918 Migratory Bird Treaty Act was unconstitutional. The U.S. Supreme Court in *Missouri v. Holland*[8] disagreed, holding that the federal government's constitutional power to sign treaties also granted Congress the power to enact laws to effectuate those treaties. The Commerce Clause didn't give Congress the authority to act, but the treaty-making power did. The birds were saved.

Environmentalists in the United States have always had to think outside the box when it comes to finding legal authority to protect wildlife and natural habitat. In the case of the Migratory Bird Treaty Act, they helped Congress discover a new power to legislate. More recently, in 1994, environmentalists helped the Forest Service use the Endangered Species Act to protect not just endangered Spotted Owls but also millions of acres of precious forest habitat. Even when the letter of the law seems to say no, environmentalists often find a way of getting to yes.

Alex Sidles studies law at the University of Washington and is an active outdoorsman and writer.

NO MORE BAD BIRDS
Victor Scheffer: Changing Perceptions

Victor Scheffer. (Photograph courtesy of Seattle Audubon Society)

With the passage of the Migratory Bird Treaty Act in 1918, Congress established for the first time the federal government's preeminent right to regulate the hunting of migratory birds, in the interests of protecting them from mass extinction. The act was passed to implement a treaty signed in 1916 between the U.S. and Great Britain, acting on behalf of Canada, to save bird species that had been decimated by hunters.[9]

This was a notable victory for the budding environmental movement, but it was by no means as wide-ranging as it first appeared. Although the act fully protected songbirds that ate harmful insects, it listed other birds as game that could be hunted, though only under certain conditions to be set by the federal government. It protected most seabirds and waders but made no mention of predators, in effect allowing open season on them. Predators included raptors, owls, cormorants, kingfishers, Water Ouzels (American Dippers), and corvids. The treaty also allowed the government to eradicate birds that greatly harmed agriculture.

As part of the effort to manage the list of good, bad, and game birds, the federal government employed the U.S. Biological Survey. The Biological Survey was created in 1896 as a bureau under the aegis of the Department of Agriculture. Its original task was to take an inventory of the biota of the country. In addition to surveying wildlife, the bureau was responsible for studying more specifically how birds controlled insect pests that hurt agriculture.

Under the new law, however, the Biological Survey was called upon to help figure out which birds and other animals were injurious enough to humans to be destroyed—and to do something about it. Thus began a major effort to poison, trap, and shoot dozens of species and millions of individuals that harmed our interests, an effort that included mammals, too. The effort continues today, carried out by the U.S. Fish and Wildlife Service, the descendant of the Biological Survey.

From the outset, Seattle Audubon opposed measures to kill birds. At first, the Society focused on delisting, doing its best to remove species from both the game list and from the "bad animals" list. The treaty allowed the federal government's regulatory agents and the individual states to give more protection to any bird species listed in the treaty, and that is what Audubon tried to do.

But as our understanding of ecology developed over the ensuing decades, the Society began to shift its focus. Instead of trying to preserve individual species, Seattle Audubon *began to fight to protect functional swaths of wildlife habitat.*

Now some environmentalists are calling for even greater changes. They say we should change the anthropocentric view of wildlife that has been the foundation of human thinking for thousands of years. Wildlife should exist merely because of its intrinsic value, they believe, not because we place any kind of human value on it. Humans, they point out, are perhaps the dominant force on the planet now, so much so that we are living in what many call the Anthropocene Epoch. As the dominant species with the most impact and the most control over nature, it is incumbent on us to become good stewards. Since this is so, say these voices for ecology, then let us become stewards who care for all creatures, great and small.

One such early voice was Victor Scheffer. Scheffer received his doctorate in zoology from the University of Washington in 1936. He wrote fourteen books about marine mammals and nature, including his most famous book, The Year of the Whale, *a bestseller that fostered the conservation of marine mammals and made whale-watching popular. Scheffer died in 2011. In 2006, at age 100, he was interviewed by Seattle Audubon oral historian Noel Angell. These are his words from that interview.*

"I grew up in the Northwest, living in Puyallup at first. I entered the University of Washington in 1925 and took mainly biology or natural history courses. All the sciences at that time were in one building, Science Hall: geology, botany, zoology, and what they called bacteriology. Up on the roof they kept the Guinea Pigs for the bacteriology classes. During those years, I was what was called a teaching fellow—it's called a teaching assistant now—under Professor Kincaid. Trevor Kincaid was born in Canada—a wonderful person. He never called me anything but Mr. Scheffer, although I was his assistant for seven years.

During that period, I worked for five summers as a ranger-naturalist in Mount Rainier National Park and enjoyed learning about the animals, plants, and geology of that region.

I retired in 1969, and I've been retired for 37 years now. But shortly after retirement I was appointed by President Nixon as chairman of the new U.S. Marine Mammal Commission. I served from 1973 to 1975 in that capacity. At the same time, I had started to write books about the natural world. The first one was *The Year of the Whale,* which was commissioned by Scribner's. They wanted a lively book about whales. My first 40 pages of manuscript were too dull. They said, 'Let yourself go,' so I wrote what is called fiction based on fact. The book caught the crest of a wave of enthusiasm about seeing whales and sold a great many copies. I remember I got $40,000, which was quite a bit in those days, right off the bat.

I followed with books on the Sea Otter and the natural history of marine mammals, the fur seal of Alaska, and a kind of philosophical book called *A Voice for Wildlife.* I also wrote an anecdotal history of the environmental movement, *The Shaping of Environmentalism in America,* in which I said:

[There are] millions of people who visit wilderness for plain delight. And there are many others who have never set foot in a wilderness and never will, yet cherish the thought that places on Earth have been set aside deliberately for the inspiration of generations yet unborn.

It has been one of my deep satisfactions to have followed for half a century the evolution of the wilderness idea. Persistently under attack, regarded as elitist by some and impractical by others, it has won a secure place in our national thought. Our wilderness reserves continually remind us that we are a society which, by saving a material heritage, has saved a moral one.[10]

My thinking was shaped by my parents, of course. My father joined the Bureau of Biological Survey of the Department of Agriculture in 1910 at a salary of $1,000 a year. His title was simply 'expert.' The Biological Survey was not in the business of compassion in those days. His first job was to go to Arizona and organize crews to poison the prairie dogs with a strychnine and saccharine mixture sprinkled on oats, which they scattered about. It seems that the ranchers' horses would occasionally get injured by stumbling into a prairie dog hole, plus the prairie dogs ate the grass which God had ordained for the ranchers.

My father did not like that—what he called the killing game—and eventually he got a much happier job in Puyallup at a branch of Washington State College [now WSU]. It was called the Western Washington Experiment Station. His assignment was to study the food habits of 'injurious' animals: pocket mice girdling orchard trees in winter, Mountain Beavers damaging tree farms and domestic rhododendrons, flickers pounding on the walls of buildings and waking people early in the morning, and various other 'nasty' habits of wild animals.

Growing up, I knew I was not cut out to be a businessman. Maybe a penniless poet, but not a businessman. That's why I studied biology. I joined Seattle Audubon in 1934. I suspect that it was partly to meet some wholesome girls, because I didn't know much about birds and really wasn't awfully interested in them at first. I've always been more interested in mammals than birds. I guess I was looking for kindred spirits. Yes. And I saw them.

Joining Seattle Audubon was a little more rewarding than joining a hiking club, I think, because we have a different mission. I don't know, it just seemed more rewarding to go out and learn birds by their calls, for example, and their flight behavior so that you could identify them at a distance, and to realize the complex strategies that birds have to survive in different habitats.

But Seattle Audubon was more than just a club for bird-watchers. Audubon was early on against predator control by government agencies. We had bounties on predator species in those days. There was even a $5 bounty on the little ordinary Harbor Seal, for example. You shot it and cut off the snout and let it dry, and then you brought it to a district agent, and you got $5 for it.

We were against bounties on principle, but also because it's easy to get skulduggery in the operations. Hunters would make snouts from other parts of the skin. You could get three or four snouts from the same animal, for example. We were also against the importation of non-native birds. There was some sort

A VERY GOOD YEAR

In 1922, the U.S. Biological Survey reported to Congress that it had had a very good year. It had killed 77,185 Coyotes, and 2,826 Bobcats and lynxes. In Washington State, it had killed 155,500 jackrabbits. All the prairie dogs in six counties of two states had been poisoned. The agency employed 105,000 men, who helped spread more than 1,000 tons of poisoned grain and laid out 1,229,000 poisoned baits. Rodents and Coyotes were at the top of the kill list, with no real science to make anyone realize that killing Coyotes only encouraged more breeding, and that the Coyotes were the best control of rodents, much more effective than poisons, fumigation, traps, and bullets. Numerous permits were issued to allow farmers and hunters to shoot American Robins and Band-tailed Pigeons, robins because they ate fruit, pigeons because they ate grain.[11]

LISTERS

Almost immediately after the Migratory Bird Treaty Act was passed in 1918, Seattle Audubon began efforts to get as many bird species protected as possible by the Department of Agriculture (at the federal level) or the Department of Game (at the state level). Protecting birds to a higher degree than the treaty called for was perfectly allowable but required the approval of federal or state regulatory agencies.

In some cases, that meant changing the hunting season of a game bird, or eliminating it altogether. In other cases, it meant defending a "bad bird" that supposedly deserved extirpation by showing how beneficial or innocuous it really was, thus justifying a switch to the "good" column. For raptors and owls, it meant getting them new protections, for under the Migratory Bird Treaty, raptors and owls were not considered at all. They were predators, not deserving of any protection.

One of the most persistent advocates for birds in our state was Emily (Mrs. Neil) Haig, President of Seattle Audubon from 1952 to 1956 and

thereafter Chair of the Conservation Committee. Her special project was the Mourning Dove, a bird that was classified as a game bird by the treaty but not hunted in Washington. It went onto the state game list for the first time in 1952, through the lobbying efforts of hunters, who asked for and received a designated hunting season and bag limits. Within months of the change, Haig began writing letters against it, forming coalitions, sending out thousands of pamphlets, acting as the voice of the dove.

In a letter to one state senator, she wrote: "[People] said at one time that there were millions of the lovely Passenger Pigeon, and [hunters] kept on killing them, and now not one is left. Do we have to wait until only a few remain of any species before taking action?"[12]

In another letter, written after she had been lambasted at a hearing, Haig wrote: "The perfectly stupid remarks of the Game Department spokesman at the hearing 'that the doves would get so thick they would fly in your face' is about as much thought given to the subject as they dare....This is not a silly idea of a few misguided individuals; it is the voice of intelligent, decent citizens asking to be heard thru [sic] a maze of smokescreened propaganda put out by the minority to win their point...It is no fun to stand up under the barrage of smooth and misguiding words, but it is certainly not going to make us give up. P.S. One more statistic. The robins have one or two nests a year with four eggs each. They have never been a game bird and yet their numbers remain stable....Robins are certainly not flying about in anyone's face."[13]

Despite decades of effort, Haig ultimately lost the battle. The Mourning Dove is still on the game list, with a season running for two months in the fall and a daily bag limit of fifteen birds.

Haig and Seattle Audubon had greater success with a campaign to save raptors. In 1961, Haig persuaded then-Representative Daniel Evans to introduce a bill in the state legislature that would put raptors and owls on the protected list. The bill never came out of committee. So Evans approached the State Game Commissioner, asking him to protect raptors.[14] Four were put on the protected list: Cooper's Hawk, Sharp-shinned Hawk, Northern Goshawk, and Prairie Falcon. Haig was grateful to Evans for his work but knew it was just a start. Other birds needed her help, and she gave it. By 1972, nearly all raptors and owls had been added to the protected list. Haig died in 1978.

Prairie Falcon. (Photograph © Doug Schurman)

of quail, as I recall, that was introduced into Northeastern Washington purely for the enjoyment of hunters. The game department did not ask the populace, the whole people who owned the wildlife, 'Do you want this to happen or not?' It was a kind of innocent error on the part of the huntin', shootin', trappin' outfit.

Many years later, we have gotten an anti-steel-trap law, which was fought by the trappers and by people who wanted to use the steel trap to get Mountain Beavers out of their gardens. We advocated live traps, taking animals way out into a territory where they couldn't do any harm and then turning them loose.

Seattle Audubon is a voice that has weight. I can't imagine the Northwest without an Audubon Society. It has a wonderful reputation for goodness when it comes to the environment. It's almost a word in the dictionary, isn't it? The Audubon Society. Above all, Seattle Audubon stands for the study and preservation of nature.

In my book on the shaping of environmentalism, I defined environmentalism, which was new to people at that time, as the art and science of studying humankind's natural basis of support

EXCERPTS FROM THE MIGRATORY BIRD TREATY OF 1916

The United States of America and His Majesty the King of the United Kingdom of Great Britain and Ireland and of the British Dominions beyond the Seas, Emperor of India, being desirous of saving from indiscriminate slaughter and of insuring the preservation of such migratory birds as are either useful to man or are harmless, have resolved to adopt some uniform system of protection which shall effectively accomplish such objects and to the end of concluding a convention for this purpose ... have agreed to and adopted the following:

The high contracting powers declare that the migratory birds included in the terms of this convention shall be as follows:

1. Migratory Game Birds [subject to regulated hunting]

    (a) *Anatidae* or waterfowl, including brant, wild ducks, geese, and swans.

    (b) *Gruidae* or cranes, including little brown, sandhill, and whooping cranes.

    (c) *Rallidae* or rails, including coots, gallinules and sora, and other rails.

    (d) *Limicolae* or shorebirds, including avocets, curlew, dowitchers, godwits, knots, oyster catchers, phalaropes, plovers, sandpipers, snipe, stilts, surf birds, turnstones, willet, woodcock, and yellowlegs.

    (e) *Columbidae* or pigeons, including doves and wild pigeons.

2. Migratory Insectivorous Birds [completely protected]:

    Bobolinks, catbirds, chickadees, cuckoos, flickers, flycatchers, grosbeaks, humming birds, kinglets, martins, meadowlarks, nighthawks or bullbats, nuthatches, orioles, robins, shrikes, swallows, swifts, tanagers, titmice, thrushes, vireos, warblers, waxwings, whippoorwills, woodpeckers, and wrens, and all other perching birds which feed entirely or chiefly on insects.

3. Other Migratory Nongame Birds [completely protected]:

    Auks, auklets, bitterns, fulmars, gannets, grebes, guillemots, gulls, herons, jaegers, loons, murres, petrels, puffins, shearwaters, and terns.[9]

while steadily applying what we learned toward perpetuating those bases. Of course, that's a very anthropomorphic look at the environment. Some religious people would say that the environment should be saved even though there were no people. That is a nice idea.

The guru of the wildlife movement was Aldo Leopold. He was a hunter, trapper, and fisherman with the Forest Service. He believed that nature was a resource for us to use. Then he got pneumonia down there in New Mexico and nearly died. He was laid up for a long time, and he had time to think about the real climax uses of wilderness land. He and Bob Marshall, among others, founded the Wilderness Society in 1935. It's still very strong. It led to the passage of the Wilderness Act of 1964.[15] Aldo Leopold brought the word 'ecology' into

Left: Golden-crowned Kinglet, an insectivore fully protected by the Migratory Bird Treaty. (Photograph © Joe Sweeney) Right: Double-crested Cormorant, a protected but "injurious" bird that eats fish, including salmon. Wildlife Services, a division of the Department of Agriculture, was issued a permit in 2015 to kill 3,489 cormorants on East Sand Island in the Columbia River, ostensibly to protect salmon.[16] Seattle Audubon continues efforts to stop this policy. (Photograph © Thomas Sanders)

the public vernacular. It was a scientific term, meaning the study of the relationships of organisms in the environment.

But ecology is also the science of studying, in one way or another, man's place in nature. When humans first developed respect amounting to reverence for this peculiar species that we are, we also developed a reverence for the incredible complexity, beauty, and wonder of nature. We need to remember that, because thereby we will be inclined to take any action we can to defend nature against waste, pollution, and poisoning.

As population grows in the world, we waste the environment. But how you control population without getting all tangled up in religion, I have no idea.

I am a religious person myself in the sense that I have a binding philosophy, which is the Latin origin of 'religion,' but I'm not a theist or a deist at all. I think the human race has the privilege and responsibility of taking care of itself, being itself, following the Golden Rule. We may be hit by an asteroid. Who knows? But it's fun trying to be the best we can be in the meanwhile.

I think it's kind of chicken to place responsibility for our welfare on imaginative sources out there somewhere,

supernatural forces. We are animals, although very beautiful and specialized animals, unbelievable animals, and the challenge for us is to be the best animals we can.

If I had to have a motto on my wall, it would simply read, 'Be kind.' Kindness is the acknowledgment that we are all caught up together in a kind of a sensual and spiritual biomass, and we must recognize that we—through kindness—we are all one kind."

YOU SHALL NOT CUT
Emily Haig: Helping to Save Olympic National Park

Emily Haig in 1970. (Photograph © University of Washington, courtesy of University of Washington Libraries, Special Collections, POR763)

When you look at a pristine rainforest such as the Hoh in Olympic National Park, do you see the forest or the trees? More precisely, should ancient forest ecosystems be viewed as a sustainable crop of trees to be harvested every few decades, or should forest ecosystems be preserved intact as living museums of flora and fauna, symbols of the wilderness that existed from coast to coast before Europeans arrived?

This is a question first raised more than 150 years ago. It still rages today. One stage where this conflict played out was Olympic National Park. Emily (Mrs. Neil) Haig, President of Seattle Audubon, was a lead actor in the drama.

Already by the mid-1830s, artists and authors such as George Catlin[17] were working to change people's minds about the nature of wilderness. Wilderness, to these romantics, was not something to be conquered and used, but something to be wondered at and saved. The first National Park, Yellowstone, came out of that new viewpoint. Yellowstone was created by Ulysses S. Grant in 1872, over the protests of mining interests, ranchers, hunters, and loggers, who got their legislative representatives to introduce numerous resolutions to reduce the size of the Park. They failed.[18]

In 1906, under the leadership of President Theodore Roosevelt, Congress passed the American Antiquities Act, which allowed the President to set aside public lands by proclamation. The act was passed out of concern that antiquities hunters were despoiling ancient ruins that stood on public lands. But the language in the act, which said it was intended "for the protection of objects of historic or scientific interest," gave the President great power to save environmentally sensitive lands as well. Roosevelt did so in 1909, proclaiming the creation of Mount Olympus National Monument and setting aside 615,000 acres of wilderness and prime old growth forest.

There followed three decades of attempts by environmentalists to convert the National Monument into a National Park. Seattle Audubon was part of that effort, with members writing endless letters, buttonholing numerous legislators, publishing and distributing thousands of brochures, constantly trying to educate the public and our representatives about the beauty, wonder, and real value of the rainforest.

Finally, in 1938, another President Roosevelt, FDR, signed into law the act that created Olympic National Park.

Seattle Auduboners were jubilant. But not for long. We soon realized that commercial interests, especially timber companies, still viewed all those giant trees enviously, with dollar signs in their eyes. For decades after the Park was established, supposedly protected stands of old growth were systematically clear cut and hauled away, over the futile protests of conservationists.

One illuminating act in this drama involved Governor Arthur B. Langlie, who was very interested in helping the timber companies log the most lucrative parts of the Park. His idea was to shrink the Park boundaries, thus opening up big stands of old growth that could be sold. As a governor, he had no authority to do this, but he and his timber supporters figured if he put together a committee, held hearings, and later reported to the President that the people of the State of Washington wanted and needed this, it would happen. Under pressure, Langlie allowed Emily Haig, Rosamond Engle of the Seattle Garden Club, and Polly Dyer of The Mountaineers to join the committee, which was heavily stacked with big business representatives. In 1953, after eleven months of deliberations, the committee was ready to

recommend in favor of shrinking the Park. Haig managed to get permission to write a minority report, which she authored, reportedly with the help of Dyer.

The minority report refuted nearly every point made by the majority. Langlie refused to release it. It lay buried until, on April 13, 1954, the Port Angeles Evening News *got hold of a copy and published it verbatim.[19] That was the end of Governor Langlie's effort to shrink the Park. Since then, no attempt to seriously shrink the Park has succeeded, but the battles continue to this day.*

Minority Report

We, the undersigned members of the Governor's Olympic National Park Review Committee, after a careful review of the oral and written testimony of some fifty-five witnesses at three public hearings, a tour of the disputed Park areas and consideration of some 220 letters from individuals and groups, are of the opinion that: The boundaries of Olympic National Park should remain as they are.

We submit the following report as a basis for arriving at our conclusions:

1. The rainforests of the Olympic National Park should take their place alongside other national scenic wonders, as a unique resource that is just as real and just as important to the nation as are the natural materials that can be weighed and valued and used for economic ends.

2. Olympic National Park fulfills cultural and recreational needs in preserving a sample of the rapidly diminishing wilderness which once clothed the Northwest.

3. The half million visitors to Olympic National Park in 1953 demonstrates the need of adequately providing unimpaired natural areas for the enjoyment of present and future generations.

4. Of the 220 letters received by the committee containing 307 signatures, 300 were in favor of retaining the present boundaries of the park, [amounting to] a percentage of 98.

5. Increased leisure time, increasing population and per capita wealth, together with greatly improved travel facilities saw over 45 million visitors to the National Parks in 1953 which demonstrates the need of these areas.

6. Olympic National Park in comparison with other American and Canadian National Parks and Monuments, is not too large, being only twelfth in size.

7. Commercial interests have not sat-

GETTING HER GOAT

Emily Haig was a masterful political advocate who believed in the power of letter-writing. Every Monday, she would host a letter-writing party in her home, training others to write effective messages to elected representatives, corporations, and bureaucrats. During her terms as Seattle Audubon President and later Chair of the Conservation Committee, she led the fight for many causes besides the salvation of Olympic National Park. One of her fiercest battles was her effort to save the Mountain Goat from hunters.

The issue was not completely supported by environmentalists. Mountain Goats are native to parts of the Cascades but were introduced to the Olympics. In 1924, four animals from Banff were released; in 1929 and 1930, eight animals from Alaska were released.[20] By 1959, goats in Olympic National Park had increased to an estimated total of 700. Environmentalists worried that the non-native goats were destroying sensitive alpine habitat; some thought they should be removed.

Haig was aware of these facts but rarely mentioned the goats of the Olympics, possibly because she saw no need to advocate for game living in National Parks, where they are protected from being hunted. Instead, she focused on the preservation of Mountain Goats statewide, as she did in this letter written January 15, 1957, to Fred Seaton, Secretary of the Interior:

"We have tried in this state to save the few remaining Mountain Goats native to this state and four other states but get no help from the game department who only think that ALL wildlife should be harvested. Many of us feel that these goats should never be killed as they are more of an attraction to the tourist when they become conscious of not being hunted. Killed from mountain areas with high-powered rifles, many unable to be retrieved, and then only used for a trophy. Isn't it about time that we become civilized enough to leave the trophy era of the past live in the past. Just to kill something for that purpose is not even good sport and only the National Fish and Wildlife can prevent this 'harvesting.' Nature when left alone keeps its own balance better than man, and it takes outstanding conservation leadership to stop some of these things....It is time to put a curb somewhere.... With all good wishes to you and your fine staff for a successful term in the field of conservation of our heritage, I am, very sincerely yours, Seattle Audubon Society Past President and now Conservation Chair, Mrs. Neil Haig" [21]

isfactorily demonstrated their assertion that the logging of some 230,000 acres of the Park's rainforests is essential to maintain the present and future economy of the Olympic Peninsula.

8. On the contrary, competent forestry authorities predict a bright future for the forest products industries of this region.

9. The commercial forest saw timber outside the park is considered by authorities to be underestimated [by] at least 20 percent and that within the next thirty to fifty years there will be an annual growth far in excess of any past or foreseeable demands.

10. Cutting National Park timber is not the solution to the problem of stabilizing and maintaining the economy and employment of the Peninsula. More effective and permanent alternatives exist in a better defined and dynamic application of proven modern forestry practices on the commercial forest lands outside the Park, which contain over 60 million board feet of saw timber and some 1.3 million acres of second growth. Authorities consider forestry practices up to now

Left: Mountain Goat. (Photograph © Paul Bannick) Opposite page: Hoh Rainforest, Olympic National Park. (Photograph © Loren Mooney)

as having merely scratched the surface of potential wood resource utilization.

11. Some of the alternatives to cutting Park timber are:

(a) make commercial forests more accessible, to accomplish a more balanced timber harvesting budget, better fire and insect control, better salvage of decadent old growth, logging waste and utilization of second growth thinnings,

(b) more modernization of mills to handle smaller logs with less waste,

(c) more pulp mills to utilize the large volume of pulp species which consisted 70 percent of the Olympic forests,

(d) more emphasis on integration between mills and within mills to utilize by-product wastes,

(e) more emphasis by the forest industries on chemical, pulp and wood use research to increase end-product manufacturing and markets,

(f) a forest land purchase program which will assure Peninsula logs for Peninsula industry,

(g) a sound public carrier transportation line along the western Peninsula,

(h) more facilities to house and entertain the growing tourist trade.

12. There is no present log shortage and as time goes on wood resources will increase to insure a steady economy in this region, without cutting the forests of Olympic National Park.

13. It is considered significant that the Washington State Federation of Labor consisting of 780 organizations with some 300,000 members, the International Woodworkers of America National C.I.O., the General Federation of Women's Clubs with its 6 million members and the National Council of Garden Clubs with 300,000 members are opposed to any boundary changes of Olympic National Park.

14. Grazing lands within the park valleys have always been the winter feeding grounds of the Roosevelt Elk herds, one of the two unique attractions for which the Park was established. To preserve these elk herds, the valley lands should be retained within the Park.

[Signed]
Mrs. Neil Haig
Earl Hartley
Jack Hollingsworth
Mrs. John [Polly] A. Dyer
(Mrs.) Rosamond P. Engle

OLYMPIC NATIONAL PARK TIMELINE: A 125-YEAR BATTLE OVER WHO OWNS THE FORESTS

MARCH 3, 1891: The Forest Reserve Act (technically, An Act to Repeal Timber-Culture Laws, and For Other Purposes) was signed into law by President Benjamin Harrison, allowing the President to set aside Forest Reserves from lands in the public domain. This act was the first to state clearly that forest lands could be set aside in reserves for use by the public, and title to the lands could not be sold or granted to private owners within the Reserves. [26 Stat. 1095][22]

FEBRUARY 22, 1897: President Grover Cleveland created the Olympic Forest Reserve by proclamation under the authority granted by the Forest Reserve Act. The Reserve encompassed 2,188,800 acres. [29 Stat. 901]

JUNE 4, 1897: Angry about Cleveland's proclamation (which created 21 million acres of Forest Reserves nationally, including the Olympic Forest Reserve), Congress revoked them all in an appropriations act. The act gave the government until March 1898 to dispose of these lands. Any not disposed of reverted to Forest Reserve, as the Olympic Forest Reserve eventually did. The act also gave the President the power to resize Forest Reserves by proclamation. [30 Stat. 36]

1900-1901: President William McKinley reduced the Olympic Forest Reserve by 721,920 acres. [31 Stat. 1962 and 32 Stat. 1981]

1902: An influential report, *Forest Conditions in the Olympic Forest Reserve, Washington*, by Arthur Dodwell and Theodore Rixon, was published by the Department of the Interior's U.S. Geological Survey, announcing that only 10,289 acres of the Olympic Forest Reserve had been logged. The report estimated that 2,883 square miles of marketable timber remained in the Reserve.[23] Timber companies began to look for ways to acquire logging rights.

FEBRUARY 1, 1905: The National Forest Service was created, under the aegis of the Department of Agriculture. All Forest Reserves, including the Olympic Forest Reserve, were transferred to a department whose philosophy was the sustainable harvesting of forests, not the preservation of intact ecosystems.

JUNE 8, 1906: The American Antiquities Act was passed. This act gave the President the power to proclaim public lands as National Monuments to be preserved if they had historical or "scientific interest." Politicos immediately began efforts to repeal the act. [34 Stat. 225]

LATE 1906: The Mountaineers was founded and quickly began to lobby for the preservation of old growth forests in the Olympic Peninsula, among other sites.

MARCH 2, 1907: President Theodore Roosevelt restored the lands withdrawn from the Olympic Forest Reserve by McKinley, except those settled by homesteaders. [34 Stat. 3306]

MARCH 4, 1907: Angry that Western states bore the brunt of the new set-asides, Congress passed a bill prohibiting the creation or expansion of Forest Reserves (except by act of Congress) in Oregon, Washington, Idaho, Montana, Colorado, and Wyoming. [34 Stat. 1271]

MARCH 2, 1909: Mount Olympus National Monument was created by proclamation of Teddy Roosevelt under the authority of the American Antiquities Act, setting aside 615,000 acres of the Olympic Peninsula mainly to protect habitat for Roosevelt Elk. Timber and mining interests began efforts to reduce the size of the Monument or eliminate it altogether. [35 Stat. 2247]

1910: After McKinley reduced the size of Olympic Forest Reserve, timber companies began moving to buy virgin old growth through the use of the Timber and Stone Act of 1878. [45th Congress, Sess. 2, ch. 151, 20 Stat. 89] Under this act, public lands deemed unfit for farming could be sold to individuals for $2.50 per acre, up to a limit of 160 acres (similar to the Homestead Act limits). By 1910, timber companies had used fraudulent means to acquire 523,720 acres of forest formerly in the Olympic Forest Reserve.

APRIL 17, 1912: President William Taft reduced the size of Mount Olympus National Monument. [37 Stat. 1737]

MAY 11, 1915: President Woodrow Wilson reduced the size of Mount Olympus National Monument. [39 Stat. 1726]

AUGUST 25, 1916: The National Park Service Organic Act passed, creating the National Park system. Preservationists were elated, until they discovered that the director, Stephen Mather, had decided to implement a predator elimination program that heavily damaged the ecosystems of National Parks. Future directors would encourage logging in the National Parks. It became clear that the National Park Service was not committed to the preservation of National Parks as pristine wilderness areas. [39 Stat. 534]

JANUARY 7, 1929: President Calvin Coolidge reduced the size of Mount Olympus National Monument. [45 Stat. 2984]

AUGUST 26, 1931: A highway (now U.S. Route 101) was completed, encircling the Olympic Peninsula and opening its western side to logging. The highway also opened the area to tourists, key to the movement to preserve the ancient forests.

JUNE 1933: President Franklin Roosevelt by executive order transferred the National Monuments to the National Park Service. NPS officials rejected the transfer of Mount Olympus National Monument because they preferred to abolish the Monument and turn it over to timber companies. They forced the issue in November and lost. The Monument was assigned to the Park Service, which was told to shield it from logging. The Park Service did not.

1935: Bills were introduced in Congress to create Olympic National Park. All were rejected.

SEPTEMBER 30–OCTOBER 1, 1937: Roosevelt toured the Olympic Peninsula and announced his support for a large National Park. Opposition to the idea of converting Mount Olympus National Monument into a National Park died, and opponents then focused on the idea of keeping the proposed Park as small as possible.

JUNE 29, 1938: Congress established Olympic National Park, consisting of 682,000 acres (more than double the size of Mount Olympus National Monument), with a provision to expand it by proclamation, not to exceed 892,000 acres. [52 Stat. 1241]

JANUARY 2, 1940: FDR added 187,411 acres in ten parcels and authorized acquisition of a coastal strip. [54 Stat. 2678] The National Park Service continued to push for logging in the new Park, using World War II as an excuse. Logging continued in the Park under a plan called "salvage logging," supposedly to remove sick and dying trees but in reality leading to clear cuts. Logging was opposed by environmental groups, including Seattle Audubon.

THROUGHOUT THE 1940'S: Timber companies lobbied to change the boundaries of the Park, freeing up old growth forests for cutting.

1942 AND ONWARD: Congressionally brokered land exchanges gave the National Park Service title to lands within the Park that had belonged to private or government landowners, in exchange for federal lands elsewhere. Significant exchanges occurred in 1942, 1958, 1987, and 1992.

1948: Olympic Park Associates was founded as a nonprofit citizens' conservation organization to defend against logging old growth forests in the Park and against reducing the Park's size.

JANUARY 13, 1953: President Harry Truman added the Queets Corridor to the Park. [67 Stat. C27]

MAY 1953: Washington State Governor Arthur Langlie appointed a committee to recommend to Congress changes in the Park's boundaries, reducing the size of the Park and opening vast areas to logging.

APRIL 13, 1954: Emily Haig and Polly Dyer's minority report against reducing the size of the Park hit the press, and Langlie threw in the towel. However, logging continued in the Park under the direction of Superintendent Fred Overly.

JULY 4, 1984: The Washington State Wilderness Act established wilderness areas within National Park boundaries, meaning that roads could not be developed nor forests logged. [98 Stat. 299]

NOVEMBER 7, 1986: Congress revised the boundaries of Olympic National Park and Olympic National Forest, granting to the Secretary of the Interior for the first time the right to acquire parklands by purchase, donation, bequest, or exchange without further Congressional authorization, an important step. [100 Stat. 3527]

NOVEMBER 12, 2008: Olympic National Park completed its General Management Plan, which calls for expansion of the Park through purchase of land from "willing buyers." The measure continues to be opposed by logging interests. [73 Fed. Reg. 219, p. 66919][24]

Hoh Rainforest, Olympic National Park. (Photograph © Loren Mooney)

THE OWL AND THE LITTLE SEABIRD
Tom Campion: Saving Ancient Forests

The haunting call floated through the night forest, coming from all directions and no direction, filling the spaces between the cathedral trees before wafting into the mysterious dark. Some people say the call of the Northern Spotted Owl sounds like a dog barking, but this is untrue. It is, rather, the call of the wilderness itself, wild and ancient, as ancient as the trees that tower in old growth forests from California to Alaska—cedar, fir, hemlock, and spruce, the chant of species that have sheltered the owl throughout the misty veils of time. Ineffably beautiful to some. Timber and board feet to others.

As early as 1972, scientists were becoming alarmed at the rapid disappearance of the northern subspecies of the Spotted Owl from its historic range. They learned it was because the ancient forests where the owls lived were being cut down at a ferocious rate.[25] They also learned how completely dependent Spotted Owls are on the specialized habitat of ancient forests, and how complex this ecosystem really is.

Prior to the 1970s, old growth forests were often characterized as dead or decaying. Timber companies said old growth forests were ecological deserts filled with old trees that had reached the end of their days. They said it was better to cut down the giants while they could still be useful for something.

In reality, we were learning that ancient forests support a web of life so vast and interrelated as to be almost unfathomable. It is an ecosystem diverse, robust, alive. And five billion board feet of its apex trees were getting chopped down every year in Washington. The Spotted Owl was well on the road to extirpation here.

It was not alone. Another bird was also on the way out in Western Washington. This was a seabird, the Marbled Murrelet, which had evolved to nest preposterously in ancient forests. Females use flat beds of moss on wide, old growth branches to lay their one egg. When the egg hatches, both parents fly as far as 50 miles to saltwater to bring back fish for their chick until the baby can

Tom Campion. (Photograph courtesy of the Campion Advocacy Fund)

fly on its own to the sea. As the giant trees with wide enough branches were felled, so too did the murrelets' population fall toward extirpation here.

But this is not just a story about humans destroying habitat for their own needs, oblivious to the paradise of nature. It is also the story about people fighting to save nature by changing the very way we look at the world. For something happened in the 1960s and '70s that opened our eyes. Maybe it was the book Rachel Carson wrote about pesti-

cides killing our songbirds,[26] or the one Paul Ehrlich wrote about overpopulation.[27] Maybe it was the astronauts circling our planet, taking photos, showing us how small and isolated Earth really is.[28] Possibly the civil rights and anti-war movements encouraged people to believe their activism could change the world, and on April 22, 1970, some 20 million demonstrators across the nation who hoped so turned out for the first Earth Day.[29]

Whatever was in the air back then, Congress passed bill after bill in a legislative whirlwind that seems miraculous today: The Clean Air Act went into effect on December 17, 1963. The Wilderness Act was passed on September 3, 1964, setting aside millions of federally owned lands to be free of human influence. The National Environmental Policy Act (NEPA) passed on December 23, 1969, requiring federal agencies to incorporate environmental considerations into their planning for major actions. On July 9, 1970, the Environmental Protection Agency (EPA) was established. On October 2, 1970, the National Oceanographic and Atmospheric Administration (NOAA) was created. The Clean Water Act was passed on October 18, 1972. The Marine Mammal Protection Act was passed on October 21, 1972. On December 31, 1972, DDT was banned. On December 28, 1973, the Endangered Species Act was passed. On October 22, 1976, the National Forest Management Act (NFMA) was passed, requiring the federal government to preserve viable populations of native vertebrates in all our National Forests.[30]

These were the legal tools forged by the environmental movement that have been used ever since to protect the Earth. They are the foundation of newer laws and regulations designed to mitigate our impact on nature, as we have slowly come to realize that if we are to survive, we cannot consume nature at will. We must conserve it.

To do so often means that we have to make the difficult choice between long-term preservation or short-term gain.

Nowhere is this clearer than in the fight to save the last of our ancient forests. Tom Campion has been an avowed warrior in this fight for nearly 40 years. He joined Seattle Audubon in 1977 and served on the Conservation Committee and various ad hoc forest-oriented committees, helping to jump-start the Society's years-long efforts to save the Northern Spotted Owl, the Marbled Murrelet, and the habitat they call home. Campion's efforts, and those of many other Seattle Audubon staff and volunteers, were joined by other environmental groups and helped by law firms including Earthjustice and the Washington Forest Law Center. Their weapons were legal, administrative, political, educational, activist—and effective.

"My first wife, Lorna Smith, and I did a lot of hiking in the late 1970s. We hiked all the trails in the Mount Baker-Snoqualmie National Forest. I wasn't a birder per se, and Lorna was more interested in the marine environment, especially Protection Island. But we both loved the ancient forests.

I remember after one hike, I walked into the District Ranger's office in North Bend and asked to speak to the ranger there. He came out with his Ranger Rick hat on. A short, stocky guy. I said, 'How much of your old growth are you going to save?'

He said, 'Oh, we've got Asahel Curtis natural area up there at Snoqualmie Pass with 300 acres. The rest will probably be on some harvest schedule or other, at some point.'

It was ridiculous. I couldn't believe it. I decided to get involved, and I started learning about the issue. The big picture was, the annual cut of our National Forests back in the late 1970s and early '80s was 11 billion board feet, every year. Half of it was coming out of Western Washington and Oregon. The timber companies were liquidating the last of our ancient forests. Most of the old growth they were cutting was low elevation, where they had access to roads or could

LITTLE BIRD, BIG BATTLE
by Chris Karrenberg and Linda Murtfeldt

Although the Marbled Murrelet (MAMU) has been known to humans for thousands of years, nobody knew where it nested. They only knew it appeared year-round in saltwater from California to Alaska to dive for fish, as other alcids (small seabirds) did. In winter it was black and white. In summer it became oddly marbled in brown and white, one of only three species in the world known to molt this way. No one knew why.

Then in 1974 in California's Big Basin Redwoods State Park, south of San Francisco, a tree pruner named Hoyt Foster was climbing near the top of an old growth Douglas Fir and came upon a nestling sitting on a wide branch. It was unlike any other forest bird he had seen before—it had webbed feet! Before Foster could grab the young bird and wrap it up to carry to an expert, the chick dropped 150 feet down from the tree and plopped, unhurt, onto the ground below. There, it was rescued by a ranger and later that day was identified as a Marbled Murrelet. At last we knew where and how Marbled Murrelets breed and raise their young: in ancient forests miles from the sea.[31, 32]

Marbled Murrelets nest in temperate rainforests along the Northwest coast in redwoods, Douglas Fir, Western Hemlock and Sitka Spruce hundreds of years old and hundreds of feet tall. Nest sites can be up to 50 miles inland. These huge, old trees must have branches wide enough for nesting platforms at least eight inches wide, and be heavily covered with mosses and lichens. The Marbled Murrelet does not construct a nest for its one large egg (nearly as big as a chicken's) but simply lays the egg on the mosses. After one month of brooding by the parents, who fly back and forth between the sea and the nest, the one egg hatches as a large, fully downed chick that is soon

Chris Karrenberg and Linda Murtfeldt are members of Seattle Audubon's Conservation Committee and have long been involved in MAMU conservation efforts.

able to be left alone during the day. Then for another month, the parents take turns flying back and forth between the sea and the forest with small fish to feed the chick and keep it warm at night. When the chick grows and loses its downy feathers, it simply drops down off its nest in the tall tree and flies (for the first time) nonstop to saltwater, using streams and rivers as guides. When it reaches saltwater, it immediately begins to "fly" underwater to begin catching small fish and plankton to eat.

Even though the Marbled Murrelet was listed as a threatened species in Washington, Oregon, and California in 1992, it is becoming more and more of a rare bird. We have lost an estimated 30 percent of our MAMUs since 2001. The population estimate for the entire state of Washington is now only 7,494 birds, and that's been declining by 4.4 percent every year over the last decade.[33] That means next year alone we will lose 350 individuals. That doesn't give the species much time left. Historically we used to have a population ten times greater than this.

The solution to preserving the species is simple: Save the trees, save the bird.

While most Northern Spotted Owl habitat occurs on federal lands, a significant amount of MAMU nesting habitat occurs on state lands managed by the Washington Department of Natural Resources (DNR). This is particularly true in Southwest Washington, which is a critical area for MAMU recovery, as it contains much of the remaining high quality nesting habitat and the best opportunities to grow additional habitat. However, the DNR is charged with conflicting mandates for the land it manages—it is supposed to maximize revenues through timber harvest while protecting and restoring wildlife habitat, water quality, and recreational opportunities. One reason why DNR maximizes timber revenue is because of an archaic article in the State Constitution that mandates cutting forest, including old growth, to fund school construction, rural libraries, and hospitals. That law may have worked in 1898 when there was a sea of trees, but now, with most of the

old growth trees gone, a K-12 population exceeding one million in our fast-growing state, and constant demands for more school construction and rural services, it provides only a fraction of the money needed.

To try to deal with these conflicting mandates, DNR has been managing state forest lands under an interim plan called the Habitat Conservation Plan.[34] Ideally, this plan was designed to allow for logging while supposedly conserving several old growth obligate species such as the Marbled Murrelet and Northern Spotted Owl, as well as species that uses this ecosystem in its life cycle, such as Bull Trout and salmonids. Far from saving these species, this plan allows DNR to get permits from the U.S. Fish and Wildlife Service (which administers the Endangered Species Act) to log stands of forest that directly support Spotted Owls and nesting Marbled Murrelets, even if it means the birds may be killed.

Seattle Audubon has been on the front lines of MAMU protection for decades, fighting government agencies and timber companies in and out of court to stop unsustainable logging and clear cutting. Timber interests have mounted continuous attacks on the MAMU's endangered status, tried to change management plans, attempted to pass amendments to the current Habitat Conservation Plan, and tried to change critical habitat designations. Seattle Audubon has fought against all these attempts, as we also advocated for innovative alternative funding sources in the legislature, such as the Encumbered Lands Act.[35]

In addition, Seattle Audubon has been pressing for the long overdue Long-Term Conservation Strategy (LTCS) that DNR is supposed to enact to supplant its nineteen-year-old interim plan. Under pressure, the DNR commissioned a science report published in 2008 which developed a scientifically credible conservation strategy for MAMU.[36] However, protecting threatened wildlife clearly isn't the priority, according to Peter Goldmark, Washington State Commissioner of Public Lands and head of the Washington DNR. "This is a science team report only," he said. "It's not proposed as a plan because, first and foremost, our major responsibility is a fiduciary interest to supply revenue for the trust beneficiaries."[37]

Goldmark's comment illustrates the conflict of interest that happens when the same agency charged with supplying revenue through timber sales of trust forests is also charged with the recovery of species that depend on those forests. As Wyatt Golding, attorney at the Washington Forest Law Center, said, "[This] highlights the difficult position that well-intentioned DNR land managers are in. Timber interests pursuing profit put massive political pressure on the DNR, and they do so while hiding behind schoolchildren." [38]

In the meantime, schools aren't winning, the Marbled Murrelet isn't winning, and humans aren't winning, as more and more acres of a truly magnificent forest ecosystem are lost and fragmented.

Marbled Murrelet nest high up in an old growth tree. (Photograph © Nick Hatch, Pacific Northwest Research Station)

build new roads. They were destroying the ecological diversity of the Mount Baker-Snoqualmie, Gifford Pinchot, and Olympic National Forests.

At the same time, there was a graduate student, Eric Forsman, who was studying this bird called a Spotted Owl back in the early 1970s. Nobody knew much about the owl then. People did know it lived in the forest, but it was mysterious. We didn't know its biology, or where it nested, how many birds there were, or even if the population was going up or down. Eric went out into the field in Oregon forests and started doing censuses. He discovered that the Spotted Owl was totally dependent on ancient forests, that it was in big trouble, and the reason was habitat loss due to logging. The Spotted Owl used low elevation old growth forests, which were exactly what the timber companies were cutting. The owl was right in the sweet spot of controversy: You going to cut trees? Then you're going to lose the Spotted Owl.

I started going out into the field myself to see if I could find Spotted Owls in Washington. I wasn't a big birder back then, though I've gotten better since, but I was fascinated. I wanted to learn. So I went out with different people from Seattle Audubon and with state and federal

agency biologists, too. At first I took a recorder with me so I could play owl calls with a loudspeaker. But one biologist, Bill Stern, taught me how to call owls. Do you know how you call them? They bark like a dog.

There was one place we went where we tried to find owls along Forest Service roads out of North Bend on the North Fork Snoqualmie. Some of the habitat was clear cut, but there was a stand in there of 30 or 40 acres that hadn't been altered by cutting or by fire in over a thousand years. I remember. It was in 1979. The Forest Service tried to sell that stand to timber companies to be cut. They called it the Fly Timber Sale. We repeatedly went up there and called for owls. We thought if we found Spotted Owls in that stand, we might stop the timber sale.

The first owl we heard, I didn't see. It was around one in the morning. It was pouring rain. We'd worked our way up and down this Forest Service road with a state game biologist named Steve Sweeney. I'll never forget. All of a sudden, an owl called. We tried to find it. We were tromping through the middle of forest. It was wet and dark. I had a flashlight, but I kept tripping over Devil's Club and roots on the ground. It called again. We

Spotted Owl pair. (Photograph © Doug Schurman)

never saw it. We were at the tree where it was calling, and it was 30 or 40 feet up.

We made it back to the car, an old beat-up Volkswagen bug, one headlight out. I held the flashlight out the window as we drove. When we got home, that same day I called the Forest Service and told them we had found a Spotted Owl in the middle of the Fly Timber Sale area.

Seattle Audubon's Board voted to make an administrative appeal against the sale. The fight went on for years.

Eventually we had to hire an attorney. The issue was cumulative effects of harvesting in the lower part of that drainage, including private land. The whole lower drainage of that watershed had been cut by Weyerhaeuser, and the Regional Forester finally ruled that the Forest Service had to consider cumulative effects on the entire watershed when making sales of timber in the National Forests. So we beat them on that sale.

I remember the attorney's bill came

to about ten grand. We had no money to pay for it. Well, I had an idea. I work in retail. I've been doing that since I was a kid in the eighth grade in 1961, when I took a ten-day backpack trip in Olympic National Park with a group of other kids. We had tarps, a tent, crappy backpacks. We ate some kind of mush for breakfast and had sardines and dried apricots for lunch. I started catching fish and selling them to the big kids for a buck apiece.

At the time of the Fly Timber Sale, I had already quit working retail at Penney's and had opened my first Zumiez store in 1978. I sell teenage clothes. Zumiez is the largest action sports retailer in the world, currently.

I got a volunteer named Linda Wilkinson to do a pen and ink drawing of a Spotted Owl, and I had it put on tee shirts. Seattle Audubon sold ten grand worth of those tee shirts to pay the attorney's fees.

That was just the start. There were other people who worked with me on this—Dave Galvin, Bob Grant, Jed Marshall, Rick Rutz, among others. Rick was especially effective in following the Forest Service's convoluted process and figuring out how we could use legal tools to push for old growth protection.

Meanwhile, I organized other people

to call owls. We worked the areas north of Mount Rainier, including White River all the way up to the Snoqualmie Ranger District and Darrington. In 1976, the National Forest Management Act (NFMA) was passed, with a line in the act that said you have to have viable populations of all the major native vertebrate species in the National Forests. That was the sweet line for guarding Spotted Owls. If timber cuts eliminate Spotted Owls from a ranger district, the watershed, or forest, you're violating NFMA. You can't keep doing it. You need to cut less old growth. As the Forest Service came out with their plans to manage old growth timber sales and keep viable populations of Spotted Owls, we kept fighting them by turning up with reports of calling owls. They got sick of us because we were controlling the agenda.

But you see, the Forest Service works for us. They work for me and you. Right? The National Forests are public. We were saying to them, 'Come on, guys, this is not how we want them run.' Of course, the cuts are all set by Congress, with a budget to harvest a certain amount. The timber companies had their fans in Congress, and at that point, timber was a huge part of the economy in Washington. The timber companies were complaining about job losses because of the Spotted Owl. It became very controversial. But most of the job losses in logging were happening anyway because of technology upgrades. More efficiency in harvesting logs meant the timber companies needed fewer jobs. A lot of loggers blamed the owl.

But here's the thing. I was growing Zumiez stores in every timber town in the Northwest in the 1980s across the American West. While loggers were complaining about how the owl was driving down business, I was opening stores in Yakima, Wenatchee, Mount Vernon, Bellingham, Spokane, Portland, Eugene. In all these timber towns, my business was going through the roof because what we found is that people want to live around public lands. The economy was evolving. New businesses were coming in, and timber didn't mean as much as it used to.

You look at the Pacific Northwest now, and it's a world-class job engine. It's not just that public lands are good for the outdoor industry, action sports, and family activities, although those are important economically. You surf at public beaches, snowboard in ski areas on public lands, skate in public parks. But even more important, conservation is great for the economy because protected lands are where people want to live. They want to be able to look at the mountains and the forests, to go there and spend money in the towns nearby. They're buying gas at the local gas station, Twinkies in the 7-Eleven, beer, and binocs. They're all spending money for the things they love to do. Throughout America, but specifically in the American West, people want to be around nature. We need it in this disruptive world of globalization and technology. It's meaningful. That's a story you don't hear, but it's proven to me. I'm a business guy. I employ thousands of people. I know this to be a fact from my 38 years of running Zumiez.

People say the Spotted Owl keeps declining, and now it's because Barred Owls are moving in. They say it might be too late to save the Spotted Owl. It's true that the Spotted Owl populations are going down. Back when my kids were little, I'd take them up to call owls. We had a van, and we'd sleep overnight in it. I'd call owls at 1:00 or 2:00 in the morning. I remember one time I was with some different guys up in the Upper Clearwater and the West Fork White River. I had three responses of Spotted Owls in three stops about a third of a mile apart. Owls used to be all over there. I doubt there are any left now. I haven't heard a

Spotted Owl in 20 years.

But that's where the long view comes in. A hundred years from now may seem long to us, but that's just a blip of time, a blink. That grove in the Fly Timber Sale was untouched for a thousand years. If we do this right, if we continue to do what we've done since I started working on this with Audubon, the Spotted Owl will come back. If we hold Clinton's Northwest Forest Plan and the Roadless Rule[39] and protect the forests that are growing into early maturity so they can mature into old growth, then the Spotted Owls that are doing better in northern California and southern Oregon will come back up here again, all the way into southern British Columbia in Canada.

This is a long-term fight, and it's really important that we stay in it for the long term. We shouldn't be afraid. I love a fight. That's how I built Zumiez. Keep pushing until someone tells you no, then keep pushing more. Make the sale.

Right now, for example, I'm working to save the Arctic National Wildlife Refuge. I like to work on the big picture. The attraction to me is the protection of large chunks of landscape. Back in the

Opposite page: Old growth in the Hoh Rainforest. (Photograph © Loren Mooney)

A GRAND DESIGN: THE NORTHWEST FOREST PLAN

On April 2, 1993, newly elected President Bill Clinton came to Oregon to conduct hearings at a Northwest Forest Summit. The summit was designed to fulfill one of his campaign promises, namely, to settle disputes between environmentalists who wanted all the remaining old growth forests preserved, vs. the timber companies and their allies who wanted old growth logging to be preserved. The disputes had been going on for more than 80 years, ever since the budding environmental movement noticed how rapidly old growth forests were disappearing.[40]

A turning point had come three years earlier when environmental groups, including Seattle Audubon, pushed the federal government to list the Northern Spotted Owl as threatened or endangered, as defined by the Endangered Species Act. The owl was chosen to represent all the old growth species under threat because it is completely dependent on old growth habitat for its survival. Spotted Owls live their whole lives in old growth forests. Thus, by protecting the owl, we would be protecting the forests. In 1988, the Northern Spotted Owl was listed as endangered by the State of Washington.[41] In 1990, it was federally listed as threatened. The battles escalated. Clinton wished to broker a solution.

After taking testimony in 1993, the new President did something unprecedented. He convened a team of experts to study the laws and hot-button issues and make a recommendation for a long-term plan. Convening a team of experts was not new, of course. Politicians have been doing that for years. What *was* new, however, was that Clinton's team consisted of inter-agency representatives who for years had resisted working together within the Administration. These included the two agencies that managed most of the lands in question: the National Forest Service and the Bureau of Land Management. Also new was the speed with which Clinton demanded a resolution: He gave the committee three months. But what was truly eye-popping was Clinton's directive to come up with a long-term plan. By long-term, he meant a plan that would govern forestry practices on federal

lands for the next 100 to 200 years.

The team drafted ten optional plans, and on July 1, 1993, the agencies agreed on a "Forest Plan for a Sustainable Economy and a Sustainable Environment."[42] Officially, this action was called a Record of Decision. It came to be known as the Northwest Forest Plan.

The plan affected 24 million acres of federally owned land, the area defined as the range of the Northern Spotted Owl. The plan was guided by five principles established by Clinton:

- National Forests are to be managed for both humans and ecology. Timber sales should go forward as long as the cuts preserve the overall health of the forests.
- Wildlife, including fish, need to be protected and therefore their habitat needs must be taken into account.
- Decisions about logging and other economic practices should be based on solid, credible science.
- Timber sales should be predictable and sustainable such that they will not degrade the environment.
- Federal agencies must work together collaboratively to make sure these things happen.

Following these principles, the plan acknowledged that approximately 30 percent of federal lands within the range of the Northern Spotted Owl had already been set aside by Congress for various purposes (National Parks, Wilderness Areas, National Monuments, Wild and Scenic Rivers, National Wildlife Refuges, and Department of Defense lands). This amounted to 7,320,600 acres. The plan divided the remaining 70 percent of federal lands occupied by Northern Spotted Owls into six categories:

- 30 percent was designated as Late-Successional Reserves, defined as old growth forest that would be preserved specifically for Spotted Owls and other species dependent on this habitat. These "other species" included the Marbled Murrelet, another threatened species identified as an obligate old growth species, due to the fact that these little seabirds required ancient forests in which to nest. Late-Successional Reserves would not be logged for timber, although thinning and salvage operations would be allowed. The lands in this category amounted to 7,430,800 acres.

- 6 percent was designated as Adaptive Management Areas, i.e., areas that would be logged but also used to develop new strategies for sustainable yield that would meet undefined social and community objectives. These lands amounted to 1,521,800 acres.
- 1 percent was designated as Managed Late-Successional Areas, i.e., areas that have been identified as the territory of Spotted Owl pairs, as well as buffer areas surrounding each pair's territory. These lands amounted to 102,200 acres.
- 6 percent was administratively withdrawn because these areas were already designated for uses other than timber (recreation, for example). These lands amounted to 1,477,100 acres.
- 11 percent was set aside as Riparian Reserves, i.e., lands lying within the Spotted Owl range that are not old growth forest. These lands are generally found along rivers, streams, and wetlands and cannot be logged. Many of these areas need protection for fish. They comprise 2,627,500 acres.
- 16 percent was called "Matrix," a made-up term that simply identifies stands where most of the logging will occur. These lands amount to 3,975,300 acres.

Recently, the Regional Ecosystem Office (REO, the inter-agency group responsible for monitoring the plan) released its long-awaited draft report on the 20th anniversary of the plan. The report ostensibly addressed one main question:Was the plan working?

In terms of habitat conservation, the report gives a qualified yes. The original plan had allowed for a certain percentage of lost habitat due to logging and wildfires. The loss due to wildfires was about 2.5 percent per decade, which had been predicted. Unfortunately, some areas within the plan suffered disproportionate losses, mainly dry areas that are more subject to wildfires. The loss of such habitat in Washington was more than 7 percent per decade. Losses from logging were much less than had been predicted—25 percent less, in fact. This was due to legal challenges preventing or delaying

cuts. Of great concern was the continuing loss of habitat on private lands abutting federally owned Spotted Owl habitat. Owls don't know about property lines, and an honest evaluation of habitat loss must take into account the fact that dispersal of young owls might be negatively impacted by these losses. Eventually, growth of protected younger stands of trees will replace habitat lost to logging and wildfires, but not enough time has passed for that to happen yet. For now, net habitat loss continues to occur—the loss over the past 20 years has been 1.5 percent.[43]

In terms of Spotted Owl populations, the REO has yet to release findings of its 20th-year analysis. However, the fifteenth-year analysis showed the picture was far grimmer with regard to Spotted Owl preservation than it was for habitat preservation. Spotted Owls continued to decline at significant rates, up to 7.1 percent per year. Part of this is due to continued habitat loss. But even in places where habitat was stable or had increased, owl populations continued to fall.[44]

It is thought that a big cause of continued decline might be the fact that Barred Owls have invaded the Spotted Owls' habitat. Barred Owls are eastern cousins of Spotted Owls. Originally, they were confined to their range in the East and Midwest by the Great Plains, which blocked them from expanding westward. However, over the past century, as people spread out across the continent and built towns and cities, the Barred Owls followed. Unlike Spotted Owls, Barred Owls are not fussy about their diet or their breeding requirements. They eat a wide variety of prey, including Norway Rats, common in cities. They don't mind the presence of people nearby and can nest in any kind of tree. They are aggressive on their territory. When their range expanded to include

old growth forests in the Pacific Northwest, they began to out-compete the native Spotted Owls, killing them, driving them away, or hybridizing with them and diluting their gene pool. Basically, when Barred Owls move in, Spotted Owls disappear.

In 2014, the U.S. Fish and Wildlife Service began shooting Barred Owls in Spotted Owl habitat. The jury is still out as to whether this will work. The hope is that Spotted Owls can hang on long enough for their habitat to regenerate, as young stands of protected forest age into suitable habitat.

late 1990s, I was working in D.C. to get Clinton to do something big on his way out the door. It was all very political. His legacy ultimately became the Roadless Area Conservation Rule, which started with the ancient forest fight right here, which Seattle Audubon was right in the middle of. That eventually saved 58 million acres of ancient forest in the American West.

In this kind of fight, you take what the opposition gives you, and it becomes an opportunity. There's always something. Years ago, it was the feather trade and the Whooping Crane. You take what the opposition gives you, and you get in the fight. There will be new things. Climate change is the one we're talking about now, and it's a big issue. But I don't understand how anyone could be cynical about it. We could never have dreamed when we started this back in the 1970s that within 20 years, we would have a Roadless Rule and so much of the last ancient forests in the American West would be protected.

As long as I've been doing this work, and as long as our country has been around, we figure things out. We shouldn't be depressed. We should be full of hope."

ANCIENT FOREST TIMELINE: A HISTORY OF BATTLES TO PRESERVE THE LAST GIANTS

FEBRUARY 1, 1905 The Transfer Act passed, creating the U.S. Forest Service and putting all National Forest Reserves in its charge. [33 Stat. 628] From its inception, the Forest Service saw its mission as the management of National Forests for sustainable timber harvest, not for the preservation of intact ecosystems.

FEBRUARY 7, 1936 When Mexico signed onto the Migratory Bird Treaty that we had already established with Canada, the Spotted Owl was added to the list of migratory birds that the treaty protected. The Mexican subspecies of Spotted Owl is migratory; the Northern subspecies in Washington is not. However, the treaty made no distinction about subspecies, and so all Spotted Owls were added.[45]

JUNE 12, 1960 Multiple-Use Sustained-Yield Act passed, directing the Forest Service to manage National Forests for multiple uses, not just for logging. Those uses included wildlife preservation and recreation. It was the first time such non-timber uses of National Forests were codified into law. [74 Stat. 215]

SEPTEMBER 3, 1964 Wilderness Act passed, creating the legal designation of wilderness as protected areas to be as free as possible from human influences. [78 Stat. 890]

DECEMBER 23, 1969 National Environmental Policy Act (NEPA) passed, requiring federal agencies to prepare an environmental impact statement (EIS) before they took major actions that might significantly affect the environment. [83 Stat. 852]

MAY 19, 1971 State Environmental Policy Act (SEPA) passed, requiring all state agencies to ensure that environmental values are considered before they take action. [1971 Wash. Sess. Laws 1st Ex. Sess. Ch. 109]

MARCH 3, 1973 Endangered Species Act (ESA) passed. Not only did this law set up categories of species at risk, but it included a broader definition of "taking" (i.e., killing) than the Migratory Bird Treaty had established in 1916, when the treaty was signed. "Taking" now included harassing and harming listed species. This meant that from now on, habitat destruction could be considered an act of taking if the destruction was enough to affect survival of the species. [87 Stat. 884]

FEBRUARY 14, 1974 Washington State Forest Practices Act passed, delegating control of state forest practices to a board, including elected officials, the general public, and timber industry representatives. The timber industry pressed for exemptions from SEPA, which were granted, creating conflicts between these two laws and their goals. [1974 Wash. Sess. Laws 1st Ex. Sess. Ch. 137]

OCTOBER 22, 1976 National Forest Management Act (NFMA) passed, requiring the Secretary of Agriculture to develop Land and Resource Management Plans (LRMPs) for every National Forest, individually. [90 Stat. 2949] The intent was to manage the forests as ecosystems rather than as individual trees to be cut or not, so that viable populations of native vertebrate species would be conserved. The "viability clause" was key because it meant the Forest Service could select indicator species to help plan habitat preservation, but it could not design its plans for the needs of just that one species.

DECEMBER 1978 The Oregon-Washington Interagency Wildlife Committee, a group established to make recommendations for Spotted Owl management, recommended the adoption of 300-acre Spotted Owl Habitat Areas (SOHAs) around known nests. These would be old growth groves left untouched. The implication was that these circles would be enough habitat to preserve Spotted Owl reproduction.[46]

OCTOBER 14, 1983 Seattle Audubon appealed the Fly Timber sale. [See pp. 23-25 above.]

JULY 3, 1984 The Washington State Wilderness Act passed, designating some 1.2 million acres of National Forest lands in the State as protected Wilderness Areas. [98 Stat. 299]

1984 The Forest Service released its LRMP for our region, inviting public comment. Environmentalists objected to much in the plan, including the notion of SOHAs, which would theoretically fragment the forest in patterns that did not meet the biological needs of the owls.

NOVEMBER 28, 1986 Green World, a small environmental advocacy group based in Massachusetts, petitioned the Fish and Wildlife Service to declare the Spotted Owl endangered.

JULY 31, 1987 Seattle Audubon and 28 other environmental groups, fearing that Green World's standing and petition were weak, petitioned Fish and Wildlife to list the owl. On December 23, 1987, the Forest Service announced it would not list the owl. [52 Fed. Reg. 48554]

NOVEMBER 17, 1988 The environmental groups sued. Fish and Wildlife eventually did list the owl as threatened.[47]

DECEMBER 12, 1988 The Forest Service issued a Record of Decision—an administrative act—to sell several tracts of old growth forest for timber, based on guidelines that it said were adequate to meet NFMA requirements to preserve the viability of species in the ecosystem.[48]

FEBRUARY 8, 1989 Seattle Audubon filed suit, claiming that the Forest Service, in its Record of Decision, had not complied with its mandate to protect the Northern Spotted Owl. [*Seattle Audubon v. Robertson*, 503 U.S. 429 (1992)]

APRIL 25, 1989 Fish and Wildlife announced its intent to list the Northern Spotted Owl as threatened, under the Endangered Species Act, prompting Congress to add a rider to an appropriations bill that allowed timber companies to keep cutting old growth for one year. (Section 318; see below).

OCTOBER 23, 1989 Congress passed an appropriations bill which included Section 318, directing the Forest Service and Bureau of Land Management (the two agencies responsible for public lands within the known range of Northern Spotted Owls) to sell 5.8 billion board feet of timber from old growth forests in Washington and Oregon. [103 Stat. 701, 745-50] This sale applied only to fiscal year 1989 but could be renewed for another year. Known Spotted Owl habitat was to be preserved, but Congress decided (not scientifically) that there was enough habitat left in the National Forests to sustain Spotted Owls. Seattle Audubon sued over this "Rider from Hell" but ultimately lost. The timber was cut.

MAY 1990 A group of agencies known as the Interagency Scientific Committee to Address the Conservation of the Northern Spotted Owl (ISC) released its proposal to protect the owl. It replaced the notion of SOHAs with the idea that larger blocks of protected habitat (Habitat Conservation Areas, or HCAs) would work better. Each HCA was supposed to hold 20 pairs of owls and be separated from the next HCA by a maximum distance of twelve miles, effectively protecting 7.7 million acres of ancient forest, including 3.1 million acres of harvestable timber. Yet the report also acknowledged that this strategy would result in the loss of up to 50 percent of the owls before habitat and owls reached equilibrium.[49]

JUNE 26, 1990 U.S. Fish and Wildlife Service listed the Northern Spotted Owl as threatened. [55 Fed. Reg. 26114]

OCTOBER 1990 The Forest Service released its plan to conserve the Spotted Owl while allowing timber sales of old growth to go forward. The plan was poorly conceived. It did not include an environmental impact statement (EIS) as required by the National Environmental Policy Act (NEPA), nor did it state standards or guidelines for how timber sales were to be carried out while also preserving Spotted Owl habitat (as required by the National Forest Management Act (NFMA).

FEBRUARY 26, 1991 In *Northern Spotted Owl v. Lujan*, a suit joined by National Audubon, the court ruled that Fish and Wildlife was compelled to designate critical habitat for the owl, as required by its ESA listing. Fish and Wildlife had claimed that it was impossible to determine critical habitat for the owl. [758 F.Supp. 621 (W.D. Wash. 1991)]

MARCH 7, 1991 In *Seattle Audubon v. Evans*, Seattle Audubon sued the Forest Service for taking the position that since the Spotted Owl was now listed as threatened, the Forest Service no longer had to make any plans to maintain the viability of the species as required by NFMA. Judge William Dwyer ruled in favor of Seattle Audubon, saying, "The duty to maintain viable populations of existing vertebrate species requires planning for the entire biological community—not for one species alone. It is distinct from the duty, under the ESA, to save a listed species from extinction." On May 23, 1991, Dwyer enjoined the Forest Service from making further timber sales until it came up with standards and guidelines to ensure the viability of the owl and the ecosystem. His decision fell like a bombshell on the timber industry and government agencies. Nothing like this had ever happened before. [771 F.Supp. 1081 (W.D. Wash. 1991)]

JANUARY 31, 1992 The Forest Service released its plan to comply with Dwyer's ruling. Two months later, on March 3, 1992, it released a new Record of Decision, in which it adopted the recommendations of the ISC. [57 Fed.Reg. 8621]

JULY 2, 1992 In *Seattle Audubon Society v. Moseley*, Seattle Audubon sued the U.S. Forest Service for not complying with NEPA in providing a final EIS in its ISC-based plan. The court enjoined the Forest Service from further timber sales until it came up with a viable plan to protect the owl. [98 F.Supp. 1484 (W.D. Wash. 1992)]

SEPTEMBER 28, 1992 The Fish and Wildlife Service listed the Marbled Murrelet as threatened. [57 Fed. Reg. 45328]

APRIL 2, 1993 President Bill Clinton held the Northwest Forest Summit in Portland, Oregon, to work out a compromise to end all these disputes among timber interests, environmental groups, and government agencies. After the conference, Clinton ordered the agencies to develop a plan, which they released on July 1, 1993. It came to be known as the Northwest Forest Plan. [See sidebar on pp. 26-27 above.]

APRIL 13, 1994 The Forest Service released its management guidelines pursuant to the court's findings that they had violated the NEPA process. The new guidelines incorporated Alternative 9, the alternative with the least protection for owls.

DECEMBER 21, 1994 In *Seattle Audubon Society v. Lyons*, Judge Dwyer accepted the Forest Service's Alternative 9 as the bare minimum to meet NEPA and NFMA requirements for logging in Spotted Owl habitat. Dwyer warned that any deviation toward more logging would not be tolerated. [871 F.Supp. 1291 (W.D. Wash. 1994)]

JANUARY 12, 2001 The U.S. Forest Service under Clinton's directive administratively established the Roadless Area Conservation Rule, prohibiting road construction on 58.5 million acres of National Forest lands, effectively blocking logging from those areas.[50]

AUGUST 1, 2007 In *Seattle Audubon Society v. Sutherland*, Seattle Audubon and Kittitas Audubon asked the court to enjoin logging on private lands held by Weyerhaeuser, under the Forest Practices Act. The court agreed to enjoin logging of four "circles" of Northern Spotted Owl habitat, a total of 56,000 acres. DNR was not enjoined from issuing permits to log 200 other circles because Seattle Audubon was unable to show they were occupied by Northern Spotted Owls. In a later settlement, the State Practices Board established a Policy Working Group to recommend measures to conserve the owl on non-federal lands.[51]

SEPTEMBER 2008 A government-sponsored science team released its recommendations for DNR's management of ancient forests on the Olympic Peninsula and in Southwest Washington to preserve Marbled Murrelet nesting habitat. The report recommended that 176,000 acres of DNR lands be managed to preserve "high-quality nesting habitat," basically in perpetuity.[52]

NOVEMBER 10, 2009 The Northern Spotted Owl Policy Working Group (established as a result of the *Seattle Audubon Society v. Sutherland* decision) released its recommendations for managing Northern Spotted Owl habitat on private lands, within parameters that included voluntary incentives for conservation; science-based decisions; sustainable logging; and control of invasive Barred Owls.[53]

FEBRUARY 10, 2010 The Northern Spotted Owl Policy Working Group released its final report to the Forest Practices Board.

NOVEMBER 1, 2013 President Barack Obama released his Climate Change Executive Order directing federal agencies that manage forests to factor in the carbon sequestration that forests—especially ancient forests—contribute to mitigate climate change. [Exec. Ord. 13653, 78 Fed. Reg. 66817]

CURRENTLY The Forest Service is in the process of taking public input on revisions to the Northwest Forest Plan.

RIVER WILD, RIVER FREE
Richard Rutz: Elwha Dams

Richard Rutz. (Photograph © Rebecca Hoff)

It started so small—an expired license, a missed deadline, a bureaucratic oversight. Mistakes easily corrected, you would think, and yet they ended in the largest removal of dams in our history.

The Elwha River flows from a snowfinger that points down from the Olympic Mountains deep in Olympic National Park. The Elwha Snowfinger is a perennial snowfield that continuously feeds the Elwha as it flows 45 miles to empty into the Strait of Juan de Fuca. The river's rush of cold water used to produce some of the biggest salmon in the world, salmon that sustained the Lower Elwha Klallam Tribe from time immemorial.

All that ended in 1913 with the completion of the Elwha Dam, the ill-constructed dream of a Canadian-born entrepreneur who came to Port Angeles in 1890 to make his fortune. Thomas Aldwell was a brash young man who looked at the river and saw dollar signs. He staked a claim for a homestead at the point where the river rushes through a narrow gorge, the perfect place for a dam. Quietly, he bought up other property, too, until he controlled all the land around the future dam. Then he went looking for investors. The town of Port Angeles was wildly enthusiastic about the notion of a dam that would produce cheap energy to power all kinds of industries, but especially lumber and paper mills. Eastern investors became equally enthusiastic, and soon Aldwell had enough money to begin building.

The dam went up slowly, shoddily, and illegally—Aldwell managed to get the cooperation of the Washington State fish commissioner, Leslie Darwin, to overlook a law that required dams to be built in such a way as to allow fish to go upriver.[54] Unfortunately, Aldwell cut too many corners during construction, and the lower part of the dam gave way in 1912, opening a huge hole in the dam. Undaunted, Aldwell had the hole plugged with whatever he could use—boulders, mattresses of fir logs, soil, and gravel. None of it was footed into bedrock as it should have been, but the hole was closed and the dam became a functioning hydropower facility. In 1927, another dam further upriver, the Glines Canyon Dam, was built.

These two dams furnished power to a mill in town. But the dreams of glory that Aldwell had envisioned—Port Angeles a major industrial hub and Aldwell the hero—never materialized. Such dreams blessed Seattle and Tacoma instead, and Port Angeles remained a small, rather isolated town.

Fast forward 50 years and there begins a strange, almost surreal tale of valor, vision, and grit whose unlikely hero was a bespectacled biologist with a passion for wilderness and a fearless disregard for the powers that be. Richard Rutz was the Science Advisor for Seattle Audubon and a member of the Conservation Committee. He became interested in energy issues that had begun to fester in Washington during the 1970s, when government experts forecast ominous energy shortages in our region.

At that time, the last of the major dams in the region had been built. It was clear that no new big dams were going to solve the crisis. The Bonneville Power Administration, which operates 31 federal hydroelectric projects in the Northwest, had reached the end of its ability to expand its production of cheap power for customers throughout the region. Other alternatives seemed equally dismal. Resistance to nuclear energy, always high in Washington State, was growing stronger, as cost overruns began to derail the efforts of the Washington Public Power Supply System to build five nuclear power plants, three at Hanford and two at Satsop.[55]

People's fears of an energy shortage were fed by the oil crisis of 1973, which was created by OPEC countries choking off supplies. People waiting in long gas lines made no distinction between gas in their cars and electricity in their homes. It was all just a big energy crisis to them. What to do?

In 1978, Congress passed the Public Utility Regulatory Policies Act (PURPA), whose purpose was to promote energy conservation and the development of more renewable energy sources.[56] PURPA provided favorable terms to companies that produced electricity from renewables. It also enabled non-utility developers to produce power for use by customers of public utilities.

PURPA unexpectedly set off a gold rush among energy suppliers, as they looked for any river or stream they could get a license to dam. Talk started flowing about how the utilities were going to apply for scores of licenses to build new dams. Environmentalists were appalled. To deal with the flood of license applications and figure out which ones, if any, could be opposed, Seattle Audubon delegated a subcommittee on energy to look into it. Rick Rutz served on that subcommittee and volunteered for several other environmental groups. His research turned him into an expert on the environmental studies and licensing process for dams.

"I'm trained in biological sciences. I have a Ph.D. in zoology, with a minor in genetics and biochemistry. I'm not an attorney, but I can read technical literature and understand it, interpret findings by other people, and apply them to new situations. It's kind of like reading a recipe. There are all these directions, but if you can read them properly, you can cook. In the same way, there are many rules governing energy projects, and it's all in heavy language, but if you can read it, you can find out all sorts of things.

When PURPA was passed, one purpose was to force public utilities to purchase power from alternative producers, and not just from big power plants. But it had the unintended consequence of encouraging big utilities to look for small hydro developments. All of a sudden there were applications for dams everywhere—over 70 applications for development in the Snohomish River basin, 40 in the Skagit basin, and 30 in another. Many were in places we considered to be important for wildlife, potential wilderness designation, and recreational uses.

Fighting these applications taught me a lot about how the system works. One thing I learned was how important the licensing process is. Putting dams on federal waterways requires a license under the Federal Power Act of 1920.[57] But the licensing process is hostile to public participation. It's conducted in a quasi-judicial manner, and to participate effectively, you need to formally intervene in the process, arguing standing and setting forth your arguments in a legalistic way.

I spent a lot of time tracking these applications, researching them, and filing for interventions. I became aware of the fact that one of the provisions of the Federal Power Act prevented the Federal Energy Regulatory Commission (FERC) from giving licenses longer than 50 years. In the Congressional discussion for the act, it said the purpose of the 50-year limit was so that people didn't get a permanent lock on a dam. The government might change its mind, in which case they would take away the license, and the project would have to come out.

In 1983, I was working with Don Parks of the Boeing Employees Alpine Society and Alpine Lakes Protection Society. We were studying timber harvest reports for the Olympic National Forest as part of the technical work in support of what would become the Washington State Wilderness Act of 1984. As we looked at the north part of the forest, Don said, 'The Elwha, that's where those

stupid dams are. We should have blown those things up years ago.'

I thought, 'I don't know anything about those dams. I should look them up and see what's what.' So I did, and I found that there were two dams on the Elwha, one on the Lower Elwha 4.9 miles up from the river's mouth on the Strait of Juan de Fuca, and one 11.5 miles up in Glines Canyon. The original license for one had expired in 1977, and the two dams were being operated conjointly, so they both needed to be licensed. But the owners hadn't moved very fast on licensing and relicensing. They didn't want to do anything for fisheries mitigation. It was money. So in 1977, FERC just gave them a temporary one-year license for a piddling amount of money. After that, the owners didn't have to do anything to keep getting an extension except file an annual report.

With my experience from other hydro proceedings, I thoroughly examined the situation, and the legislative and legal records. In doing so, I came upon information that I used to put forward a completely new idea and rationale, based on the following:

1. The Federal Water Power Act was amended on March 3, 1921, to exclude licensing of water power

projects in National Parks or National Monuments without Congressional authorization.[58]

2. On June 29, 1938, Congress passed an act that established the Olympic National Park.[59] While the construction and licensing of the Glines Canyon Dam predated the establishment of the National Park, no 'grandfathered' nonconforming use was provided for in the act.

3. In 1983, the Yakima Indian Nation, state and federal agencies, and National Wildlife Federation petitioned the Ninth Circuit Court of Appeals to set aside a new license granted for the Rock Island Dam. In 1984 the Court rejected FERC's positions, voided the new license, and among other things found that 'relicensing involves a new commitment of the resource' and is 'more akin to an irreversible and irretrievable commitment of a public resource than a mere continuation of the status quo.'[60]

By these findings, I reasoned:

- Relicensing is a not a continuation of an old license, but a new proceeding and new commitment of the resource;

- Under the 1921 Federal Water Power Act, relicensing, like licensing, cannot occur within a National Park or Monument without Congressional authorization;

- The establishment of the Olympic National Park did not provide for the continuation of the Glines Canyon Dam. No Congressional authorization for licensing the dam in the Park existed;

- The Federal Power Act of 1920 provides that a nonfederal hydro project on U.S. waters must be licensed.

Therefore, FERC had no authority to relicense the Glines Canyon Dam. Without a new license, by law the dam must come out.

I'm not an attorney, but this was my reading of the laws and the legislative history. I shipped this around to various people, and most attorneys I talked to said, 'That's not what the law says. You're not an attorney. You're wrong about this.'

Most people told me I was misguided, wrong, or insane. That was actually a fairly common response. 'You're crazy, Rick. This is the craziest thing we ever heard of.' This included many people in the environmental community, who feared political consequences from trying to remove working dams. But enough

people were supportive of my reasoning for me to proceed. Importantly, if correct, there was a duty to proceed in order to prevent an unlawful relicensing of a dam within a National Park.

In 1983, it looked like FERC was going to proceed with the real licensing. Various agencies and the Lower Elwha Klallam Tribe wanted to intervene in the process. In hydropower licensing, FERC places a notice in the Federal Register. If you want to intervene, you have 30 days to file. If you file in time, you are automatically a party to the proceeding. If you file even one day late, you're 'out of time,' and you are excluded from the proceeding unless you are expressly granted intervention.

Permission is hard to get, but the thing is, if you're one day late or two years late, it's all the same. FERC wanted the relicensing to go ahead without any trouble. They didn't want anyone to become a party to the proceeding. But nothing much had happened since 1977, so allowing people in would not hold up or harm the proceeding. Furthermore, in 1983 there was no way to get the dams relicensed without the Tribe being part of the proceeding.[61] Once FERC allowed the Tribe in, they had to allow in the agencies, too. The upper dam was in the

Olympic National Park, so Parks wanted in. Fish and Wildlife wanted in. So did the Bureau of Indian Affairs.

We wanted in, too. This river was the biggest drainage in the Park, and it was totally closed off to fish down at mile 4.9. The fish populations were just going down, down, and down. They were in danger of dying out in the river. So I felt this needed to be pushed. Everything that I'd done in reading regulations and technical information and the law said this reasoning was correct. Yes, it was an unexpected result. It had big implications. But that didn't make it wrong. Just unexpected.

I took my reasoning to various conservation groups with interests in the Olympic National Park. I realized this was going to be politically big if we went forward with it. It was something that would probably end up in court. FERC and the owners were going to fight. I needed to get groups with standing to come in on this. Seattle Audubon was one of them. An intervention on this relicensing had very big fish and wildlife considerations. Restoring the health of the Elwha River for the Olympic National Park was about as big as those get. Seattle Audubon could show that it had a long-standing interest in visiting and using the Park and in advocating for it. I ran my idea past John Lundin, who was Seattle Audubon's Legal Advisor. He thought it was worth trying. But the Board wasn't so sure. They had a big debate, but in the end, they voted in favor of intervening. So I had my first group onboard. Subsequently, Friends of the Earth, Olympic Park Associates, and the Sierra Club-Cascade Chapter joined in the motion to intervene.[62]

So now we were four. We filed for intervenor status, and in May 1984, we were granted intervention. We were a party to the proceedings.[63] Being a party means that if FERC takes an action that you don't like, you have the standing to sue for grievance. That's really important. Also, as a party you must be provided with copies of everything.

The interventions by the Lower Elwha Klallam Tribe and the four conservation groups were the first to petition for dam removal in a FERC proceeding. Once we were a party, we started making requests. We wanted studies of this issue, we wanted studies of that approach. We wanted an Environmental Impact Statement (EIS). We wanted the EIS to have dam removal as a full alternative. That was critically important: It had never before been formally considered. In FERC's first EIS proposal, dam removal was excluded as an alternative from further consideration because they said it was not a feasible alternative. But of course it was feasible—it had to be. All things wear out and must be removed or replaced eventually. FERC would be capricious and irresponsible to allow dams in streams if they couldn't safely be removed. Removal became a full alternative only when we threatened to take it to court.

Lower Elwha Dam and powerhouse, 2005. (Photograph by Larry Ward, Lower Elwha Klallam Fisheries Biologist; courtesy of DancingBear, Wikimedia)

After the interventions were granted, the conservation groups, the Tribe, and the agencies gradually established a working protocol. The agencies and Tribe worked on fisheries measures and protocols. The conservation groups and the National Park Service were the leads on wildlife, recreation, and Park issues among others, with the Tribe providing support. In political matters, the main load for convincing the Congressional delegation to back (or not hinder) the effort to remove the dams fell totally on the conservation groups and the Tribe. We and the Tribe also had the main work of countering moves by the dam owners to undermine or circumvent the process.

In addition to the illegality of licensing the upper dam, the conservation groups took issue with the safety of the Lower Elwha Dam. When under construction in 1912, it had failed, blowing out a 100-foot hole beneath the dam. The hole was filled with whatever material came to hand at the time.

I had company people yell at me in public meetings about how irresponsible I was, saying the dam was unsafe, and how I was needlessly alarming people. But the EIS was supposed to review the footings of the dam, as well as the dam itself. To do that, it was necessary to take core samples. The company would not allow its engineers to take cores through the material underneath the dam. Why? Because no one knew what was in there. When the dam failed in 1912, the construction workers had dumped whatever they could to plug the hole. The fact was, nobody knew how stable the dam was, and if they drilled cores through there, the engineers worried it might destabilize the dam. We confronted the owners about this, and their rhetoric went down.

However, the owners still claimed the dams were necessary because of the power they supplied to the local mill. They claimed that if the dams were removed, the mill would become uneconomic, and people would be put out of work. They went to Representative Al Swift, the Congressman from the district, and convinced him that he should introduce a bill that would authorize FERC to issue a license, no matter what.

It was a threat we had to counter. When we learned about this, we decided to reply with the "Creative Solution" strategy that was conceived by Jim Baker of Friends of the Earth. All of the power of the dams went to one paper mill, which had an energy-intensive pulp-grinding process. The mill was old and had made no capital improvements to conserve energy. The likelihood was, in a mill of this size and with this kind of industrial process, energy conservation opportunities could be found that would completely obviate the need for the power contribution of the dams. Swift had been a lead sponsor of the Pacific Northwest Electric Power Planning and Conservation Act.[64] We met with him and told him that we would agree to a conservation audit of the mill by Bonneville Power Administration—not a friend of ours—and would abide by their findings. We were convinced that enough energy conservation would be found. We also observed that if the owners were not willing to have the audit performed, they might be lying or hiding something. Swift met with them and asked them to conduct the audit, and they refused. Swift then told them that there would be no legislative fix, that they would have to fight it out in the FERC proceeding or in court. (Later, after the fighting was over, such an audit was performed, and conservation opportunities in excess of the power supplied by the dams were indeed identified.)

Meanwhile, FERC officials had decided they did not agree with my reasoning, and felt they had authority to relicense the upper dam. Representative John

Conyers requested the Office of the Solicitor General and the General Accounting Office of the federal government to review our arguments, which they did. They supported my conclusions and those of the agencies and Tribe. Even so, FERC announced they were planning to relicense the dams anyway, despite everything we had done. We filed notice that we were going to court for enforcement of the Federal Power Act. That precipitated a crisis, and the Washington Congressional delegation swung into action. In 1992, Congress passed the Elwha River Ecosystem and Fisheries Restoration Act,[65] which said the dams would have to come out. But while we had won the main issue, the Congressional delegation did not want to force the owners to pay the costs of taking out the dams. The government would have to pay to remove them.

Now we had to get the money appropriated—a hundred million dollars. The main way environmental projects are funded is through the Land and Water Conservation Fund. Lots of people want that money. So every year we had to have our Congressional delegation

The Elwha River today. (Photograph © Steve Ringman, Seattle Times)

lobby for an appropriation from that fund. Some years the government didn't allocate any money to us. When they did, the money went into an account, but then that became a worry because as it grew, it became a target. Other groups said, 'We could use that money instead of them. They're never going to get there.' So each year we had to fight to defend what we had, plus get more.

Because Congress did not make the companies pay for removal of the dams, it fell to the conservation groups and the Tribe to lobby Congress over the years to appropriate the money. While it took us nine years to get the bill to remove the dams, it took another nineteen years before we had the money to let the contract for deconstruction.[66] What finally put us over the top was the recession. Congress passed an act in 2009 which said there were a lot of communities that were in dire straits, and some monies would be available to help communities out, but they had to compete for it. One of the things that gave you points was if your project had environmental benefits.[67] Representative Norm Dicks looked at our project and said, 'The North Peninsula is as hard hit as anybody, and this has got the best environmental benefit

you can imagine,' so in one fell swoop we were able to acquire the rest of the needed money.

I didn't consider the fight to be won until the government let the contract for the company to actually start deconstructing the dam. The day they announced that the contract had been let was the day I celebrated. It was a great victory.

But fighting and litigation are actually the smallest part of what we do. They're the last resort, really. People think environmental groups are ready to litigate at the drop of a hat, but quite the opposite is true. Most of the things that get done are things that nobody sees. You go to meetings. You talk to people. You write letters. You advocate for things, and you do all this for years. You can't just show up at the last minute and make demands.

You hope what you're doing will lead to some desired conclusion, but most of it is work you can't even put your finger on and say, 'That was formative,' or 'That letter I wrote produced this result.' Most of what you do—you never really know the outcome of your effort. You may never see anything come of it. Maybe nothing does come of it. In the worst

case, you may lose. But you certainly would have lost if you hadn't done anything. There's nothing inevitable about any of this. Working for the environment is hard. You have monied interests against you. It's difficult to mobilize people. It takes money and resources that often you don't have.

Hardest of all, you can never say, 'We've won and now we're done.' If you save something from being developed, it's still there potentially to be developed. You can destroy something forever. But save it forever? Politics can change it all.

What keeps that from happening is the fact that enough people care. What preserves the environment is a commitment by people to save the things they feel are important, that enrich our lives and other people's lives. To me, the Elwha River was one such thing, a place worth caring about, a place worth fighting for.

Things like this aren't started by government agencies or political leaders, they're not miracles, and they aren't grand experiments. They are done because people work hard and refuse to be put off. They are done because the public makes them happen.[68]

Long live the Elwha!"

SAVING NATURE, ONE PIECE AT A TIME
John W. Lundin: Martin Miller Fund

Consider the planet and all it holds: 7.4 billion people; an estimated 8.7 million different species with a biomass of 4 billion tons; an atmosphere with a mass 5.67 trillion tons; and oceans, lakes, and streams with a volume of water that would fill more than 3 million cubic miles.

Amid all the living things, all that hot air, all those miles of water, one human being amounts to less than the proverbial drop in a bucket. Can a single person make even a dent in the world's problems when the world is so unimaginably large? Indeed, can any one make any difference at all?

For architect, conservationist, and poet Martin Miller and a team of dedicated Seattle Audubon members, the answer to these questions is a most emphatic yes. Years ago, they got together to establish a fund to buy critical habitat and preserve it in perpetuity. Working with other environmental organizations and land trusts all across the state, the Martin Miller Fund has helped preserve more than 31,000 acres of habitat. Forever. Here, in the words of long-time committee member John W. Lundin, is their story.

John W. Lundin. (Photograph courtesy of Constance Sidles)

"Martin Miller was an architect who had retired from government work and had bought 32 acres of forested habitat out near Carnation. He was a bit of a recluse and lived by himself out in the woods where you couldn't see any other houses. He had built his own house on the top of a hill and was quite proud of the work he had done. He was dedicated to environmental values and conservation, loved his land, and wanted to leave his estate as a legacy.

In the spring of 1985, he decided to find an entity that would take his estate when he died and use it to acquire more conservation and habitat land. He was interviewing a variety of nature and environmental organizations in the Northwest, and he just appeared one day in the Seattle Audubon office.

Dick Butler was Chair of Seattle Audubon's Sanctuary Committee at the time and happened to be in the office when Martin came in. He took Martin under his wing. Martin didn't have a lawyer, but I was Seattle Audubon's Legal Advisor then, so Dick called me to come in and meet Martin.

Martin didn't have a will. He had some loose ideas of what he wanted to do. We told him about Seattle Audubon and what we'd already done. We were quite involved in acquiring habitat land at that time through several programs our Sanctuary Committee had put together. The best-known project we had was Carnation Marsh out east of Lake Washington.[69] We had bought the marsh and expanded it several times. Martin liked that idea, but he left our office without making a commitment.

According to the Board minutes of the time, about a month later, Martin let us know that he had made us his legatee.[70] He had hand-drafted his will, and the essence of it was, he gave the bulk of his estate to Seattle Audubon, with a number of restrictions on its use. We were to establish a fund and use its earnings to buy land that would be conserved in perpetuity. The will required Seattle Audubon to form a committee of a minimum of seven Audubon members chosen by the Board for their expert ability to evaluate and select habitat projects. The fund had to be kept in the most conservative, safe investments, like a bank account. It could be used only to buy property. None of the money could be used to manage property, not even to fence it, put up signs, or do anything to improve it.

So all of a sudden we had this bequest, and we had to think about what to do with it. The Board decided to accept Martin's estate, even though some of the terms seemed so restrictive and might make it difficult to achieve Martin's objectives in the long run.

About a year later we got a call from the sheriff's office. Martin had died after an encounter with a neighbor.[71] The sheriff's officers were going through his papers and found his will, so that's why they called us.

Dick, who had been named executor of the will, recruited volunteer probate lawyers to open probate, and ultimately, Martin's property was sold. This resulted in Seattle Audubon obtaining $527,000 to be used to protect land.

An interesting thing about the sale was, over the years, we've been approached by a lot of people who want to give us property, but they usually want

QUALITY OF LIFE

by Martin Miller

It is not a fulfilling life which contains so many "I remember whens" as a substitute for experiences with nature. "I remember when there was a meadow of wildflowers here." "I remember when there was a forest there." "I remember when clean rivers were full of fish and eagles and hawks soared and nested." ... "I remember when the air was so clear that the mountains seemed near and stars were distinct."

If we continue to accept destructive actions, our progeny may never have their experiences in nature, and may even be denied their "I remember whens."...

Those who did and are doing the desecration lose their temporary importance and will not be remembered. But I would rather not have their legacy. [I would rather] participate in activities to protect, enhance and rehabilitate natural ecosystems. We need not

Martin Miller. (Courtesy of Seattle Audubon Society)

accept the comment,..."It used to be such a wonderful natural place." Rather let's say, "My God, thank you for these creations. We will protect and save them for the survival of all life forms in nature, and in your name." [72]

us to keep it as habitat because they love it. Martin loved every bit of his land, but he didn't require that we keep it. He said, 'No, if you want to keep it, you can, but if you want to sell it and use the money to acquire land elsewhere, go ahead.' He was really motivated to save nature in the broadest sense.

When SAS formed a committee in 1988 to manage Martin's bequest, we divided the responsibility into two areas. We had one committee to administer the funds themselves and make investment decisions, and another committee to evaluate the wildlife habitat value of projects submitted for grants. The latter committee was and is composed primarily of members with wildlife habitat expertise, and uses criteria developed by the committee to select worthy projects. The membership of the habitat committee has been very consistent ever since.

The committee felt, almost from the beginning, that we had too limited powers under the will to achieve long-term objectives. Given the rate of inflation, if you hold your money in a savings account, the actual amount will be reduced every year. We wanted to grow the money, not see it shrink. So ultimately we went to court to ask a judge to broad-en the investment base but still keep it within the conservative objectives and management that we felt Martin would have approved.

We were also limited to buying fee title to property itself under Martin's will, so we asked the judge to authorize us not only to buy real property, but to buy conservation easements and other sorts of less-than-full-title interests in property, and to clarify our right to purchase properties in partnership with other entities. That was a big step.

We felt that these provisions were consistent with what Martin wanted, but they gave us more flexibility in meeting his long-term objectives. A bequest of $500,000 sounds like a lot of money—and it is, of course—but it wouldn't even come close to buying most of the single properties that we have helped to purchase over the years. In addition, buying conservation easements is far cheaper than purchasing the fee title itself. Conservation easements allow certain kinds of uses that are acceptable for conservation purposes in the long run, but they absolutely prohibit subdividing, developing, or converting the land into something that would be inconsistent with its conservation values.

The court order also permits us to fund properties where incidental uses, such as scientific, educational, or recreational, may occur, so long as the habitat committee's experts determine that those incidental uses will not interfere with the primary purpose—permanently protecting the site's wildlife habitat value.

This flexibility has helped us fund a variety of projects, both small and large, throughout Washington State. They include a heronry on Vashon Island, a night eagle roost on the Skagit River, the Loomis Forest in the Okanogan, old growth forests in several locations, a peat bog on Vashon Island, property at Moses Coulee in Douglas County, and a site near the mouth of the Humptulips River in Grays Harbor County. We have helped preserve habitat along the Elochoman River in Wahkiakum County, along Elk Creek in Clallam County, and in the Tarboo Creek watershed near Hood Canal in Jefferson County. We've also helped preserve parts of a wildlife corridor on Bainbridge Island, and parts of the Yakima River wildlife corridor at Snoqualmie Pass, among many other critical projects.

We've never gone out and initiated land purchases ourselves, but sometimes we have solicited proposals from other entities who identified valuable land to acquire in areas in which they work and have expertise. In the beginning, no one had ever heard of the Martin Miller Fund, so we had to advertise it in the environmental/conservation/land trust community, which we did. But now, we're generally known by the land acquisition organizations, so they know to contact us.

Oftentimes, entities don't approach us until they have acquired some right to purchase already. They may do a purchase and sale agreement that has to be closed in a specific time, such as six months. They'll raise money from their members and get some funds from a government entity, but often they'll need up to $50,000 or more to close the deal between the time they sign the sale contract and the closing date. So there's often a limited time frame that we have to respond to such requests.

As required by Martin's will, the habitat committee drafted criteria for selecting projects. These criteria help us identify projects that meet the will's requirements, and they give potential applicants some guidance about what we would fund. The criteria were thoughtfully done by some very savvy people on the committee. The applicant has to do a thorough inventory of the land's flora and fauna and describe its value as habitat property. We require an applicant to give us a large-scale map showing where in the community the potential property is located, as well as a small-scale map of the site itself. We ask for information about surrounding land uses that might in the long term affect the site. Since we typically fund just a portion of a project, we ask where the other funds are coming from, how they're to be obtained, and how our grant would fit in with the larger project funding. We insist on getting binding legal restrictions to limit uses to preserve the site for habitat or conservation purposes.[73]

Our committee meets on an as-needed basis to look at proposals. Most of the committee members, as I said, have been on it a long time. Bob Sieh, the Chair, has been on the committee from the beginning. He's a lawyer. He coordinates the review of the applications and uses his legal skills to evaluate the legal aspects of the proposed purchases. Ken Brunner, Fayette Krause, and Martha Jordan have also been on the committee from the beginning. Ken was the Endangered Species Coordinator for the U.S. Army Corps of Engineers, Seattle District. Fayette was the Washington Land Steward for the Nature Conservancy. Martha has led efforts for years to preserve habitat for the swans that winter in Washington. Herb Curl has been on the committee nearly from the beginning—he is a scientist who used to work for NOAA and has served on the Seattle Audubon Society Board as Science Advisor. Dick Butler, an attorney and long-time member and former President of Seattle Audubon, has served for many years. Kate Sternberg has, since 1998, brought to the committee her scientific expertise and extensive public and private sector experience in wildlife assessment and conservation. Marc Boulé, a wetlands biologist who worked for private consulting firms, was an initial and valued member of the committee until his death in 2014. Calvin Douglas, a professional wildlife biologist with years of experience, is a more recent addition to the committee but has been an active participant. Lorna Smith is our newest member. She has years of experience in wildlife and natural resource conservation planning for both public

THE OTTO PRESERVE: A PROJECT OF THE MARTIN MILLER FUND

by Mira Lamb

On tiny Lummi Island among the San Juan Islands stands a former farm known as the Otto Preserve. Located on the Pacific Flyway, this 104-acre parcel provides habitat for many migratory and resident birds. Raptors such as Bald Eagles and Peregrine Falcons soar and swoop above thrushes, warblers, and other songbirds. Northern Flickers, Rufous Hummingbirds, Olive-sided Flycatchers, and Marsh Wrens—all listed by the U.S. Fish and Wildlife

Service as Birds of Conservation Concern—also call the property home. Currently, the Otto Preserve is undergoing several transformations: its pastures and meadows are reverting to join its already-existing mixed forest, and an emerging scrub-shrub wetland will serve as a haven for waterfowl such as Mallards, Wood Ducks, and Ring-necked Ducks. In the coming years, the Otto Preserve will play a vital role in wildlife preservation as development displaces native species elsewhere on Lummi Island and on the mainland in Whatcom County.

The Otto Preserve also holds historical and scientific value. Geologists from Western Washington University, for example, have

discovered 160 million-year-old intrusive rocky outcrops on the site, which are rare in Northwestern Washington and the only ones of their kind in Whatcom County. From these ancient relics, the scientists hope to discover how new volcanoes shape the land.

The preservation of the Otto Preserve was spearheaded by the Lummi Island Heritage Trust, but also made possible by the joint efforts of federal agencies, environmental organizations, and private individuals. Funding was provided by the Martin Miller Fund and the U.S. Fish and Wildlife Service. Organizations such as the Wildlife Conservation Trust and North Cascades Audubon Society, as well as the Lummi Island community also raised funds and greater awareness for the project. Ultimately, the acquired property was placed under a conservation easement with the San Juan Preservation Trust to protect this precious land in perpetuity.

Today, the Otto Preserve is an important educational resource for Lummi Island. It's a place where visitors can explore and learn about the preserve's ecological importance, starting their visit at the old farm shed, which has been transformed into an information center and base of operations. Thanks to the dedication of the conservation community, the Otto Preserve will always be a haven for native plants and wildlife and a place where people can experience them.

Above left: A trail through the Otto Preserve. (Photograph by Ed Lowe, © Lummi Island Heritage Trust) Author Mira Lamb was a Conservation Volunteer at Seattle Audubon Society who worked on various projects from 2012 to 2015. She now studies anthropology and neuroscience at Grinnell College in Iowa.

and private entities. I've been on the committee from the beginning too. I'm not a scientist. I'm a lawyer, so I depend on the expert analysis that our scientists give. And they're terrific. I love seeing them go through the criteria, evaluate the flora, the fauna, the significance. It's enlightening.

Sometimes the process of selecting land or easements to purchase is competitive because of the number of projects we evaluate, and sometimes not. Partly, it depends on how much money we have to spend. According to Martin's will, we can spend only the earnings and the increase of the fund. Over the years, we have had other donations to the fund, so that has helped it grow. We welcome all contributions to the fund and encourage people to consider donating to it as a way to invest in our area's future.

The Martin Miller Fund is partially invested in stocks, and there, the earnings go up and down. We've had times when the fund has shrunk a little bit, and we've had relatively little cash to spend. We've had other times when there's quite a bit of cash in the fund. When the expendable part of the fund is built up, we'll sometimes contact conservation groups and say we have some money to spend if they're interested. They love getting calls like that.

I think the Martin Miller Fund has had a significant impact in Washington State. For example, one of the largest grants we made was $50,000 to the Loomis Forest Fund to help preserve 25,000 acres of forest in north-central Washington. We were part of a $16.5 million effort that was spearheaded by the Northwest Ecosystem Alliance (now Conservation Northwest) that transferred school trust lands to the status of a natural resource conservation area.

One of the smallest purchases we made was five acres to expand the Otto Preserve-Eliot parcel on Lummi Island, working with the Lummi Island Heritage Trust. The Otto Preserve protects prime wetland and forest on the island. The parcel we helped buy protects the northern edge of the wetland. It's a small piece of property, but the local impact is very important.

Another such example is the work we did with the Capitol Land Trust in the Olympia area. The Martin Miller Fund participated in one or two of the land trust's projects. The projects were very small and limited, and probably you could go to a dozen counties and see comparable land. But within the context of what's important around Olympia, these small parcels matter.

We're just one of many actors seeking to preserve valuable habitat land in Washington. It really takes all of us working together to be able to make a dent, to slow down the development that is taking place at an ever-increasing pace. I mean, you look at what's happening to our city, to our state, and all along the West Coast with population growth and with intensification of uses. Land is being gobbled up at an amazing rate. If we're going to save at least a portion of it, it's going to take concerted action from everyone.

You or I, sitting here, could live minimal lifestyles, and it's not going to have any influence on big issues such as global warming. But look at what one person did with a fair-sized estate in the mid-1980s. He dedicated everything he ever acquired to this fund.

Working with other entities, the Martin Miller Fund has participated in 20 or 30 different projects in fifteen different counties throughout Washington State. We've leveraged Martin's legacy way beyond the dollars he bequeathed to us to make a real impact."

NATURE IN RESERVE
Lillian Forsman: Wildlife Refuges & Bird Sanctuaries

Earth Goddess Series-3, *oil on canvas by Mita Brahma. Many cultures have embraced the idea of an Earth Mother who cares for nature, an appropriate image to represent Seattle Audubon's continuing efforts to create and support bird sanctuaries and wildlife refuges. (Artwork © Mita Brahma, reprinted here with permission. For more of Brahma's art, see her website at www.mitabrahma.com.)*

Throughout the latter half of the nineteenth century, Americans gradually came to understand that the seemingly unending stretches of wilderness that had characterized the continent when Europeans first arrived were not, after all, infinite. It was entirely possible for humans to kill every one of the billions of Passenger Pigeons that had flowed torrentially overhead. It was conceivable that the millions of bison that filled the legends of the West could be exterminated right down to the last cow. Uniquely beautiful natural wonders could be bought by private citizens, who could and did deny access to the public.

People began to rethink the use of public lands. Instead of seeing them as resources to be privately exploited or owned, we began to think of them as belonging to everyone, in the sense that everyone should be able to share their bounty and beauty, including future generations. Starting in the late 1800s and rising to a peak in the teens of the next century, interest in designating public lands to save nature rose sharply, fueled in part by hunting clubs and birders.[74] President Theodore Roosevelt, an immensely popular and admired man, freely used his bully pulpit to advocate for habitat preservation. Not only that, he took practical actions, too. By executive order, he established seventeen wildlife refuges while in office.[75]

At first, the idea of setting aside lands as parks or refuges was closely tied to the desire to preserve wildlife for human exploitation: hunting, fishing, and timber. This idea still drives many of the decisions we make about how we manage public lands. But another idea began to take hold at the same time: that wildlife should be protected for its own sake.

Seattle Audubon supported both ideas. On the one hand, a system of wildlife refuges could address preservation at the national level, where whole species could be saved, especially ducks, geese, and swans. At the same time, sanctuaries established at the local level could preserve habitat and birds within urban areas, ensuring that wild birds would always be a presence in the city.

In 1938, Lillian Forsman, President of Seattle Audubon, wrote an essay intended to build support for National Refuges. She did so at the height of the Great Depression, when it was easy to make the argument that people were more important than birds. And yet, with the help of conservation groups such as Audubon, President Franklin Roosevelt managed to set aside $14.5 million to build up the refuge system originally begun by Ulysses S. Grant in 1868. At the end of her essay, Forsman lists the Refuges that were established in Washington State, Refuges that to this day continue to provide habitat for birds and respite for us.[76]

"There is a little book called *Wildlife and the Land: A Story of Regeneration*, which contains a record of the activities of the Bureau of Biological Survey to recover and conserve our American bird life.[77] Special emphasis is placed therein upon the relation between wildlife restoration and land rehabilitation and use. The special Committee on Conservation of Wildlife Resources which was appointed by the President in 1934 needed such a report to determine its recommendations of a legislative program which would perpetuate our wildlife resources.

The Committee found, as had the Bureau before it, that a restorative program had become necessary because, unfortunately, many species of migratory waterfowl were threatened with extinction. One of the main causes of this waterfowl mortality was the drainage craze that swept our country some years ago when the reclamation of much swamp land occurred, supposedly for the benefit of the farmers. In reality many of these drainage projects were unsuccessful because the land proved unfit for farming. The chief results became barren landscapes, dust storms, drought and disaster for the birds, for they were deprived of millions of acres of their natural breeding and feeding habitats.

Up to 1933, the Bureau had acquired 99 Refuges with over one and one-half million acres of land where it was endeavoring to build upon the scattered remnants of seed stock by rehabilitating these lands so that they produce and maintain wildlife. In 1934, eight and one-half millions were made available to the Bureau for waterfowl restoration. This was a far greater sum than had ever been given before for the purpose. The following year six millions more were given to continue the program.

When the President's Committee began functioning, a great amount of material was examined bearing upon the needs of restorative measures for waterfowl, upland game, song and insectivorous birds, and mammals. Methods and plans were carefully sifted. When the report was completed the Committee made definite recommendations, calling for 25 millions for acquiring of lands and an additional amount for developing of them. Although these amounts were not allotted, the report was endorsed by many interested conservation groups and the work was given much publicity. Thus the restoration idea which the Bureau of Biological Survey had been advocating for many years was given a tremendous impetus.

THE FIRST SANCTUARY:
SEWARD PARK

You wouldn't think it would that easy to steal a 250-year-old Douglas Fir more than 150 feet tall, transport the log through city streets, and sell it somewhere for cash. But log poaching was one of the reasons Seattle Audubon decided to advocate for converting the city's newly acquired Seward Park into an official bird sanctuary.

The sanctuary movement was a hot topic of conversation in the early 1900s. Cities in many parts of the nation were creating sanctuaries to preserve habitat for wildlife within city limits. President Theodore Roosevelt had left office in 1909, having created seventeen Wildlife Refuges in rural areas, so it made sense for urbanites to want to preserve nature in their own backyards as well.

Here in Seattle, the desire for open spaces and nature took form in the City's first Comprehensive Plan in 1892, when Seattle Parks Superintendent E. O. Schwagerl proposed that the City buy Bailey Peninsula and turn it into a park. That plan was shaped by the Olmsted Brothers, the famous landscapers who were hired by the City to create a parks and boulevard plan in time for the Alaska-Yukon-Pacific Exposition in 1909. The City bought the peninsula in 1911 and named it Seward Park. It contained some of the finest old growth forest left in Seattle.[78]

But there were problems. Not only were tree poachers active in Seward Park, so were game poachers—and feral cats. Seattle Audubon decided that if the Park were made a bird sanctuary, not only could feeding stations be set up in winter to feed wild birds, but perhaps the community could lobby for more active enforcement of the poaching laws, and maybe the cats could be killed off, too.

The Society began to press for sanctuary status in late 1916, but action by the Parks Department was tabled when President Woodrow Wilson asked Congress to enter World War I in April 1917. In 1919, Parks Superintendent J. W. Thompson agreed to make Seward Park Seattle's first official bird sanctuary.[79] Eventually, Washington Park Arboretum would be made a sanctuary, too.

The rationale for these two sanctuaries is eloquently expressed by Seattle Auduboner Edwin J. Johnson, in the April 1940 issue of *The Seattle Wren*:[80]

"We Americans, in our mad haste to promote economic security, have neglected to assist nature in coping with her problem of advancing civilization. Every acre of tilled land excludes some form of natural floral and fauna. This steady encroachment by man is rapidly depleting and threatening with extinction many species of animal life. Therefore, it becomes necessary that certain areas in closely populated centers be used to encourage propagation of bird life. This can be accomplished only by persistent activity on the part of nature-loving groups and societies to make the general public 'bird conscious'....The stimuli for such public interest must originate in organizations such as the Audubon Society."

Above: Seward Park in 1926. (Photograph courtesy of Seattle Municipal Archives)
Opposite page: Montlake Fill at sunrise. (Photograph © Doug Parrott)

The sanctuary plan had many aspects. Boy Scouts agreed to construct and put up birdhouses. They and other youth groups, as well as Seattle Audubon members, agreed to supply up to ten feeding stations with seed. Berry-bearing plants and other natural sources of bird food were planted by Audubon members. Concrete bird baths were established by the Parks Department. Kids with BB guns were banned from the Park. Although Audubon was denied the right to kill feral cats, a cat licensing law was passed by the City.[81]

It was hoped that if cat owners were required to buy licenses for their pets, they would take better care to keep them indoors, especially during daylight hours in the birds' breeding season.

Poaching of birds was still a problem in 1924, however, when F. W. Cook, the Corresponding Secretary of Seattle Audubon, was asked by the Society to write a letter to the King County Game Commissioners, in which he made the following claim, on the basis of little, if any, evidence:

"An active Supervision of Alien shooters and trappers—Italian and Japanese—principally the former, is much needed, also an excessive shooting license to be paid by such Nationals. It is believed that much of this indiscriminate shooting has been done to augment a scanty food supply, as their action is not confined to the killing of game birds, but any bird or animal met with."[82]

The overt racism expressed in this letter is shocking to us today, but it is part of our history and should be remembered. It is a reminder of how things used to be, how things are today, and how far we still have to go.

The Malheur Migratory Bird Refuge in Oregon has recently been enlarged by 64,717 acres which is rapidly being restored to a wilderness condition. Two Civilian Conservation Corps camps are maintained on the area and are doing splendid work in improving it.

In the State of Washington, the Turnbull Migratory Bird Refuge, once the site of an unsuccessful drainage project, is being restored to its original condition by the construction of several dams which will stabilize the water level so that the great numbers of waterfowl that formerly nested there will, it is hoped, return to nest again.

The Willapa Harbor Migratory Bird Refuge is [currently] being established to protect waterfowl using the Pacific Flyway. This refuge will ultimately contain 5,446 acres.

Other wildlife refuges in our State, all under the jurisdiction of the Bureau of Biological Survey, are as follows: Dungeness Spit, Quillayute Needles and Flattery Rocks Migratory Bird Refuges in Clallam and Jefferson Counties; Lenore Lake Refuge in Grant County; Copalis Rock in Grays Harbor; Smith Island in Island County; Conconully in Okanogan; Jones Island in San Juan; and the Columbia River Migratory Bird Refuge, Walla Walla County."

INSPIRATIONAL

Seattle Auduboners were passionate about the idea of nature as a refuge, as this essay by Cecil M. Baskett in 1934 shows:[83]

Recreation is Nature's greatest tonic to man. Lavish with her varied offerings, she has endowed the universe with vast playgrounds convenient for his use.

Particularly partial was she in her plans for future Washingtonians. Within the boundaries of their present commonwealth, she built a wonderland.

In that plastic era of her greatest activities were moulded the Cascades and the Olympics, projecting examples of Nature's imposing handiwork, and, with their exalted peaks and verdant valleys, they stand today a perpetual monument to her characteristic foresight.

That was Nature's part.

Man has done his by building metropolises at the gateways to this realm of constant pleasure. Into the depths of this promised land he goes forth for sport and recuperation.

How fortunate are we, who live at the very portals of such an area of beauty and diversion!

Between suns, we are conveyed into its midst.

And tired man, who seeks the great outdoors, finds the silent places.

CARNATION MARSH AND THE SANCTUARY STORY

In March 1965, roughly two years after Seattle Audubon officially became a branch of National Audubon (formally accepted in February 1963),[84] William Goodall, the Western Representative of the National Audubon Society, came out to talk to the Society about National's policies and goals. Among them were National's desire for local branches to acquire lands for sanctuaries.

Goodall's timing was good. The Tritle family had just offered to give Seattle Audubon title to a property near Three Tree Point to turn it into a bird sanctuary. An ad hoc committee, the Nature Center Committee, chaired by Mrs. Howard (Nell) Behr, decided the property was suitable, and so the Society got its first sanctuary, named the Tritle Cliff Sanctuary.[85]

Soon other property owners began to offer parcels too, and the Nature Center Committee got busy evaluating them. Not all donations were accepted. National Audubon had advised us that a minimum of 50 acres was needed to create a viable sanctuary. Consideration also had to be given as to the ecological value of a given property, the affordability of taxes and liabilities, the costs of maintenance and possible development of access, and the possibility of future sale for cash.[86] Some bequests of property demanded that the Society never sell it, even though the property in question did not always meet the standards that National Audubon had recommended. Sometimes we refused such bequests, and other times we accepted them. Our properties began to accumulate, but not in a way that resulted in a bird sanctuary for us.

To handle this issue, a Sanctuary Fund was begun in 1965.[87] It proved to be a popular fund for legacy donors and for people who wanted to memorialize lost loved ones. But there were questions raised by the Board about our priorities and whether refuge management fit our goals. In September 1970, the Board voted to fold the Sanctuary Fund into the Publications Fund, where the money could be used to publish books.

The dream of our own sanctuary lived on, however, and people continued to donate money to buy one. In February 1976, for example, former Seattle Audubon President Walter Hagenstein left a bequest of $500 for this purpose, and the Sanctuary Fund was started up again. We looked around at other Audubon chapters, and at National too, and it seemed like everybody was acquiring sanctuaries. National had 63 scattered around the country.[88] The Audubon Society of Portland had had a sanctuary since 1930; San Diego, a much smaller chapter than ours, had had a sanctuary since 1965.

At the same time, many conservationists at Seattle Audubon worried about the pace of development encroaching on prime bird habitat. One such place

was Carnation Marsh, a part of extensive wetlands along the Snoqualmie River near the town of Carnation. Housing was growing rapidly there and attempts were being made by private developers to drain the wetlands. Conservation Chair Dave Galvin asked the Board to set up an ad hoc committee in 1979 to explore the feasibility of buying the Marsh. Also on the committee were Rick McGuire, John Lundin, Jim Anderson, John Huskinson, and Harold Laws.

The possibility of owning our own nature reserve suddenly became more real when Doris Jelliffe left a bequest of $48,000 to the Sanctuary Fund in September 1980. This bequest, and subsequent fundraising efforts on the part of the Sanctuary Committee and the Board, as well as generous donations from several Audubon members, resulted in Seattle Audubon buying 30 acres of Carnation Marsh in 1984.[89] Plans for the Marsh were ambitious. The Sanctuary Committee wanted to raise enough money to build a boardwalk and viewing station, perhaps even a nature center that would "accommodate both members and the general public for educational programs and bird walks."[90]

These plans, and the Board's continuing success in buying critical parcels around Carnation Marsh and in other areas on the East Side[91] impressed Martin Miller, a conservationist who lived nearby and who wanted to leave his estate to an organization dedicated to preserving habitat. He chose Seattle Audubon. In 1987, we received his bequest of $527,000 (see "Saving Nature, One Piece at a Time; John W. Lundin: Martin Miller Fund," pp. 38 ff above).

Seattle Audubon set up two committees to administer the fund and make recommendations to the Board about how best to save habitat. They decided the Martin Miller Fund wasn't big enough to buy enough land to make much of a difference statewide. Instead, they suggested that Seattle Audubon form partnerships with other environmental organizations to share the cost of significant land purchases or, even more effective, to buy conservation easements.

Through this strategy and the monies in the Martin Miller Fund, Seattle Audubon helped save many thousands of acres of critical habitat all over Washington State. We began to realize that having a nature reserve of our own such as Carnation Marsh, was not as necessary for our preservation goals as we had thought.[92] What mattered was the act of preservation itself, saving the land until we could find entities who would manage it for wildlife in perpetuity.

On December 30, 2010 we conveyed title of 89.06 acres of Carnation Marsh to King County.[93] Thus between Seattle Audubon's efforts and the County's, 182.25 acres of prime marsh habitat were saved. By granting title of our Carnation Marsh to the County, we achieved what we had wanted all along: to save the Marsh from development, make it accessible to the public, and help the resident and migratory birds who depend on it. A great success.

A WAKE-UP CALL FOR BIRDS
Carolee Colter: Northwest Shade Coffee Campaign

Carolee Colter. (Photograph © Neil M. Berg)

It starts as a trickle, just as the crocuses begin to fade in mid-February. One day the land is bleak and bare, the skies gray, empty but for a few black crows flapping to who knows where. The next moment, a living jewel flashes by, emerald and amethyst, catching the light, shining it back into our dazzled eyes. The first Violet-green Swallow of spring has returned. It is the harbinger of a rivulet of neotropical migrants beginning to wing their way north. The earliest arrivals come even before the sun can warm the land: Tree Swallows and Mountain Bluebirds, glowing sapphire blue; Say's Phoebe, a quiet carnelian. As the days grow longer, the stream of birds flowing north becomes a river: Rufous Hummingbird, Savannah Sparrow, Common Yellowthroat singing their little songs. By mid-April, the river swells into a flood, billions of birds all rushing north in flocks so dense they appear on radar. By June, they are done, the last migrants thrilling our souls with their beauty: Black Swifts slashing the sky like black scimitars, and Common Nighthawks flashing their white-striped wings like fencing masters saluting. In fall the flood reverses as birds flee the coming winter and return to the tropics.

It is a pattern as old as time. For as long as birds have been birds, some have always migrated. And yet in our corner of the world, it is a new phenomenon, geologically speaking. Twenty thousand years ago, Seattle lay under a mile of ice. No sound broke the silence except the whoosh of the wind and the creak of the glaciers. As the ice retreated and plants returned to the land, the birds from the tropics returned, too.

Neotropical migrants are thus a symbol of the resilience of nature.

They are more. In past decades, the numbers of migrants have fallen steeply, each year the number of birds growing fewer. Habitat loss is the culprit. Thus, migrants are also a symbol of the fragility of nature. To survive, neotropical migrants need thousands of miles of good habitat, some in their winter homes, some in their summer breeding grounds, and some along the way. If habitat fails them at any stage in their lives, they die.

And so migrants are also a symbol of the connectedness of the world. The warblers we host in the U.S. in April are the same birds who grace the tropics of Mexico, Central and South America in November. They unite us as no other living creature does.

One of the most ardent Seattle Audubon activists to realize this fundamental truth is Carolee Colter. In 1996, she and a team of other volunteers spearheaded the formation of a coalition of birders, scientists, writers, artists, growers, and retailers to unite literally over a cup of coffee. The Northwest Shade Coffee Campaign was designed to bring together growers, roasters, retailers, and consumers to promote shade-grown coffee, an ecologically friendly product that helps preserve neotropical habitat for birds.

It may sound like a small—perhaps even trivial—action, but it is not. Coffee as an annual commodity is worth $100 billion worldwide, with an annual yield of more than 4 million metric tons of beans produced in the New World. Almost all the countries that grow coffee commercially are in the developing world, where coffee is an important cash crop. For decades, most coffee was grown on small family farms under the shade of a mixed canopy of trees and shrubs. This habitat was not natural, but it was very good for birds. Then in the 1970s, small farms began to get displaced by large agribusiness plantations that cleared out the canopy and replaced it with rows and rows of sun-tolerant coffee. The plantations had discovered that coffee grown in this way was less labor intensive. Today, most coffee is grown on such plantations. The resulting deforestation has been devastating for neotropical birds. Of the 50 countries with the highest rate of deforestation, 37 are coffee growers.[94, 95]

Colter realized that if retailers could be persuaded to source shade-grown coffee, and if consumers could be persuaded to buy it, the potential for helping neotropical birds would be real and dramatic. It was her way of saving the world.

"It was in 1984 on a whale-watching trip to Baja California that I became obsessed with birds. Watching Blue-footed Boobies plunge 50 feet headfirst into the Sea of Cortez to catch fish and then try to escape from Magnificent Frigatebirds pursuing them like pirates, I realized why people went birding. I decided I would, too. I joined Audubon in 1985, mostly to get the magazine with its pretty bird pictures. Also that year, I read a small article in the *Seattle Times* headlined, 'Quick Decline Predicted for Migratory Birds.' It was a story about the decline of migratory warblers and other migratory songbirds due to tropical rainforest deforestation. I felt sad and angry too—I had just successfully identified my first warbler (a Yellow), and now they were going to disappear.

But I didn't see what I could do about a problem so vast and intractable. Things kept getting worse. In the summer of 1988, I read a devastating article about how radar maps of migrants flying across the Gulf of Mexico showed the numbers of birds were only half what they had been 20 years before. I sat at my desk with my head in my hands, feeling overwhelmed with despair. *Earthcare Northwest*, Seattle Audubon's newsletter, was lying in front of me. I picked it up and saw an announcement: 'The Conservation Committee is looking for new members.' Without any further thought, I dialed the number, which happened to be the home of the Chair, Melanie Rowland. I told her I wanted to get involved.

'What are you interested in?' she asked me.

'Is anyone working on migratory songbirds or tropical rainforests?' I said.

'No,' she said. 'Why don't you come to our planning retreat this weekend? You could start your own subcommittee.'

The last thing I had in mind was to start my own committee! But with the encouragement of Seattle Audubon,

I eventually did start the Tropical Forests Committee. We developed the idea that we would write a series of articles in *Earthcare Northwest* and also in PCC Natural Markets' newsletter, which had a wide audience and had ageed to do this. So we divvied up the subjects to research, and we wrote articles. We wrote about rubber, aluminum, hydroelectric dams, Brazil nuts, gold—more topics than I can remember. Eventually we wrote so many articles that we put them together into a booklet. We also created a slideshow around these topics and took it to show anyone who was interested.

TURKEY VULTURES ARE NEOTROPICAL, TOO

Usually when people think of birds that benefit from shade coffee plantations, they think of neotropical songbirds. But another species also benefits from such habitat, the Turkey Vulture. These large, graceful flyers pass through Central America on their way to and from their wintering grounds as far south as Venezuela and other parts of South America. One researcher who has studied them for over 40 years is Diann MacRae. MacRae is the founder of the Olympic Vulture Study and past chair of the Hawk Migration Association of North America. Here are some of her thoughts.

"While southeastern Turkey Vultures in America are not known to migrate, those in the West, North, and southern Canada do. They take the easy route down through the States, continuing into Mexico and through Central America into South America: no water crossings! Arguably the world's largest migration route for birds of prey follows a lowland route through the State of Veracruz, Mexico. Annual counts are taken parallel to the line of flight: one from a tower in the pueblo of Chichicaxtle and the other atop the Hotel Bienvenido in Cardel. Turkey Vultures number over a million every year.

Bird-friendly coffee plantations are in the mountains all through Mexico and Central America. Plantations are often planted in three levels: a canopy of mixed forest shade trees, then a layer of various fruit trees such as avocado, banana, or mango and, finally, the shorter coffee plants. This is important habitat for Turkey Vultures for several reasons. Local nesting Turkey Vultures often leave fledged young on the outskirts of the plantations where they wait impatiently in the shade for parents to return with food. The migrating flocks settle in the acres of trees to roost for the night. Hungry Turkey Vultures with their sense of smell can detect edibles in the understory, although they tend not to stop and eat often on migration. These forested areas also provide sanctuary where migrants can feel safe on their sometimes up to 15,000-mile journey.

'Our' Pacific Northwest Turkey Vultures migrate in the fall through September until early October. They are often seen in flocks of 400 or more. One late September day not long ago, we had over 1,100 vultures in a few hours crossing from Vancouver Island to Salt Creek on the north Olympic coast, one of their longer water crossings. Their effortless flight, drifting from thermal to thermal, allows them to cover 200 miles in a day. Not too long a trip to Veracruz for these soaring experts."

Turkey Vulture. (Photograph © Doug Schurman)

Most often we were invited to speak at elementary schools. I gave a lot of presentations. I saw that young children of all ethnicities and in every neighborhood in Seattle had a visceral connection with the animals of the rainforest. They cared. They would ooh and aah over the pictures of jaguars, butterflies, and macaws and take very seriously the idea that the rainforest was being destroyed because of the products we were using.

The following year, Hazel Wolf and I from Seattle Audubon, a representative from the Seattle Rainforest Action Group, and a person who worked for the Lummi Nation organized a conference. We invited indigenous speakers familiar with deforestation: Native Hawaiians, Modocs, Yakamas, Lillooets, and two Lacandon Mayans. From that arose another group of volunteers.

We got connected with Russell Greenberg from the Smithsonian Migratory Bird Center. He was doing research in Chiapas, where he found that a lot of the birds we see here in Seattle need intact rainforest in Mexico and Central America in the winter. Only a few of our Northwestern migrants go down into South America. It's mostly the East Coast migrants who do that.

Russell was working with a conservation group in Mexico called Pronatura Chiapas. They were doing intensive educational work with local people about conserving rainforest by using it in sustainable ways—sustainable wood-cutting, for example, and reforesting cut-over slopes. We decided to help Russell in his work as much as we could. In 1991, a group of us participated in the annual Birdathon, but we donated all the money we raised to Pronatura. We raised a lot. It was in the five figures. Later some of our volunteers went to Chiapas to meet the people from Pronatura. They took a bunch of used binoculars and scopes with them to give to the scientists there, who couldn't afford optics.

Russell's research began to show that coffee plantations seemed to be the most important variable for habitat preservation for neotropical migrants. As I came to understand it, in Central America and Mexico, there is very little land in preserves. Most of the landscape is completely used. It may seem like a natural landscape, but in reality, it's pretty much all working land. Traditionally, a lot of the land was used to grow shade coffee, which was grown under a canopy of trees and shrubs. The mixed canopy isn't

natural, but it mimics the natural forest, and it's great for birds.

In 1994, we brought Russell to Seattle to publicize the results of his research, that migratory birds were finding a safe winter haven in coffee plantations but that new methods of coffee growing—sun-tolerant coffee grown on large plantations that cut down the canopy—were threatening that haven. We hoped that in a coffee town like Seattle, we might get a hearing for this new message. We got Russell on NPR, and had him give talks at the University of Washington and a couple other venues. The *Seattle P-I* interviewed him, too. He and I were on the front page. I guess it was a slow news day!

Starbucks was beginning to make a name for itself in those days, and so was Seattle's Best Coffee. We met with their sustainability officers and marketing people and tried to push the idea that they should buy shade coffee. We told them, 'You could really make a big difference in where you source your coffee.'

I would say we were met with some interest, but we could also see nothing was going to come of it. I had had this fantasy: We would meet with high enough people in these big companies, and they would take our idea and run with it. That did not happen, at least initially. So the publicity that we were getting about urging coffee-drinkers to buy shade coffee ran into a problem. There was nowhere consumers could buy it.

But in 1996, we stumbled into a successful model: the Northwest Shade Coffee Campaign. It was really more of a coalition than a campaign. Thirty coffee companies that carry at least one line of shade coffee and sell in the Pacific Northwest paid dues to be members of the Campaign. A core group of ten volunteers did the work of promoting their shade coffee. We wrote articles, created graphics, set up a website, and staffed tables at public events. Helen Ross, Seattle Audubon's Conservation Coordinator, fielded the phone calls from people who wanted to know where to buy shade coffee. She also worked with media and other conservation groups to promote it.

The founders of the Campaign were all passionate about their commitment to quality coffee, to the environment, and to social justice. They didn't always agree about how to go about achieving our goals. Our discussions were pretty lively. My role was to find common ground and keep the group focused on our purpose

of publicizing the benefits of shade coffee. It took a lot of hard work and energy. And I don't even drink coffee!

One day, I got a call from a man on Bainbridge Island who had read one of our articles. He was involved with the Sister Islands Association and worked with Bainbridge's sister island of Ometepe in Lake Nicaragua. His group was importing shade coffee beans grown by the islanders. Some high-level birders had gone to Ometepe years before and reported that there was great avian biodiversity on Ometepe. They thought it was because of the 150-meter-tall canopy over the coffee plantations. Ometepe became part of the Northwest Shade Coffee Campaign. The islanders would harvest their coffee and ship the beans to Bainbridge to be roasted. The growers on Ometepe didn't have the capital to build their own roasting facilities. Volunteers on Bainbridge would have the beans roasted by Pegasus Coffee, a local roaster, and then

Poster courtesy of wildlife artist Ed Newbold. Newbold was a member of the Northwest Shade Coffee Campaign and continues to promote shade coffee in his store at First and Pike at the entrance of Pike Place Market. (Poster © Ed Newbold)

sell it. All the proceeds would go back to Ometepe. We used to joke about it at Seattle Audubon, that Ometepe coffee was the most environmentally correct coffee in the world. Eventually Seattle Audubon carried it in the Nature Shop.

Our volunteers began finding other sources of shade coffee. Russell Greenberg helped us with that. We made lists of where consumers could buy shade coffee in different parts of the country. We passed out the lists to other Audubon chapters so they could tell consumers in their areas, too. Then one day, the *New York Times* ran an article about our efforts. We began to get calls from everywhere. It became almost too much for us to handle.

Eventually we got our own funding and hired a part-time coordinator. We left Seattle Audubon to carry on by ourselves. One of the lessons I learned from Seattle Audubon was, as an activist, you go where the energy is. A project that generates a lot of energy motivates people to volunteer. Your project might not be exactly the same as the mission of the parent organization, yet it inspires people to get involved. I will always be grateful to Seattle Audubon for helping with shade coffee. On each step along the way, there were always people to support us. Hazel Wolf, Helen Engle, Bob and Eleanor Grant, Gerry Adams, and Gene Hunn were all incredibly supportive when I really needed them. So were our volunteers.

There was a time, for example, when I went to Chiapas. I traveled from San Cristóbal to Palenque through unbelievable amounts of clear cuts and devastation. I came back depressed by what I had seen. But the people on the committee said, 'We hear you and understand that you're discouraged. But we aren't. We're going to keep working.'

That was fantastic. They really believed in the vision behind the Northwest Shade Coffee Campaign, that we could use the market to promote values that are good for the environment.[96]

One of our volunteers told me about returning from a day of staffing a coffee booth at a fair. She saw a Western Tanager in her yard when she got home. She said she felt the bird had appeared there to thank her.

Whenever I see neotropical migrants myself, I feel the same way. It is always a gift to see them, and I feel like they are thanking me for whatever I can do to save their habitat."

Left: Seattle Audubon volunteer Alison Wysong holds a bag of Seattle Audubon's Centennial Blend Coffee, a dark roast prepared specially to celebrate our Centennial. It's a blend of Guatemalan beans, certified shade grown, fair trade, and organic. (Photograph courtesy of Constance Sidles) Right: A mother Anna's Hummingbird finishes feeding her chick. (Photograph © Paul Bannick)

EDUCATION: SHARING KNOWLEDGE

KIDS MATTER
Kate Thompson: Junior Audubon Club

OCTOBER, 1911
5 Cents a Copy

Above: This cover of Boys' Life Magazine *dates to 1911.* Boys' Life *was—and still is—the official magazine of the Boy Scouts of America. Beginning in 1919, as part of our Junior Audubon program, Seattle Audubon volunteers began to mentor Boy Scouts who wanted to earn their birding and nature badges. Later, Girl Scouts and Camp Fire were added to the program. (Courtesy of Boy Scouts of America)*

Any organization that manages to reach the ripe old age of a hundred knows at least one thing for sure: You can grow that old only if you stay young.

In other words, to survive in the long run, organizations must find a way to bring in new members, especially the younger generation, who will one day step into the shoes of those who went before. New blood is vital.

The National Audubon Society (then called the National Association of Audubon Societies) realized this early in its history and in 1910 began a national club for kids called Junior Audubon Club. The idea was to enroll as many children as possible into a club, send them pins and bird cards to collect, and get them to sign a pledge not to hurt birds. The pledge was important, as a lot of children owned air rifles from an early age and often shot small birds for fun.

In August 1916, after Seattle Audubon was recognized as a Society by National Audubon, we were given the responsibility of distributing Junior Audubon Club materials throughout the state. Often these materials were supplied by the national organization, but sometimes Seattle Audubon printed them at our own expense.[1]

The first President of Seattle Audubon, Mrs. Charles (Minnie) Crickmore, took a great interest in Junior Audubon Clubs, as did the first Secretary-Treasurer, Miss Kate Thompson. They looked for ways to open up the clubs to more children. Often, the key was to persuade elementary school teachers to enroll their entire classes in a club.[2]

Another successful way to get kids to join was to offer Junior Audubon talks and activities in public libraries. Individual Seattle Audubon members were encouraged to "adopt" a library and offer a program each month. By 1922, there were eight branch libraries participating in Junior Audubon. Kate Thompson, Minnie Crickmore, and Mary Compton, who became Seattle Audubon's second President, each adopted a library. There, once a month, they would hold a Junior Audubon meeting. Often they would show lantern slides of birds and other animals. Sometimes they brought study skins to show the kids as well. The library program was very popular and always attracted a good audience.[3]

The total number of children participating in Junior Audubon Clubs was impressive. Statewide, Seattle Audubon helped serve more than 9,200 kids. Nationwide, the number of clubs grew to more than 10,000 by 1955, with a membership that exceeded 400,000 kids.[4]

On October 14, 1955, Seattle Audubon launched a new program: Junior Audubon Society. It was an attempt to convert what had been a club structure into more of an educational program. Adult members of Seattle Audubon were enthusiastic and volunteered to introduce kids to high-level nature and conservation activities, including the rescue of injured birds, construction and installation of birdhouses and feeder stations (to be maintained by the kids themselves in Seattle

parks), field trips with adults, and classes taught by experts.

It was a smart move, as interest in Junior Audubon Clubs began to fade nationwide during the 1970s. Seattle's Junior Audubon Society—and its focus on broad educational programs for kids—became a model for National Audubon Society, which eventually converted its clubs into a program called Audubon Adventures. Audubon Adventures launched in 1984 and has since served more than 7 million students.[5]

Meanwhile, our own Junior Audubon Society gradually faded out, to be replaced by educational programs targeted to specific age groups: Nature Camp (for kids in first through third grades, fourth through sixth, and seventh through ninth) began in 1982;[6] Finding Urban Nature (FUN, an in-class program for third- and fourth-graders) began in 1986; and BirdWatch (for high school students) launched in the 1997-1998 school year. BirdWatch has now broadened its membership to include middle school students under a new program called Young Birders.

The programs may change over the years, but Seattle Audubon's commitment to young people remains the same. We know that teachers of children are also shapers of the future, because what kids learn to love early in life, they will love all their lives.

TREE SWALLOW (young and adult)
Published by the National Association of Audubon Societies

Above: New Juniors received six bird cards, a pin, and other materials. New cards would be issued periodically. Each card had a beautiful painting of a bird species on one side and its natural history on the other. (Courtesy of National Audubon Society)

Note: These two essays, "Our Junior Clubs" and "Invitation," were written by Kate Thompson for Seattle Audubon Society's newsletter, *The Seattle Wren.* "Our Junior Clubs" was published in April 1940; "Invitation" in July 1934. Kate Thompson was one of the founding members of Seattle Audubon and served in many capacities, including state-wide Chair of Junior Audubon Clubs, and Secretary-Treasurer and President of Seattle Audubon. She was an elementary school teacher for 40 years and took a great interest in helping children learn about nature, giving numerous talks and leading many bird walks.

Our Junior Clubs

"Twenty-nine years ago the National Association of Audubon Societies began sending out materials to Juniors. The dues in the Junior Audubon Club were ten cents. For this, each member received six bird leaflets, a bird button badge, and every club of 25 or more was sent *Bird-Lore* magazine.

In the past few years the quality of the materials furnished has been greatly improved and a large amount of extra helps are sent to each club, the last being *News on the Wing,* a publication for and by the Juniors. This comes to them four times during the year. However, the dues remain the same. This is possible because of the National Society being heavily endowed.

What has our Society done to help in this great movement? For four years we have had a supply station for our state and have mailed the materials to clubs. Some of the leaders tell us what the leaflets and buttons meant to them years ago when they were Juniors.

One young man writes: 'You may recall that you sent bird material to me when I was in Bellingham. I had a large club there but as I was only fifteen years of age, I couldn't accomplish very big things. I hope I did someone some good, at least enough to rouse them to protect our feathered friends. I am now older by three years and burning with zeal to teach others the way to gain true joy from the loving book of nature.'

How many Juniors do we have in Washington? We have enrolled over 9,200. Since last September, 80 clubs have been organized with 2,132 members.

Many of these groups are in remote corners of the state. Knowing the scarcity of bird literature in these regions, we are especially pleased to aid these bird enthusiasts."

MERITING A BADGE

In 1934, for a Girl Scout to earn a Bird Finder badge, she had to prove to four adult examiners that she could:

1. Know the parts of a bird.
2. Make a careful study of 25 birds that she has personally observed.
3. Make a list of the birds seen on one day in the field.
4. Study the English Sparrow [i.e, the House Sparrow] and tell briefly why it is an example of an unfortunate introduction of a bird to our land.
5. Show she has made use of some device to attract birds to her school or home.
6. Find out some general facts about the life history of birds.
7. Tell what the Audubon or other societies are doing for the protection of birds in danger of extermination and what a Girl Scout may do to protect birds.
8. Know the bird laws and refuges of her state; locate some of the larger bird refuges of the United States; keep up to date as far as possible with any international agreements which may be made.[7]

Above: The Girl Scout Bird Finder merit badge, as awarded from 1925 to 1938. (Photograph courtesy of Girl Scouts of Greater Atlanta Archives)

Invitation

"Nature extends her perpetual invitation to all people to attend her continuous pageant. The only requisites for the most advantageous places to view the passing spectacle are a seeing eye, a hearing ear, and an understanding heart.

Unlike man's clumsy efforts to furnish entertainment, there are no repetitions, no dull seasons—each day's performances are fresh from the Creator. The early morning hours are more completely filled with soul inspiring concerts and 'inciting moments' that lead to all-absorbing drama.

And what are some of the scenes on this enticing stage?

Wild geese from Mexico flying over on their way to the Arctic, their faint, melodious honks falling down to us earthbound creatures as they pass on into the northern twilight.

Vivacious little Seattle Wrens, in the wildest swampy woods or in the heart of the city, singing their many songs.

Twittering swallows feeding little ones on telephone wire nurseries.

Water Ouzels flitting over the turbulent mountain streams, the wild songs sounding above the roar of the torrent. Sandpipers twirling over mudflats.

Gray skies shedding silver mist over spruce thickets from which comes the long-drawn whistle of the Varied Thrush, rivaling in mysterious and melancholy sweetness the pipes of Pan.

These brave spirits in feathers enliven outdoor days with many experiences to store in memory's casket."

Not every Junior Audubon activity was about birds. Especially after the youth group was reconfigured from a Club into a Junior Society, kids learned about ecology, botany, zoology, even astronomy. Instruction involved classes taught by experts (including a tide pool class taught by Dixy Lee Ray in 1968), after which the kids went on field trips to test their knowledge of such things as web and wildflower identification. (Photograph © Doug Plummer)

YOU'LL HAVE FUN
Janet Sawyer: Finding Urban Nature

All children, especially the very young, are scientists on a mission—they must figure out as quickly as they can how the world works, including both the laws of nature and the intricacies of culture. Children do so mainly through experimentation. Drop a hammer on your foot, and you begin to appreciate gravitational physics. Draw a crayon stick-family on your parents' white wall, and you learn a bit about adult psychology. Flush a toothbrush down the toilet, and you get your first inkling about black holes, or at least small vortices. It's no accident that a two-year-old's favorite word (after "no") is "why?"

By the time children enter elementary school, they are capable of learning about the world second-hand, from books and lectures. But their first love is still hands-on experimentation. Maybe that will always be so,

even into adulthood, though many of us adults lack a child's courage to try just about anything new without fear of failure.

In the 1980s, Seattle Audubon began to look around for a way to serve children. Junior Audubon Clubs, sponsored by National Audubon, had faded out by this time, partly due to lack of interest on the part of kids, but also due to the growing discomfort of teachers to ask their students to pay dues.[8] Seattle Audubon's junior program, called Junior Audubon Society, had also declined by this time, as children became more interested in spending their leisure time on organized sports, video games, and after-school programs rather than membership organizations. It was clear that if Seattle Audubon wanted to engage kids, we

would have to change our approach.

The Education Committee, chaired by JoAnn Riecke, became intrigued by a science program for inner-city children conducted by the Denver Audubon Society. Denver Audubon had become concerned about the lack of nature programs and opportunities for inner-city children. In 1985, it launched a pilot program called Urban Education

Above: Anonymous student's watercolor and pencil portrait of Janet Sawyer. (Courtesy of Janet Sawyer)

Project, which involved volunteers taking kids outdoors to explore nature in their own neighborhoods. The program was offered in a variety of settings, including community centers and schools that had after-school programs.[9] In 1988, Denver Audubon received a grant of $380,000 from the National Science Foundation to do outreach to other cities. The NSF recognized that ever since the Soviet Union's launch of Sputnik in 1957, the government had spent millions of dollars on attempts to improve science literacy in the public schools, but results had been disappointing. The NSF hoped that Denver Audubon's program might get urban kids excited about science by showing them the natural world right outside their doorstep and by getting them involved in hands-on projects that were fun as well as educational.[10]

Riecke spoke to Denver Audubon about its program and realized this was our chance to invent our own version of Denver's experiment, with seed money from the NSF and the real possibility of raising funds from those Seattle Audubon members who cared about childhood education. She approached the Board with her idea, and on August 10, 1989, the Board approved.[11] FUN (Finding Urban Nature) was born.[12]

Although it took its initial idea from Denver, our FUN program soon achieved an

identity all its own. For one thing, Riecke and the Education Committee decided that it would work best if we took the project directly into schools during the school day, instead of offering it as an after-school or community program. That meant we had to get buy-in from the Seattle School District, from individual principals of schools, and of course, from the teachers themselves. To be successful, we had to tie our program directly to the State's requirements for science education, so the teachers could fold FUN into their curriculum. FUN would not succeed if it became a stand-alone, add-on program. It had to feel to the teachers like Seattle Audubon's efforts completely integrated their learning goals into our program offerings.

Thanks to succeeding generations of Education Managers at Seattle Audubon, as well as to the Coordinators they hired, that did happen. FUN became one of the most successful and long-lasting programs Seattle Audubon has ever run. FUN will soon celebrate its 30th anniversary and can be very proud of the fact that it has given life-changing science lessons to literally thousands of young children from all backgrounds.

One teacher of such children is Janet Sawyer. Sawyer has seen what FUN can do in her own classroom, and she is glad to host it every year.

"I've been working with the FUN program here at B. F. Day Elementary for 20 years now. My very first year of teaching here, I started working with FUN. I was teaching a class of third-, fourth-, and fifth-graders. The FUN program was already running in our school. A former colleague of mine who is now in Olympia, Mabel Atkins, was a birder, and she brought FUN to B. F. Day. I joined her team when I started to teach. She had a classroom of fourth-graders, and she invited me to partner with her.

B. F. Day was a diverse school back then. Although it still is, we had special programs then for homeless children. Predominantly, it was a site where we welcomed and nurtured that population, which had special needs. One such need was transportation. The kids and their families might move around a lot from one shelter to another, but we wanted them to be able to stay in the same school. So the District made sure to provide transportation for them, no matter where they were living. We still do that, but now we also have children from many different parts of the world, and many different backgrounds.

Gratitude is an important word in my classroom. We're grateful that we're here, that we have each other to learn from, that there are so many different cultures represented in this classroom, and we can learn from that.

FUN is an amazing program that fits in with those ideas. FUN is all about getting the students outside, doing science in their schoolyard environment, but also giving them hands-on experiences outdoors and letting them learn by interacting with their peers. The kids listen

Left: A team of students sifts through leaf litter, looking for tiny insects, spiders, and worms. Opposite page: The worm unit is one of the most popular among the students. (Photographs © Janet Sawyer)

respectfully to each other's ideas and learn from one another.

Seattle Audubon visits our school eight times a year. There are four classes in the fall and four in the spring. The program provides volunteers in addition to our parent volunteers. The small group setting ensures that each voice has a chance to be heard during the hour.

Each FUN lesson starts with a leader from Seattle Audubon in the classroom guiding the students about what they'll be doing and giving them some background on the topic. Then groups head outside to our schoolyard habitat where the lesson is conducted. The kids discover, observe, share, and then apply what they're doing in the classroom to the FUN lesson of the day. Later on, we might extend the FUN lesson with writing or math activities, and we discuss our listening skills, our observational skills, and our respect for each other.

FUN covers many different areas. There are two lessons specific to birds. The one in the fall gets the kids quite

excited. Seattle Audubon brings in bird skins, which the kids get to handle. The kids make measurements and collect data on everything from hawks to owls to little hummingbirds.

In the spring, Seattle Audubon teaches a class about nest construction. Audubon volunteers bring wire frames that they give to the kids to use as a base, and then we go outside to collect nest material, which the kids weave into the wire frames. The nests all look different because the kids collect different kinds of material—leaves, grass, sticks.

After they make their nests, each group talks about how birds hide or camouflage the nests. Then each student hides his or her nest, and the other kids have to try to find it. It's a great lesson. I had one student who wanted to bury his nest. The leader had told the group that some birds build their nests on the ground, so he wanted to hide his in the ground, too. He covered up the nest with dirt and leaves, and the other kids tried to find it. He was very clever about hiding it, because no one found it. I think it might still be out there!

One lesson the kids really get excited about is the spider unit. I start by reading them a story about spiders, so they're prepared with some background information. When Seattle Audubon comes in, they first talk about different types of webs, and then they share a little about spiders. When we go outside, the kids hunt for different webs. We have vast grounds at B. F. Day, everything from concrete playground to an open play field to a rain garden. The kids might find an orb web or a cobweb almost anywhere. Once they find a web, they try to locate the spider. Next, they go into the leaf debris and try to find an isopod,

like a sowbug or a pillbug—something they can place on the web. When they do that, the spider will sense its prey and go after it to see what it is. When it finds the bug, the spider wraps it up, and the kids get to see that. It's incredible. I'll never forget the look on one girl's face when her spider went after its prey. She just could not believe she was witnessing such a thing. I remember her expression so distinctly.

Another important lesson is the worm unit. The kids go outside and look for worms to put in their pans. Some of the kids are squeamish. They don't like worms. However, they get so fascinated by the lesson that they end up picking up the worms after all. This year, I really appreciated one mom who took her group onto the cement area of our grounds, where there were few trees and much less leaf debris. The kids were still able to do all the activities that the other groups did. I loved the fact that she did that because it taught the kids that where there are fewer trees and plants, they can still find worms and spider webs.

During this last worm lesson, we didn't find as many worms as we have in the past. I shared with my students, 'Last year, every group found thirteen,

fourteen, or fifteen worms each, but this year, each group found only one or two. What were the variables that impacted this discovery?'

We had a great discussion about why that could happen, why in other years we might find triple the number of worms that we found this year. The kids eventually got to what we think happened, that the weather was so dry and hot, the worms were buried too deep underground to come out. I challenged the kids to go home and try their own yards, to see if they were different from our school's. We'll see what evidence they collect.

One of the things I really appreciate about what Audubon provides is the vocabulary they use. The kids remember the words because the vocabulary part of the lesson gives them tools they need to explain their thinking and talk about what they have learned. Their retention of material is amazing. I think that's directly related to the fact that the kids are personally involved in touching the materials and collecting them. They get to choose, find, and sort them on their own. It's part of the whole process that Audubon provides. Kids aren't just sitting in a classroom, reading things and answering questions. They're interacting with the adults, with the materials, and with each other.

You might think that taking third-graders outside would lead to them running all over and not paying attention. To keep that from happening, I do two things. First, I take them outside before Audubon starts, to get them doing some independent activities outdoors. Second, I have high expectations for their behavior. This is not recess or play time. It is class. We are scientists going outside. It helps that they love the classes. That's the hands-on piece. The scientists are always doing something, whether it's gathering materials, collecting things, sorting them, observing, sharing. They're busy and focused the whole time they're out in the field.

Another part I like about FUN is the focus on peer learning. The volunteer leaders lead the kids to talk about what they might expect to find, what they do find, and why. We try to make them more aware of what's going on around them. Part of that is to be aware of the environment, but another part is also to be sensitive to their peers' comprehension of the subject matter and lesson objective. As I said, we have a diverse classroom, and we talk about our differences. We try to be brave when we do it. Even when we go outside for FUN, the kids need to be aware and help each other to succeed.

We owe them the sharing of our knowledge, so they understand what we're trying to tell them and can apply that to the world they're going to be living in when they grow up. It will be a different place. I want to let them know that they need to think about their actions and their choices. We compost in our classroom, for example. We recycle. We're constantly talking about the things we can recycle and the things we can't.

Teaching kids about nature and the things they see when we're doing the FUN lessons makes them understand that a leaf could be somebody's meal, a bush could be somebody's home. I hope these lessons make my students more sensitive about the choices they make, because the bigger picture is that our resources are dwindling in the world. Teaching eight- and nine-year-olds about the little things they can do right now will help build their foundation and understanding of the impact they have on the world. It will help them find their own place in the world.

I love my job. I feel so grateful that I get to do this every day. I love working with Audubon. I think it's amazing they are able to come here and provide this kind of learning for third-graders."

FALL

The leaves are so red,
Falling from the trees with grace.
Then people rake them.—*Hugo Henrikson*

This haiku was written by one of Sawyer's students as an extension of a FUN lesson. Sawyer often ties FUN lessons into her academic curriculum. (Photograph of Chestnut-backed Chickadee © Paul Bannick)

OUTSIDE THE BOX
Adam Sedgley: Nature Camp

A wise outdoorsman once said, "If you want your kids to love nature, then the first time you take them into the wild, you must make sure they have fun. No miserable weather. No long slogs. No nettles. Just fun."

Adam Sedgley's parents must have known this because they showed Adam the outdoors in such a way that now, even as an adult, he is struck by wonder at the mystery and beauty of the wild.

Part of his parents' efforts involved signing him up for multiple sessions of Seattle Audubon's Nature Camp, year after year. Being in nature was a life-changing experience for the young boy, one that shaped his life, influenced his career path, and gave him a joy that still fills his soul today.

Nature Camp started in 1982, with the strong support of Education Committee Chair Wynne Brown and staffers Clare Close, Michael Donahue, and Laura Stone. Its first year was a wild success, with more

than 90 kids ages six through eleven attending day-camp sessions four days a week.[13] Sessions met initially at the Good Shepherd Center in Seattle, but the kids spent a lot of their time on field trips. That first year, they went to Carkeek Park on "Beach Day" to explore tide pools, catch hermit crabs, and observe sea pens, sea urchins, and starfish. "Meadow Day" found them in Discovery Park looking for insects, rodent runs, garter snakes, and pheasants. "Forest Day" took them back to Discovery Park to hike Wolf Tree Nature Trail and construct a trail from an ant's point of view. Montlake Fill hosted the kids for "Marsh Day," when they waded in ponds, made casts of animal tracks, and picked as many blackberries as they could eat.[14]

Camp leaders tried to bring in as many experts as possible to the classroom sessions, including a beekeeper and a snake handler, who brought in Boa Constrictors

Adam Sedgley. (Photograph © Kristi Sartnurak)

to drape on the kids and a Corn Snake to touch. Staff also got highly creative about activities that would appeal to children: an "Indian walk," where the kids had to be silent and communicate only with hand signs; "create a tree," with kids acting out the various parts of a tree; and "owl ears" to appreciate the acute hearing of owls.

By the second year, the program grew to serve 175 children.[15] Staffers Ann Hursey,

Michael Donahue, Jan Auman, and Liz Matteson continued to develop the program, refining it to fit the needs of the kids. For the younger kids, the sessions explored nature from three perspectives: "What's Up" focused on flight, namely, birds and flying insects. "What's Down" examined what's in the soil and included tracking skills. "What's All Around" focused on life in wetlands, the intertidal zone, and everything in between. For the older kids, the emphasis was on an in-depth study of natural history, with the kids meeting at a different field site every day. Their summer session culminated in a field trip to Dungeness Spit.[16]

Over the years since then, Nature Camp has expanded to serve a wider range of kids. It is offered now at Magnuson Park for grades first through ninth. Many kids return year after year, signing up for the higher-level sessions offered to older kids. Some stick with the program all the way through high school to become Junior Naturalists in a program that trains high school kids to be volunteer assistant camp counselors.

The sessions nowadays tend to focus on special areas of interest. For example, "Bugs or Bust" focuses entirely on a week of uncovering the world of creepy-crawlies. "Habitat Restoration Rangers" teaches the kids about restoration ecology and gives them a chance to do real restoration work in a park. "The Natural Artist" gives kids a week of art lessons inspired by nature.[17]

Nature Camp has changed in detail, but never in intent: The object always has been to expose city kids to nature on their doorstep, to get them excited about the wild, and to teach them about the wonders and interconnectedness of our world. The hope is that as they grow up, these children will come to love nature as much as we do and will want to take their place in the ranks of those who work to protect it. Adam is one who did.

Some of the creepy-crawlies to be observed at Magnuson Park are insects such as this Great Golden Digger Wasp (top) fighting a yellow jacket (right) over a katydid (green) that has been stung into paralysis, a dramatic life-and-death struggle for prey. (Photograph © Gregg Thompson)

"I've always loved nature. I had parents who were very supportive of my outdoor lifestyle and who always encouraged me to learn more. I got into birding at a very young age because my mom, Linda Sedgley, was one of the first employees at Seattle Audubon, so I just kind of grew up with the organization. I knew Dennis Paulson when I was a kid, and Chris Peterson, Bob Sundstrom, and Idie Ulsh. I've known them all for years.

When I was five, my mom took me to a National Audubon conference at Asilomar in California. Passionate bird conservationists gathered from around the country and, amongst the meetings and networking events, the California Condor took center stage. For the children, educators rolled out an impressive piece of cloth that was cut to represent the life-sized silhouette of the massive bird. Scientists gave presentations about the plight of the species. At that time, in the mid-1980s, there were only 22 birds left in the wild—the situation was dire. Habitat loss, DDT, electrocution from power lines, pressures from cattle ranching, and poisoning from lead shot proved too much for the dedicated scavenger.

I cried all night. I loved birds and when I learned the plight of the near-extinct species, I was heartbroken. According to my mother, I was inconsolable.

Word of my concern spread and, by the following morning, the world's experts on California Condors had assembled at our breakfast table—Ph.D. ornithologists had gathered to assuage the concerns of a five-year-old child. My mother recollects that I didn't say a word, I just held my chin barely above the edge of the table. Undeterred by my melancholic state, the scientists reassured me that they were doing absolutely everything they could to save the emblematic species.

I tell that story because it really speaks to the power of the Audubon community. To have the world's experts on the California Condor take the time to make a little five-year-old feel better shows how much they loved nature and how much they wanted others to love nature, too. It's also a tribute to the love of nature that my parents nurtured in me and which Nature Camp also nurtured as I got a little older.

I started going to Nature Camp when it was still up at the Good Shepherd Center. I was six or seven at the time—a long time ago! We had a lot of in-class sessions, but what I remember best are the field trips. We explored local parks with birders, and we went tide-pooling, too. Tide-pooling wasn't new to me—my parents used to take me to beaches in the Seattle area. I thought it was really exciting because you can unlock a lot of little features of nature that you might otherwise easily walk by. You walk over a stone, you don't see anything. You turn it over, and there's an entire ecosystem underneath. Plus, in tide pools there is lots of squishy stuff—gross things that get kids going. Even as an adult, I still tide-pool every few years when the tides and my schedule allow for it.

The most distinct class I remember was when someone brought in wolves from Wolf Haven. We were in a circle, sitting on the ground, and then the Wolf Haven people brought in two wolves. One was gray, and one was black. They were kind of accustomed to kids, I think, but they were on leashes and very skittish. So you could tell that they were still very wild. They weren't domesticated by any means. We were sitting on the ground looking eye to eye with a wolf, knowing that it still has the wild left in it. That definitely leaves a mark.

In terms of activities, the one I remember best is going on a dinosaur egg

The young Adam Sedgley with his dad, Richard Sedgley. (Photograph courtesy of Adam Sedgley)

hunt. The camp counselors would draw a small footprint in the mud, the kind that some sort of miniaturized *T. rex* would make, and they told us to follow the footprints. 'We're going to find the egg, we're going to find the egg,' they said. In the end, the egg turned out to be a watermelon.

I must have known it wasn't a real dinosaur egg. It tasted remarkably like a fruit I often ate during the summer and looked a lot like it, too. But every year, I got excited about that.

For me, though, the biggest impact of Nature Camp was being with children my own age, my peers who shared a lot of my same interests. We all came from different schools, different backgrounds, different household situations, but we were all really into nature. That's huge for developing minds.

Like I said before, my parents were always supportive of my interest in nature. I can appreciate now the sacrifices they must have made, because getting out into nature can be a logistical nightmare. It's complicated. Now that I'm an adult, I joke when my wife and I go backpacking with our friends: We spend hundreds if not thousands of dollars on gear just so we can rough it, insert ourselves into nature, almost bring ourselves close to death just so we can experience some of these magical natural areas. I was lucky to have parents who would take me out there. Not everybody can do that. When you look at what it takes to get out into the wilderness, you realize how inaccessible some of these natural areas are. It's not just that they may be hard to get to.

Michael Donahue (far left) checks out the differences between Western and Least Sandpipers while campers observe a flock of peeps during the very first Nature Camp in 1982. Campers left to right are: James Loetterle, Roland Jones, Ming Gale, and Ben Fitzpatrick. (Photograph by Laura Stone, courtesy of Seattle Audubon Society.)[18]

You have to have the flexibility in your schedule to be able to take off with your kids and go to your local or National Park, and you have to have the disposable income to do that.

One thing that Nature Camp does is make nature accessible. Nature can be found in your backyard. It doesn't have to be a drive across the state. It could be right down your street.

Because Nature Camp is a summer program, it fits into parents' schedules, obviously. If you talk to any parent, it's daycare. But it's more than that. It's also an opportunity for kids to have activities while their parents are at work. Kids have an innate curiosity about everything because they're figuring everything out. A lot of the experiences they're having, they're having for the first time, especially when you're taking them into unfamiliar territory, into a whole new world. That path of discovery—Nature Camp brings out the inner scientist in every kid. They have that innate curiosity that oftentimes just wouldn't get nurtured otherwise.

When I went to college at the University of Puget Sound, I had a chance to apply for a study-abroad program in Asia. I found out about it in the second week of college. It was a program where fifteen students got to travel around Asia taking different classes in each country. I didn't think I would be admitted because I had to ask for recommendations from my teachers, but no one knew me. My mom encouraged me anyway. She said, 'You're doing it.' And I did.

That changed my focus in school. I became an Asian studies major because of that program. But I was still interested in nature and had an environmental studies minor. I fulfilled my natural history core credits probably two or three times over.

After college, I lived in Japan for a couple of years teaching English. I was trying to figure out what I wanted to do with my life. I realized that I still really appreciated nature and the outdoors.

When I came back, I decided I was going to chase opportunities to get back into the environmental field. I volunteered for a herpetologist down in the Amazon, and I was there for three months. It was an absolute slog, but I loved it. I was doing the same type of things I had done as a kid in Nature Camp, flipping over rocks in tide pools, only now I was flipping over logs in the Amazon looking for creepy-crawlies.

Eventually I ended up back at Seattle Audubon, working on BirdNote with Chris Peterson and then was hired as the Science Associate. I stayed for seven years, growing the science program. I got to do a lot of citizen science, but I also volunteered as much as I could for the kids' programs because I knew how

important those programs were for me when I was growing up.

Now I work for Conservation International, which is based out of Washington, D.C. It's an environmental nonprofit that addresses global issues. I developed a skill set with websites and digital media. I use my skills trying to get people to care, trying to find that emotional linchpin that makes people act to conserve some of the places that we need most around the world.

I still enjoy doing field trips, but now I lead them. It's a passion for me because maybe I've seen a bird 1,000 times, 10,000 times, but as soon as I show that bird to someone who hasn't seen it before, to see the look on their faces is totally addictive. I absolutely love it. I'm seeing that bird again for the first time through someone else's eyes. I feel like I'm unlocking a little piece of nature, a little bit of the mystery.

That's what Nature Camp was for me. Someone took the time to show me the natural world and unlock those pieces of it day after day, week after week. Now I want to give that back."

A Western Sandpiper tries to capture a worm. (Photograph © Gregg Thompson)

READY TO SOAR
Emily Tompkins: BirdWatch

Emily Tompkins in the Galápagos. (Photograph courtesy of Emily Tompkins)

Despite all the mythology about the sweetness of age sixteen, when asked if they could go back in time and be teenagers again, most adults would just shudder. It's impossible to forget the awkwardness, the pangs of shyness, the fear that your voice would break at the worst moment or you'd be the only girl not invited to the senior prom. The teen years are when children make their first forays into the adult world, away from the safe harbor of parents who used to be so smart but are now so uncool. It is the time when boys turn into men, girls into women. Teens know instinctively they must figure out who they are and what they want to do with their lives, but most of them haven't a clue how.

High school counselor and Seattle Audubon past President Idie Ulsh understood this age group well. As a woman who spent her career helping teens get into college, she knew how important it is for teenagers to belong to a group that has shared interests and does cool things that are admired by

peers. Idie believed that high school teenagers could also benefit from activities that connected them to the natural world and helped them develop skills that would give them a sense of adult-level mastery. She thought a service/learning club might be just what was needed. It would be small, intimate, with a lot of mentoring by Seattle Audubon's ornithology experts and with a strong focus on learning by doing.

In 1997, Idie's dream came true: with the whole-hearted support of Executive Director Chris Peterson and a cadre of dedicated volunteers and staff, BirdWatch was launched.[19] During that first school year, BirdWatch students met monthly for presentations, field trips, and bird-banding training. It soon became clear that another purpose the program could serve was to fulfill the students' service hour requirements, which in some school districts amounted to 60 volunteer hours. BirdWatch teens volunteered to help in Seattle Audubon's

office, clear invasive plants from parks, serve as camp counselors in the City of Seattle's summer programs, and help with cleanup efforts along the Duwamish River.

Throughout its history, BirdWatch was always a small program—usually fewer than 30 teens at most.[20] This was intentional. It was felt that BirdWatch teens should have a high degree of personal contact with the adults who mentored them. It was also hoped that the teens would become leaders among their peers, spreading the word about conservation and nature, and eventually taking leadership positions as adults.

One of the early participants in BirdWatch was Emily Tompkins. Although it has been fifteen years since she first got involved with the program, she remembers her experiences vividly. They changed her life.

"I got involved in BirdWatch in ninth grade in 2000 and stayed with it until I graduated in 2004. A family friend—Woody Wheeler—had told me about it. He was a great birder and was the one who introduced me to birding. He came by for dinner with my parents one night and dropped off a flyer. It sounded really interesting to me, so I went to a meeting.

I was looking for a group to fit in with in high school. I was already very interested in birds and nature, and I was having trouble in the Seattle Public School District finding a group of my peers who shared my same interests. I was really shy, too, so for me, BirdWatch was great.

I really liked the idea of learning new skills that might translate into a career for me. Two of those skills were bird-banding and MAPS monitoring. MAPS stands for Monitoring Avian Pro-ductivity and Survivorship, a program sponsored by the Institute for Bird Populations to study passerine birds at bird-banding stations nationwide. Don Norman from the Puget Sound Bird

WHY WE HELP

Isadora (Izzy) and Kendrick Wong began volunteering with BirdWatch almost from the very beginning. Over the years they have helped many kids learn about nature, both human and wild. One girl, though, stands out for them. Izzy tells why:

"After four years in the program through high school, Rebecca graduated and went on to college. She mailed me a note, thanking me and my husband Kendrick, saying that if it hadn't been for our presence, she might not have stayed all four years. She was a girl of color, and she felt that our presence in BirdWatch as people of color too gave her the confidence, encouragement, and strength she needed sometimes to see it through. Role models for people of color, you know, particularly in environmental groups, are limited. We're growing in numbers, but we're still not that common.

The reason I point this out as an important piece is because Rebecca went on to college at Lewis & Clark, and now she's a lawyer advocating for environmental causes.

It's a big deal for kids that age to have role models. They are often lost. They're foundering. They don't know what to do. It's so significant if we adults show them our enthusiasm, that we care about the environment and about birds, and we're willing to teach them and help them. We show them by our example that they can do this, too.

We don't always know that we're making an impact, which is why it's always said of teachers and role models, 'You never know who's going to listen to you and watch you.'

I didn't think about that much when I was with the BirdWatch group, but clearly all the adults in the program made a big difference to the kids. They were all wonderful kids, too, and many of them went on to get degrees in wildlife biology or natural resources or some other environmental field. They might not have, if it hadn't been for BirdWatch, because many of the kids who started in this program were not birders.

It was certainly fun for us, too. BirdWatch was one of the best experiences of my life within Seattle Audubon, for sure.

I still stay in touch with Rebecca—we think of her as almost a daughter of our own. Her mother passed away not long after she graduated from the program, but before she died, her mom told me, 'Rebecca is always talking about you and Kendrick and how wonderful it was to have you around.'

I was very touched by that. I had no idea she felt that way. I had no idea."

Observatory helped train a bunch of us BirdWatch students about how to band birds and monitor populations. Those were practical skills that gave me an exposure to what that kind of research was like.

BirdWatch met monthly, and the meetings were quite variable. Some of them would be talks by people who were associated with the Burke Museum. Others would be presentations by local ornithologists, talking to us about everything from bird identification to conservation of birds and bird research, including how to use museum collections for research. We also practiced some activities together. For example, we learned how to take a dead bird and develop it into a study skin. We stuffed each skin with sawdust.

I hadn't known before what the skins were stuffed with.

In addition to these more formal meetings, we also had a lot of Bird-Watch-specific outings, usually connected to some sort of community service. We went out and removed brush and invasive species from sites that were overgrown, for example. I remember doing that at Carnation Marsh and along the Duwamish River.

One of the community service projects I always enjoyed was taking study skins out to show young kids. We mentored the kids during a summer outreach program where once a week, some of the BirdWatch students would volunteer at community centers. We would go out with skins and work with elementary school kids. There is just something about bringing in a real bird, even though it's dead, that really hooks people. The kids could see the actual

---

In 2001, Tompkins and eight of her fellow students in BirdWatch took a week-long trip to Southeast Arizona, where they saw a total of 161 different bird species, including Blue-throated Hummingbird (left) and Least Bittern (opposite page), a county record. (Illustrations by BirdWatch student Diana Thayer, reprinted from the June 2001 issue of Earthcare Northwest, *courtesy of Seattle Audubon Society)*

bird up close, which most of them had never done before.

BirdWatch took us on a lot of field trips, too. I had been birding before, but many of us were just learning how to bird at that point. Some had never birded at all and had to learn how to use binoculars and scopes. We went out to local parks, over to Eastern Washington, even down to the coast to look at shorebirds. We explored the State through learning about the birds that inhabited all the different kinds of habitat we have. And we went owling. It was all so cool. That's what we liked, right? Getting out and playing in the mud, working with birds and feathers, getting to touch real birds.

Senior year, I did an internship created by BirdWatch in partnership with the University of Washington, working with four graduate students in the urban ecology program. The project we were working on was tracking juvenile songbird dispersal through different environments —in urban environments and more natural environments. What I got to do was go out and set up mist nets. I'd play recordings to draw in target individuals, and then we would band them. Then we would look for nests. We did a lot of nest searching. When we found a nest, we would wait until the fledglings were just about to leave, and then we would attach little backpack radio transmitters to them. We had a big antenna, and we would go out every couple of days and track each of these transmitters.

Sometimes we would have to bushwhack through blackberry bushes and dense habitat. We always tried not to walk through anybody's backyard as we tracked some of these songbirds. Every so often we would find a bird that had died. I remember once we got a signal that looked like it was coming from underground. So we started digging and sure enough, we found this little radio tag and the songbird's feet in a sort of tunnel underground. So something had eaten the wren and dragged it under the earth, where we found it.

It was a cool project and an amazing thing to be able to put on my college resume, to say that I'd already had field research experience at the college level, working with these graduate students. I'm sure BirdWatch helped me get into college, and it inspired me to major in biology. Now I am a Ph.D. student at Wake Forest University, and I have one year left on my Ph.D. My study species is the Nazca Booby, which is a large pelagic seabird. I study a population breeding in the Galápagos Islands of Ecuador. My research has to do with evaluating how much genetic variation is available for selection to work on. I'm asking questions about the factors that maintain genetic variation for traits that are under selection, traits such as clutch size and laying date that vary from individual to individual, because selection should be eliminating less fit genotypes and eroding genetic variation over time. But certain aspects of genetic architecture, such as the same genes affecting multiple traits, can interact with selection to maintain genetic diversity.

I accomplish my research using quantitative genetic techniques. The breeding traits I focus on are affected by many loci, and we're not necessarily looking at individual genes within a genome. Instead, we're using pedigree information and statistical techniques to infer how much trait variation is due to genetic similarity between relatives vs. how much may be due to environmental effects such as sea surface temperature altering productivity or food availability.

Exposure to all those different scientists who took the time to work with us in BirdWatch certainly cemented for me an interest in science. With that, I knew I wanted to go into science right away when I began my undergraduate education. There was a direct line between learning about birds in high school, continuing to learn about birds in college, and then going on to do a graduate degree working with birds and answering these ecology and evolution questions.

But more than that, BirdWatch did a lot for my self-esteem in high school. It gave me opportunities to work independently and to work with others. A lot of the things we did felt like an adventure. BirdWatch ignited in me a passion for travel and for exploring different areas. I made a lot of good friends in the program, including Emily Sprong, our fearless leader, and that certainly carried through high school and beyond. I'm still friends with a lot of the BirdWatch kids.

After I get my degree, I want to have dual tracks in my life: teaching and research. In graduate school, I've been fortunate enough to mentor other researchers. I have also been a teaching assistant in undergraduate laboratory classes. Passing on my enthusiasm for science and for asking good scientific questions, in particular, is something that I really like to do. It gives my life meaning.

I'm also passionate about research, specifically basic research. I'm a quantitative geneticist. I'm not necessarily going to focus my laboratory around population monitoring or direct conservation issues, but I do think that basic science tells us a lot about what we need to know to be able to manage populations, particularly under climate change.

That's been a lot on my mind. I've been working on a manuscript that we're about to submit that has a climate change angle. For Nazca Boobies, my study species, there was a big dietary shift that happened after the 1997 El Niño. The boobies lost sardines, which were a preferred prey item for them, and now they're eating flying fish. Associated with that change in their diet, there's been a big change in reproductive success. Reproductive success is much lower. Survival is actually a little higher, but that drop in reproductive success means the long-term population growth rate is less than one, signifying a population in decline.

The link we made to climate change is that in the Galápagos Islands, the projected ocean warming is going to move the islands outside of the preferred temperature range that sardines flourish in. So if we look to the future, what's likely to happen is this flying fish diet will persist. Under a flying fish diet, we see that the population is going to decline.

I hope that we can mitigate to the best extent possible the damage that is going to come from global climate change. I hope that we make the most out of studying the changes that are going to happen that we can't stop right now, that we already put into motion. And I hope that we and future generations figure out the best way to manage our use of fossil fuels so that we don't lose all of the amazing biodiversity and ecosystem functioning that is present right now."

Tompkins did not want to go home from her Arizona Bird-Watch trip without seeing a Greater Roadrunner. It took the group five days to find one, but finally Tompkins got her life bird. The kids recorded the bird species they found, because they had each secured birdathon pledges as part of their efforts to raise money for the trip. (Photograph © Larry Engles)

LIFELONG LEARNING
Jack Stephens: Adult Classes

Chickadees grow new neurons every fall so they can remember where they cached their seeds. Later, when winter comes, the extra neurons fire up, and the chickadees flit from one remembered cache to another, eating all the seeds they have stored.

If only we humans could do that! We could remember where we parked the car in the shopping mall lot, where we put our glasses, why we entered that room, and what we were saying just now.

Alas. We grow our brain cells fastest when we are very young. The older we get, the slower we grow. But although we can't keep pace with chickadees' IQs, we now know that adult humans do have the ability to grow new neurons all our lives.

That means learning, for us, doesn't stop when we grow up and leave school. It is a lifelong process—one that Seattle Audubon has been feeding from its very beginning.

The first official activity of Seattle Audubon was an expert-led bird walk around Lake Burien, followed a month later by a guided walk starting at the University of Washington.[21] The walks were not just to look at birds but to teach others to identify what they were seeing. Within the first month of organizing, Seattle Audubon hosted its first lecturer, Professor Trevor Kincaid of the University of Washington, who taught an audience of 50 about the "economic value of birds."[22]

People were eager to learn almost anything to do with birds, because birds are the gateway into a deeper understanding of nature. The July 1916 meeting of Seattle Audubon, for example, featured a presentation by Miss Adelaide L. Pollock on the common birds of the Seattle area and their habits. She brought study skins and played phonographic records of bird songs.[23]

Jack Stephens feeds a chickadee. (Photograph courtesy of Jack Stephens)

The first actual course offered to members began at Broadway High School on November 4, 1917. It was the result of an effort by Seattle Audubon to partner with the University of Oregon in order to offer a year-long course on birds, consisting of 34 lessons. The lessons included topics such as "Ancestry of

Birds," "Moulting of Birds," and "Special Sense Organs of Birds." Half the lessons were given by Seattle Audubon's own Professor Kincaid.[24] The course proved so popular that it was offered many more times over the next ten years.[25]

The tradition of our own members sharing their expertise with others has continued since those early days. Now every quarter, new classes are offered, and eager participants sign up. Among the most popular of these modern courses was one taught by two of Seattle Audubon's most revered teachers, Barry Levine and Jack Stephens.

The pair offered their "Beginning Birding" class every fall or winter since 2008. There were two two-hour classroom sessions, and two all-day field trips. It was an easy, gentle introduction to the world of birding. But more than that, it was both fun and funny, as Barry and Jack would exchange jokes, tweaking and testing each other both in class and out in the field. People who have taken the class say that this dynamic duo made an indelible impression.

Tragically, it is one that will live on only in memory, for we lost Barry Levine in December 2015. Jack Stephens carries on alone now, missing his friend, missing the fun, but also knowing that birders need him, and the world needs birders. A lesson for us all.

"Barry was a good friend of mine. He'd gone through the Master Birder class, needed to give back some volunteer hours, and recruited me to help teach 'Beginning Birding'. I didn't have any background in teaching, but Barry was a professional. He taught biology at Newport High School in the Bellevue school system for 20 years. It was his idea to teach a class for beginning birders that was not about facts but process. We thought it would be impossible to run through all the birds of Washington and tell beginners enough about them that they could go out and identify the birds themselves. So what we tried to do was teach mainly critical observation—how to look at something and really *see* it, not just look at it.

For example, we'd start every class showing a flash of a bird—say, a robin—for five seconds, and then we'd ask the class, 'What color was the bill? What color were the legs? Was the head darker than the back or the same color? Did it have an eye-ring?' We would ask people to describe what they had seen so that they got used to critical observation.

We would follow that with side-by-side pictures of a robin and a Spotted Towhee, and I would tell an anecdote

Barry Levine. (Photograph © Marvin Cooper)

about a friend of mine who had a bird feeder that attracted a towhee, but she was convinced she was seeing a robin.

I told her, 'No, that's not a robin,' but she kept saying it was. We went back and forth. She was a very intelligent person who's got fine eyes. How was it she didn't see what was in front of her? How did that happen?

That was the kind of thing we'd talk about as we went through the class exercises. 'You tell me why she's wrong. Explain to me what are the differences? How do you know that's not a robin?'

You can use that process with ducks, gulls, little brown birds, or whatever you happen to come across. If you can really see what you're seeing, you can probably identify it. But for many of us, our expectations get in the way. We see what we expect to see. We all do it, but knowing that, we can account for it, we can control it.

We also talked about what to do when you see a bird you don't know. The way we taught people to look at a new bird was to start at the bill and just very methodically work their way back: bill shape and color, eye color, markings about the head, the back, belly, legs, and tail. What did they see? Just describe it.

After we talked about the way things looked, we would add other things to observe, such as behavior. For example, we had a video of a nuthatch going down a tree. We would show the video and then ask the class what they had seen. 'The bird went down!' someone would say.

There is only one thing that does that. All the other ones go up. Woodpeckers go up. Creepers go up.

Sometimes Barry and I would do this thing where I would tell him something I saw and not describe its appearance at all, just the behavior. 'I was looking at my suet feeder when a whole flock of tiny birds came and covered the feeder. It was almost solid birds. Then all of a sudden, whoosh! they all flew away. What were they?'

Barry would get it. 'Those were Bushtits,' he would say.

We tried to stay away from jargon and not talk about things like auriculars or secondaries/primaries/tertials. Our students were beginners, and they didn't need to know all that. They needed to know simpler things. Some of them would come to class with no optics. A few couldn't identify any birds at all at first. It was surprising to me. We would have an exercise where we would put up an American Robin, a bird we thought everyone would know, and we would ask the class, 'How many don't know what this is?' There would always be six or seven who didn't know.

So we would say, 'That's okay. This class is for beginners. This is why you're here.' We didn't want to make people feel uncomfortable about not knowing something. So we stuck to the basics. We

would mostly cover common birds that you could easily see around here. That's one reason we would always teach the class in the winter, because waterfowl are easy to find here then, and they're easy to see. They're pretty colorful, and they don't fly away. You can find them with your binoculars.

Sometimes, though, Barry and I would go back and forth about being too technical, like using the word 'seagull,' for example. Barry would always correct me whenever I said it. The correct term is 'gull.' Okay, I do get it. I understand. It's like calling a bison in Yellowstone a buffalo. It's not technically correct, but everybody knows exactly what you're talking about, which is the point of the spoken word, right? To communicate. Besides, 'Bison gal, won't you come out tonight?' just doesn't do it somehow.

That kind of banter made the class fun for us, and I dearly miss it now that Barry is gone. We would have that interplay. It wasn't just rote memorization of facts. We had fun with it. It was the glue for friendship.

We taught every single class together, and when Barry passed away in December, I didn't think I could do the next class. I almost canceled it. Then I

THERE'S GOING TO BE A TEST

Jack Stephens and Barry Levine taught one class called "Little Brown Birds," about how to tell apart the many different species of small birds in Washington whose dominant color scheme is brown. Such birds start out looking alike to beginners, but with practice using critical observation skills, students begin to see that each species does indeed have distinct field marks. You can identify them! Give it a try and see how you do. Answers appear upside down on the next page. (The photograph immediately to the right is © Alex MacKenzie; all other photographs are © Gregg Thompson.)

thought, 'He would want me to go forward,' so I did.

We both thought it was important to show people how to go beyond just a passing glance at the natural world. Our overarching goal was that people should love what they were doing and want to do it more.

It's possible to look at birds and not know what you're looking at and still think they're wonderful. You can do that. But if you don't really know what you're seeing, it's going to be an impediment to understanding nature. Barry used to start the class by saying, 'Our goal is to change your life. We want you to appreciate and interact with the natural world in a different way.'

One day we took the class out on a field trip to Montlake Fill. We heard there was a Tufted Duck that had shown up down there. I tend not to chase rare birds, but this one was so close that we all went. So there we were, looking at this rare duck, and a woman came up and said, 'Barry! Jack! You changed my life! I bird all the time now, and it's wonderful. Thank you so much.'

It was Alex MacKenzie. She had taken our class two or three years before, and now she is a Master Birder. We hugged. I was like, 'It works! It works!'

That was a 'whoa!' moment for me. But that's the thing with beginners—they have those moments all the time. They will see things that for us are mundane and pe-

destrian—like a Red-winged Blackbird, or a Green-winged Teal—and just be blown away. That happens over and over again. I get almost as much thrill showing somebody something new to them as they do seeing it themselves. The wonder of discovery is infectious. Seeing the world with new eyes, seeing what's been around you all the time but you just ignored it, being able to share it—that is just a ton of fun for me.

I remember another time we were out at the Skagit, and we found the Snow Goose flock that winters there. We were looking at it in a field, when all of a sudden the whole flock took off. They just blasted up and covered the sky. You can look at birds in a book. You can show

that says we have so many Passenger Pigeons here and so many caracaras there and so forth. Then we report at a meeting. The data get published and go into a database at National Audubon.

Then there is the Puget Sound Seabird Survey.[7] That was Jerry Joyce's idea. He worked with our Executive Director, Shawn Cantrell, to get money to pay for staff. Adam Sedgley was hired to begin the project. Now Toby Ross, Science Manager, runs it. It's a citizen science project to count seabirds in Puget Sound, with observers at various sites. The protocols are scientific, and so are the data. It's a popular project. People like doing it. They're happy to stand out there in the middle of winter and count birds.

The Science Committee was also involved in the Breeding Bird Atlas, which began in 1994. That was Hal Opperman's project, along with a couple of people who are no longer with us. Breeding bird atlases are sort of standard operating procedures. There's a national one. Various states do it. The idea is, in the summertime you go out and find out how many birds are breeding. The data can be used to tell us how the numbers of migrant birds change over time. Most breeding bird atlases are done on main roads. You usually drive to particular sites and record what you hear and see. That's not really scientific. Our BBA was different. We divided the state into nine-square-mile atlas blocks and had volunteers visit as many blocks as possible, finding all the breeding birds they could. Coverage statewide wasn't complete, but in King, Kittitas, Kitsap, and Island Counties, it was. It's all posted on Seattle Audubon's website now, along with another one of our projects, BirdWeb, which is an online field guide to Washington birds and their natural history.[8]

Another thing that Hal and the Science Committee were involved in was nominating Important Bird Areas.[9] These are areas designated for special consideration because they provide habitat for species at risk, species with limited ranges, or species that congregate in large flocks. We nominated several Important Bird Areas (IBAs). One, East Sand Island in the Columbia River, is actually in Oregon but close to Washington. We nominated it because of its importance to nesting Double-crested Cormorants and Caspian Terns. Seattle Audubon went to court to protect the terns in 2002. The terns were nesting then on nearby Rice Island, where they were being harassed by the U.S. Army Corps of Engineers, on the theory the birds were eating too many young salmon. We won, moving the terns' nesting colony to East Sand Island and forcing the government to make provisions for other nesting areas outside the Columbia River estuary. Another IBA in our region is Quartermaster Harbor on Vashon Island, where many Western Grebes wintered. Originally, IBAs started out as Important Birding Areas, because many birds are in great habitat, and birders show up. But we soon realized that the habitat itself needed protection. Getting it designated as an Important Bird Area will, we hope, help protect it permanently.

Citizen science at its most basic is when any citizen goes out and makes measurements of some kind. Some Audubon chapters say they're doing citizen science, but they're really birding and keeping track of the birds they see. That used to be what Seattle Audubon did in the beginning years. But now we do projects that are formal, using standard protocols with the idea that there will be publications eventually. I think that's where Seattle Audubon is unique. I have yet to run across another chapter that has a Science Committee or that does the [...]d of science we do.

Per[...]lly, I've loved nature and scien[...]nce I was a kid. When I was nine[...]en, I got a Chemcraft Kit No. 1, an[...]y brother coveted it. I said, 'Sure y[...]an have it.' He went on to become [...]emical engineer, and that kit was his [...]rt. He had a rock collection. I thought, [...] can make a much better rock collection than that.' And I'm still collecting rocks and just about anything nature-made.

We had a spare bedroom in our apartment. My brother had a chemical lab at one end, and I had a natural history museum at the other. It was really a large bookcase in which I duplicated the American Museum of Natural History. I had a Hall of Mammals and a Hall of Reptiles and so forth on each shelf. If I caught a frog, I could cast a frog out of plaster of paris, paint it, and stick it on the shelf, in the Hall of Amphibians.

When I was in high school, I started a neighborhood microscopy club. We'd go out and collect specimens, and we'd make slides. Using money from an after-school job, I bought a microscope to which I added over the years, until it was a really good scientific instrument. I still have it.

After high school, I went to Wagner College, a small Lutheran-associated school of mostly brown-baggers on Staten Island. I designed and built apparatus for collecting water samples, and was given some lab space for chemical analysis of the samples. After graduating, I went to Ohio State, to their hydrobiological laboratory, at the western end of Lake Erie. The faculty thought I was going to work on a Ph.D., but my draft board thought otherwise, and I ended up with two years of active duty in the Marine Corps. I needed a break, anyway.

Afterward, I went to Florida State. It was an ideal situation since they had an Oceanographic Institute, but it wasn't degree-granting. The expectation was that you would graduate in botany, chemistry, zoology, or something like that, and your degree would be facilitated by the Oceanographic Institute. They had several medium-sized boats, and a little lab down on the coast just south of Tallahassee, so I started to do my dissertation on the phytoplankton of this particular part of the Gulf of Mexico.

In the beginning, I'd go out in a boat by myself, but the faculty finally gave me an undergraduate assistant because they were worried I'd fall overboard sometime. I did fall in once but grabbed a line. By that time several other grad students were with me and they helped me back into the boat. I had a succession of major professors and was pretty much able to work independently.

After getting my Ph.D., I joined Woods Hole Oceanographic Institution, then taught and did research at Oregon State University, and finally ended up here in Seattle working at NOAA, where I spent the next seventeen years. I retired in the 1990s, but now I'm 'working' for Seattle Audubon. I began as the Science Advisor before the formation of the Science Committee, and have served twice on the Board and a number of committees, including the Science Committee and Conservation Committee. I need to have a job. I don't want to be someone who just goes to meetings and raises a hand every time there's a vote. I need to be more active and activist than that.

I was asked by somebody one time, why do I keep on doing stuff for Seattle Audubon? My reply, without thinking, was, 'I can't help myself.' It's an addiction. The organization can be used for good, so I want to help it, especially in conservation work and science. We're trying to change people's opinions about the values of nature and habitat in a changing world. That's something really worth doing. My way of doing it is through Seattle Audubon."

IT ALL ADDS UP
Eugene S. Hunn: Christmas Bird Count

In the late 1800s and early 1900s, after the last drumstick of the Christmas turkey had been gnawed, the final crumb of mincemeat pie spooned up, the belts surreptitiously loosened, the men did not gather round the television to watch college football playoffs. Aside from the fact that television hadn't been invented yet, men of those days followed a different tradition. They would take up their guns, choose up sides, and, in the words of Frank Chapman, curator of birds and mammals at the American Museum of Natural History, "hie them to the fields and woods on the cheerful mission of killing practically everything in fur and feathers that crossed their path—if they could. These exceptional opportunities for winning the laurels of the chase were termed 'side hunts,' and reports of the hundreds of non-game birds which were sometimes slaughtered during a single

hunt were often published in our leading sportsmen's journals, with perhaps a word of commendation for the winning side." To halt the slaughter and create a different set of values, Chapman proposed in the 1900 issue of Bird-Lore, "a new kind of Christmas side hunt, in the form of a Christmas bird-census, and we hope that all our readers who have the opportunity will aid us in making it a success by spending a portion of Christmas Day with the birds and sending a report of their 'hunt' to Bird-Lore."[10]

Thus was born the Christmas Bird Count (CBC), a citizen science effort that continues to this day. Seattle Audubon participated in CBCs from the very first. For many years, Gene Hunn ran the CBC for Audubon. Hunn is a past President of Seattle Audubon, a professor emeritus in anthropology at the University of Washington, an author, and a preeminent birder. He lives retired now in California, but a piece of his heart will always stay with us here in Seattle, as ours stays with him.

Above right: Eugene (Gene) S. Hunn out in the field. (Photograph courtesy of Seattle Audubon Society and Gene Hunn)

"The standard protocol of a CBC, which is supposed to be followed by all the counts that are formally approved by the National Audubon Society, is a circle with a diameter of fifteen miles that does not overlap any preexisting circle, though there are occasional conflicts that have been unavoidable. The center of the Seattle circle is on the old Skid Road in Pioneer Square, so the circle actually covers a lot of Puget Sound, Mercer Island, and a bit of Bellevue. There are more than 2,000 circles altogether being counted every

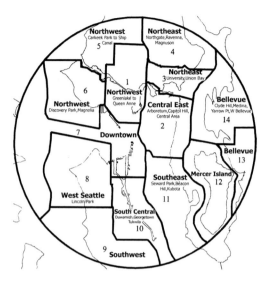

year now in the United States, Mexico, Canada, and on down to South America.

The goal is to tally all the wintering birds possible. That's kind of an odd side effect of the way things were originally established back in 1900. The official count period is designated by National Audubon. Last year it ran from December 15 through January 5. You pick one day in that period, and then you organize a team and divide up your area into sectors, because a fifteen-mile diameter circle is quite large, and you want to get as complete coverage as possible. Then, within a 24-hour period, the goal is to see

and document as many species as possible. You not only document the presence of each species, but you estimate how many individuals of each species are observed. It can become a bit of a competition among the teams at times, though that's not the real goal of the counts.

The accuracy of the count depends to some extent on the nature of the bird. So if you're counting shorebirds or waterfowl or raptors, for example, you can get a pretty accurate count because the birds are conspicuous and they're out in the open. The problem there is estimating very large numbers. If you have a flock of coots on Lake Washington, for example, then you might have 2,000 or 3,000 birds—no way are you going to count every single bird with any confidence. What I do, I count by fives, tens, or 25s, depending on how many birds I'm trying to count. You aren't going to be totally accurate, but I think it's very solid scientific data because if the numbers are really large, the count doesn't have to be accurate to the last bird.

When the crows were roosting on Foster Island, for example, we estimated up to 10,000 coming out of that roost. They would leave the roost at dawn and return at dusk, spreading out all over

the city. So we'd have a team stationed at Montlake Fill before dawn to count crows as they went over in flocks of 100 or 200 at a time in various directions.

When you're dealing with dickey birds such as Bushtits, chickadees, or sparrows, you're not going to see more than a fraction of the birds that are actually there because they're in the bushes. No way are you going to be able to count every chickadee. The best you can do is try to keep a tally as you go along during the course of the day and cover as much ground as possible. Your total will be a rough estimate of how many birds are out there that the team is able to observe in the time allowed. So you may only get ten percent of the birds, but year after year, if you have good observers and teams in the area and you cover the same territory, you can compare the numbers from year to year, even though you're really only sampling the available habitat.

The official Seattle Christmas count began in 1908, but it was sporadic and not systematically organized in the early years. It wasn't until 1919 that groups of observers went out. Before that, only individuals recorded their counts.

I moved to Seattle in the fall of 1972 when I started to work at the University of Washington. I was already a birder. It happened when I was in the Peace Corps in Ethiopia in 1965. Three of us arrived in January in Addis and got assigned to this little town in far western Ethiopia. We were pretty much stuck out there. There was no regular transportation. One of the three of us was Mike Huxley, who was a nephew of Aldous and Julian. Anyway, he was a birder, and on the weekends he would go off and come back covered with mud, raving about all these birds. I thought that sounded kind of interesting, so I managed to get a cheap pair of binoculars and a Peterson's East African bird guide and went out on my own. Then Mike's replacement arrived: Nancy. We started birding in our spare time, and the next year, after we both were back from Ethiopia, we got married. On our honeymoon we went bird-watching.

When we came home, we started going to Point Reyes Bird Observatory, which had just been established a year or so before. We'd go up there on the weekends to band birds, weigh them,

measure them, and run the nets. We fell in with the young Turks of the day. We were all in our twenties, hotshot birders you know. We would run all over the state chasing rare birds.

Rich Stallcup and Guy McCaskie were my mentors. We got in on the ground floor of a revolution in field observations. In the past, if you saw something unusual, you'd go out and shoot it and prepare the skin, deposit it in a museum, maybe write a little note for

The Auk. That was the way ornithological bird records were handled well into the 1950s and the '60s, when field birding really got going. There was a real excitement about how we can identify birds and document them by writing very detailed descriptions. Guy McCaskie was noted for being a hard-nosed critic of anything unusual, so if you wanted to maintain a good reputation, you had to provide sufficient documentation so that McCaskie would accept it.

Opposite page: Seattle's count circle is divided into fourteen sections. (Map courtesy of Seattle Audubon Society) Right: CBC counters, like these at Discovery Park, go out on count day regardless of the weather. (Photograph © Doug Schurman)

When I arrived in Seattle, the birding scene was a little casual, to put it mildly. There were a few very expert active birders, but there wasn't much in the way of communication or organization, certainly not compared to the way it is today. But I kind of hit the ground running because I'd been schooled in California about how you document rare sightings and keep records.

Phil Mattocks and I decided to get Washington birding more organized.

We worked on a revision of the state list, which we published in 1974. In the process of reviewing the old records, we looked at all the Christmas count reports, which were published by Audubon under a series of titles. We found some things we considered perhaps questionable, plus it didn't seem as if the entire circle was being covered systematically.

So Phil Mattocks took over the count in 1973 and '74. From that time on, first Phil and then myself were the coordinators and compilers. We were responsible for recording the information from the teams at the end of the day and then sorting through all that data, checking to make sure it was accurate, questioning anything that seemed out of the ordinary by going back to the initial observers, and then submitting a report for publication in the Audubon journal.

The coverage has been very systematic since then, but we have fun, too. We have a potluck at the end of the day. It's a big party. That's half the fun of it because if you see something really rare, you don't tell anybody about it. You keep

At the potluck, Henry Noble (left) and Helen Gilbert tuck into dinner while they discuss their tally from Discovery Park before reporting to the group at large. (Photograph © Doug Schurman)

it secret. Everyone sits with their teams around tables, and after we eat, the coordinator gets up and starts calling out each species from a list of all the possible species that might be observed. If you've seen that species, you raise your hand. At the end, the coordinator will say, 'Any other birds to report?' That's when you leap up and say, 'Well, you didn't mention the White-footed Albatross,' or whatever it was you saw.

In a more serious way, the tallies are all added up by the teams and submitted to a compiler. I was the compiler for a number of years. I would take all these reports and handwritten scratches and scrawls that people had made in the field and enter them into an Excel spreadsheet, which I maintained over the years. When I left Seattle, I gave it all to Matt Bartels, who compiles now.

This last year was the 116th Christmas Bird Count, so there is now a massive compilation of data. That allows us to not only track changes for the whole count, but it's possible now to go back and compare the totals for the different sub-areas as well, if you wanted to go to all that trouble.

The striking thing about the records is that the average for Seattle for count day is 120 species, plus or minus ten. That's been extremely consistent, despite the changes in land use. The highest total I think we've ever recorded is 129, and the lowest is 113. So it doesn't vary, even as the weather can vary dramatically. I think that's because we have so many people out covering the areas now, and they know what they're supposed to be looking for.

I'm sure that many species have declined in abundance since the count began, but that decline has been more than offset by an increase in the observer intensity, so there are a lot more people looking who are really knowledgeable. As the years go by, the grand total of species gradually increases because every year you might add a new bird to the historic list. The grand total is 216 species that have been recorded on one Seattle Christmas count or another.

Of course, as habitat changes, so do the birds. Christmas counts used to include Lewis's Woodpecker and Ruffed Grouse, for example. Western Bluebirds sometimes overwintered. Those birds haven't been recorded in the area on CBCs for quite a number of years. In recent years, there has been a decline in sea ducks. That's a region-wide phenom-enon. We've noticed that down here in California as well. White-winged Scoters have almost disappeared. Western Grebe populations have declined substantially, though they may have made a slight comeback more recently. But Anna's Hummingbird populations have explod-ed. House Finches did a similar thing, and of course Eurasian Collared-Doves and Western Scrub-Jays are recent arriv-als. And swans. In the early 1970s there were something like 25 Trumpeter Swans in the whole state. They wintered up in the Skagit at a lake near Mount Vernon, and now there are thousands of them. Bald Eagles, Peregrine Falcons—track their numbers and you can see the pos-itive side of our conservation efforts, to balance out the negative.

I know some friends of mine think the sky is falling, every time they talk about the environment. But I'm an optimist, I guess. I can't help it. Cities are incredi-bly diverse. In the city of Seattle, because of the parks, because of the habitat, the shoreline and the intensity of observer effort, there are close to 300 species of birds you can see here during the year, which is a large fraction of the total for the county. Urban areas don't have to be devoid of bird life. If people are passion-ate about preserving patches of habitat, they can be like oases in a desert—very attractive to birds."

CBC'S BELIEVE IT OR NOT

- Greatest participation: 224 birders in 2015, who saw 45,606 individual birds and 127 species
- Counts held during World War II: 0 (counts were suspended so as not to raise suspicion about birders with binoculars in the field)
- Number of Bald Eagles seen in 1980: 1; in 1990: 7; in 2000: 30; in 2010: 61
- Old and new names of CBC birds: Buffalo-head = Bufflehead; Desert Sparrowhawk = American Kestrel; Holboell's Grebe = Red-necked Grebe; Nuttall's Sparrow = White-crowned Sparrow
- Biggest surprise of 2015: Rock Wren at Alki
- Biggest surprise of 2014: Thick-billed Murre off West Point in Discovery Park, a first for King County
- First Anna's Hummingbird found in 1966; high count: 518 in 2013
- Most number of species ever found: 129 in 2006 (plus 2 more during count week)
- Most numerous bird found in 2009: American Crow—18,180
- Waterfowl on long-term upward trend: Cackling Goose, Bufflehead
- Waterfowl on long-term downward trend: White-winged Scoter, Black Scoter, Ruddy Duck[11]

OUR PARKS, OUR PLACE
Janice Bragg: The Neighborhood Bird Project

Most of the birds that live and breed in Seattle have a defined territory, a place where they forage for food, fight off rivals, find mates, have babies. For some, their home territory can be as small as a good-sized house lot. For others, it can span a large fraction of the city. Birds' territories are not exactly home as we think of the word, but birds do have a sense of place. They need it to thrive—and so do we.

When the Neighborhood Bird Project began in 1994, Seattle Audubon sought to expand residents' sense of place and love of nature by engaging people with their local parks. At its most basic, the idea was for people to go out once a month with an expert birder as leader to find, identify, and get to know the birds in their local parks.

Since then, the project has grown to become one of the most important citizen science efforts in the city, producing mountains of data that help scientists determine the abundance of birds in selected parks, the amount of avian diversity in the city, even the success of habitat restoration attempts. Jan Bragg has been a leader in the project from the beginning. Her special place is Magnuson Park.

"Back in 1989, I was new to the Seattle area, and I was kind of bored. My husband and I had lived six years in Switzerland, and I was used to traveling a lot. We weren't traveling here, and I didn't really know what to do. Then I saw in a Nature Conservancy bulletin that there was going to be a walk at Nisqually, led by Thero North of Seattle Audubon. Thero brought along a recording of a Virginia Rail, and when she played it, the bird walked out of a marsh. Everybody in the group went nuts because they'd never seen one, and they kept telling me this was just unreal, for me to see this on my first walk. But that isn't what really hooked me. What hooked me was that Thero heard an Orange-crowned Warbler singing, and we kept hearing the song over and over. I wondered, what would an Orange-crowned Warbler look like? After a long search, Thero finally found one, and I got to see it. I was just amazed that this tiny bird could produce such a long song. I wanted to learn more, so I contacted Seattle Audubon and saw that Gene Hunn was leading a trip to Vantage. I went along. At Ginkgo State Park he pointed out a Bullock's Oriole. I thought I had died and gone to heaven when I saw that bird. That was it.

After that, I wanted to learn as much as I could about birds. I took a bunch of Seattle Audubon classes and got into the Master Birder class in '94. It was a two-year class, and you were expected to give volunteer hours in return. One night, Ann Zavitkovsky came to Master Birders to ask for our help. Ann was a

Vice President of Seattle Audubon at the time and was very interested in conservation. The Neighborhood Bird Project was her brainchild. Ann wanted to start the project because she wanted first of all to see what was out there in the parks, but second, she wanted to get people connected to their neighborhood parks. She thought if people got interested in the birds in their local parks, that would empower them to become advocates for birds and wildlife in their communities.

The idea was that once a month, teams would compile data on the birds that we observed, using a point count. A point count is a technique used by the U.S. Forest Service. It's described in their *Handbook of Field Methods for Monitoring Landbirds*.[12] Point counts involve an observer standing in one spot and recording all the birds seen or heard at a fixed distance for a certain amount of time. For our project, the distance was a circle with a 50-meter radius. We would stand in the middle of the circle and count birds for five minutes.

To be honest, this sounded like an easy way to give back hours, plus it would help us pay attention to the common birds, something that Dennis Paulson said was important. So I signed up

Opposite page: Jan Bragg surveying a stop at Magnuson Park. (Photograph © Tim Boyer) Right: A Brown Creeper finds an insect. Creepers are one of the focal species specially targeted by the Neighborhood Bird Project. (Photograph © Gregg Thompson)

for it, and so did a bunch of other Master Birders. We started with Carkeek and Genesee Parks. The Master Birders and Gene Hunn went to the sites and literally walked around as Gene said, 'I think this would be a good place to put a stop.'

So for a year, I would drive out to Carkeek Park every month, and our team would do a point count there. Kent Slaven, Tracee Geernaert, and I were the 'captains' for Carkeek. The other early sites were the Bliner property (a large private property) and Shadow Lake Bog in Kent, as well as the Walsh property (another private piece) in Woodinville. Richard Youel was the captain at Genesee, Joe Miles and Terry Sisson were the captains in Kent/Renton, and Yvonne Bombardier was captain at Woodinville.

After a year of driving across town to Carkeek, I said to myself, 'This is crazy. I don't want to have to drive so far.' I lived near Magnuson Park and walked there nearly every week for exercise. I thought if I was going to be putting in this much time, I wanted to do it in my own neighborhood. So I started doing point counts at Magnuson every month. Eileen Bryant, Bob and Becky Benton, Herb Curl, and I were the first captains at Magnuson; Cynthia Wilson took over for me as captain at Carkeek (and continued for nearly 20 years).

Eventually, the Neighborhood Bird Project settled on covering eight King County parks and green spaces: Carkeek, Genesee, and Magnuson stayed in the project. Golden Gardens, Discovery, Seward Parks were added, as well as the Arboretum and an open space in Lake Forest Park.

We have the big parks divided up into different loops, with anywhere from five to ten stations or stops along each loop. We don't want the project to be too burdensome for the volunteers, so each loop has its own separate team. We try to have the same leaders for each loop for the sake of consistency. At Magnuson, we always meet at the same start time: 9:00 a.m. in winter and 8:00 a.m. in summer. The volunteers who show up can decide which loop they want to go on. They walk to the first stop, wait a minute, then observe for five minutes, writing down every bird they see or hear within a 50-meter radius, including birds that pass overhead. If we hear a bird but can't see it, we try to determine if it is within the circle. If it is too far away, we don't count it.

My loop at Magnuson starts at the boat launch and goes along the main drag, the old road along the lake. We walk toward NOAA as far as the off-leash area, then follow the loop south again. One stop I've kept on that loop is fairly useless: it's where the habitat was leveled in order to install the artwork, *The Fin Project: From Swords into Plowshares*. I don't see many birds there, but I wanted to keep that stop to show what happens when you take away habitat.

We have a special area where we stop, and that is the wetlands that were built where the commissary and parking lot used to be when Sand Point was a naval base. That area was not in our original loops because there was no habitat there. When the wetlands were put in, that totally changed the habitat. We added it to our survey because we wanted to have data to show if the wetlands were succeeding or not. When the wetlands were put in, there was an argument that they would fail unless they were maintained. People said the wetlands were a waste of money. We wanted to know if the plant species that were brought in would thrive. Were the wetlands functional? Would birds breed here? Would they return year after year?

To find out, we do a sweep through here, meaning, we try to count every bird in the area, not just the birds we might find on a point count. It's a separate database, but the same people do it.

Over the years, there have been a lot of people involved. Toby Ross, the Science Manager who runs the project now, keeps a database of all the volunteers. There are more than 300 in the database now, with more than 1,500 hours recorded.[13] An important volunteer we had for years was Helen Crawford. She was responsible for entering the data we collected and occasionally attended meetings of the captains and staff. That was really important because there needs to be a connection between the data entry person and the project. The person entering data has to understand what people in the field are recording.

In 1998 we tightened up the protocols. Helen Ross was the Conservation Manager at the time. She found out that for a scientific point count, the stops needed to be 200 meters apart. We had some that were only 100 meters apart and some that were 500 meters apart, because we had selected them for habitat reasons. Some were near creeks, some were in apple orchards—that sort of thing. To be more scientific, we actually went out on all the loops and measured off the stops. Unfortunately, at Magnuson, that meant we lost some of the stops we had been using. It was just heartbreaking to lose the data from those stops, considering that we were three years into what we thought would be a five-year project. So we kept some of the stops where they were, just to preserve the data. We didn't know then that we would be doing this project for more than 20 years!

When we started, the purpose was mostly to get people aware of what's in their own neighborhood. By coming once a month, instead of once a year like people do for the Christmas Bird Count, they would get to see the same Song Sparrows over and over, hear the same towhees. People would actually learn the birds. That was one of the cool things for me, to see the educational value. By seeing the same birds over and over, people get a grasp of seasonality. They learn which birds are here every single month because they're resident, which birds are here in the wintertime and which ones in the summer, and which birds are seen only on migration. For some people it takes years for them to get this, but one day they'll say, 'When do Savannah Sparrows come back? Is it April or May?' They start to see the repetition and regularity of the birds, the patterns.

CANOPY CONNECTIONS

The Neighborhood Bird Project is not the only city-wide citizen science project Seattle Audubon has started. Another started as a result of our concern about dwindling urban forest habitat within the city limits. The issue came to a head in 2007, when the City Council was about to unveil its plan to regulate tree cutting and planting. The plan called for a total canopy coverage of 30 percent by the year 2037, but Matthew Mega, Conservation Director, worried that the proposal had no teeth and would be disregarded by developers, who were cutting down mature trees at will.

In 2009, responding to pressure, the City Council created the Urban Forestry Commission, with Mega as chair. "Many people take trees for granted and still consider them to be 'pretty green things' or amenities," Mega wrote in 2010.[14] But they are not. Trees sequester enormous amounts of carbon, helping mitigate global warming. They filter water and clean the air. They moderate extreme temperatures. They provide needed habitat for urban wildlife. Mega began to think about how to build community awareness and support for trees.

In 2010, Seattle Audubon received a grant from the Department of Natural Resources to begin a pilot program in Columbia City to engage citizens in preserving and planting urban trees. Canopy Connections—the brainchild of Mega—encouraged citizens to identify their favorite trees or groves in the city and map them onto an online tree map maintained on Seattle Audubon's website. The program proved to be popular. Many people cared about the trees in their neighborhoods and volunteered to help with tree mapping. Funded in part by the Horizons Foundation, Seattle Audubon's Canopy Connections became a citywide program.

In 2013, the Urban Forestry Commission proposed to the City Council the Urban Forest Stewardship Plan, which was adopted. Enforcement is still an issue that remains to be resolved, but under the new plan, the City now actively promotes preservation of trees and has created its own tree map.[15] Other agencies and organizations have also been collecting data on area trees, as Seattle Audubon's commitment to the preservation of urban bird habitat continues.

For example, at Magnuson we have Bullock's Orioles that come back every year, usually in May. They nest, and then they leave very quickly. They're gone by the end of July or early August. I issue challenges each month when I send out reminders to the volunteers. I'll say, 'This is when we're looking for the Bullock's Orioles, so if anybody sees one, let everybody else know when and where you see it.' In the fall I'll issue a challenge for observers to find the first Common Goldeneyes coming back. In the spring, it's the swallows.

For me, one of the beauties of the project is that it's something anyone can do. A person could call up Seattle Audubon and volunteer without knowing anything about birds. Maybe somebody just likes to be outside. That person could join a team and be useful. He or she could be the scribe who writes down the observations, or the timekeeper who keeps track of the observation times at each stop. A person without birding skills could be the one who learns all the stops of a loop, so in case a new leader arrives who doesn't know the stops, he or she could be the one to help. At Magnuson, we've had many people who started out as beginning birders go on to become Master Birders.

Another thing I really like is our connection with the University of Washington. Because Magnuson is near university housing, we often get students who are here for only a short time. They want to volunteer for something, and the Neighborhood Bird Project is perfect for them. As students, they don't have that much time to give, but they're willing to do this once a month.

As I said, we didn't start out knowing how our data collecting might be used for something scientifically important. But after several years, we began to realize we had enough data to be analyzed. It could tell us important things about habitat and birds in the city.

Charlie Kahle and Alice Arnold were the first people to look at the data. Then Adam Sedgley became Science Manager, and he enlisted Eric Ward and Kristin Marshall to do statistical analyses of what we had.

But Toby is the person who really took the bull by the horns and helped get our first technical report published. First he enlisted Mira Lamb, a high school volunteer, to go through our database. Then through our connections with the University of Washington, especially the Burke Museum, he got a graduate student to analyze it. C. J. Battey is a

doctoral candidate at the Burke, and he and Toby put together a report published in 2014 called *Impacts of Habitat Restoration and the Status of Avian Communities in Seattle City Parks.*[16] In that report, C. J. wrote, 'The data from [our] surveys provide an insight into the avian diversity and abundance in urban areas and afford an appreciation of the diversity that can be found in cities, given appropriate quality habitat.'

I wish I had had that report when I testified to the City's hearing examiner about loss of habitat at Magnuson when the City wanted to put in synthetic sports fields. The biggest question the hearing examiner wanted to know was if there were any endangered species in that habitat. In my head I was screaming, 'The birds are not endangered, but what difference does that make? They're not endangered now, but they're going to be if we don't start protecting habitat.'

I realized then why data collected for projects like the Neighborhood Bird Project are so important. We have to have scientific data about the birds in our urban areas so we can do something to preserve open space and parks. With nearly 20 years of monthly surveys in our database now, the Neighborhood Bird Project is a great way to do that."

BIRDS ON THE WIRE, SCIENCE ONLINE
Tom Aversa: BirdWeb & Sound to Sage

Tom Aversa holds a Red-breasted Nuthatch. (Photograph © Terry Mihashi)

Long ago, in the dim mists of time when snail mail was just beginning to give way to email and Al Gore was starting to think he ought to get some credit for inventing the internet—in other words, the 1990s—visionaries could already see that the World Wide Web would fundamentally change the way we communicate, interact, and even perceive the world.

Some of these pioneers belonged to Seattle Audubon. Early on, members of Seattle Audubon's Bird Records Committee became intrigued with the possibilities of this new technology. They liked the idea of somehow hosting a site that would encompass an enormous amount of data about birds. Such a site could include all the records of the Christmas Bird Counts, which went back to 1908. It could include breeding bird records assembled from four counties in the state. It could provide readers with an almost infinitely large field guide to the birds of Washington, with updatable photographs, maps, and natural history descriptions far more extensive than even the most complete printed field guides. And it could be accessible to anyone who wanted to know more about the birds of our state.

The Committee—which by then had transformed into the Science Committee—took the plunge. BirdWeb launched in 2002, and Sound to Sage (the four-county breeding bird atlas) launched in 2006. Since then these two sites have received millions of "hits" and have helped

untold numbers of researchers, teachers, students, and birders of all skill levels find the information they need about the birds of Washington State.

Committee members made one other critical decision that still holds today. They decided both sites would be open source, meaning the information would be free to everyone. The costs of creating and maintaining the sites would forever be borne by Seattle Audubon alone, our gift to the world. Tom Aversa, amateur scientist and member of both the Bird Records Committee and later the Science Committee, remembers those early days.

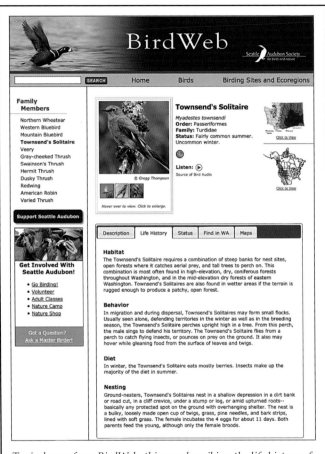

Typical page from BirdWeb, this one describing the life history of Townsend's Solitaire, with links to range maps, the bird's status in Washington, occurrence frequencies, bird song, and three different photographs to aid in identification. (Web page and birders photograph courtesy of Seattle Audubon, Solitaire photographs © Gregg Thompson; Harlequin Duck photograph © Paul Bannick)

"I can't say exactly where the idea of BirdWeb came from, but I can remember discussing it with Hal Opperman soon after Seattle Audubon's Bird Records Committee had transformed to become the Science Committee. We began to think about how we might use this new technology that was becoming available.

Seattle Audubon's Bird Records Committee was responsible for keeping records of bird sightings, running the telephone hotline, and recording Christmas Bird Count reports. Seattle Audubon had been doing that for years, but eventually the rare birds records were taken over by the Washington Ornithological Society, which vets and keeps them now.[17] When that happened, our committee decided to focus on citizen science. We became the Science Committee, with Hal as Chair, and began to flesh out the idea of BirdWeb, an online field guide.

We realized it was going to be a big job with a lot of moving parts. We would need species accounts—descriptions of each species, its status in Washington, and its natural history (diet, nesting, behavior, that kind of thing). We needed maps that showed where to find each species in the winter, summer, and during migration. We wanted to have photos showing different plumages for males and females, juveniles and adults, breeding and nonbreeding. We wanted bird songs, too.

We started recruiting volunteers.[18] Hal was the Director of Production Management. I was on that team as well, along with Ellen Blackstone, Kelly Cassidy, Brenda Senturia, Ron Simons, and Emily Sprong. Emily was also the project lead for writing. She would go to sources such as *Birds of North America,* which was not even online at that point, and other natural history sources. Then she would throw together a rough draft, and we would edit it and add status and distribution information. Hal and I did a lot of that work.

Kelly Cassidy produced the state range maps, and Kenn Kaufman's North American maps were used, too. For the bird songs, we used recordings from the Macaulay Library, a library of wildlife recordings that's part of Cornell Lab of Ornithology. Dennis Paulson donated tons of photos. He really pushed it. He had so many bird photographs, and that was critical because it was before the advent of where we are now, with digital photographs. We got photos from other photographers too, but Dennis's contribution was huge.

Chihiro Nishihara did the web design, with a lot of help from some great computer volunteers: Adam Ahringer, Kelly Crimmins, Steve Garvin, Deni Mensing, Andrea Sparling, and Shang-fan Tu. They put together a beta version, and then we all went on the site and tested all the links to assess how they were working. Then we made suggestions about how they could be improved.

BirdWeb was launched in 2002. It included 350 species of birds that occur regularly in Washington State, and notes on 100 species of rarities. Right away, people started going to the site. In fact, I remember being amazed at the amount of hits it was taking at the time. I still had dial-up at that point. The online stuff was just so new, but even then it was overwhelming to see the amount of interest in BirdWeb. That interest just keeps growing. Now I understand BirdWeb gets up to 2,500 hits a day. In 2015, the most recent

data available, it logged 499,053 visitors and 1.8 million page views.[19]

The surprising thing to me is that so many views are from out of state. I currently teach courses on North American wildlife and captive wildlife at Unity College in Maine, and I look at the sources my students use for their projects. A lot of times, they cite BirdWeb. Partly that's because when I let the students use online sources, I tell them, 'Don't go to Joe's blog or something like that to get information. Go to good scientific sources.' BirdWeb is a reliable source, but even though it's supposed to be just about Washington birds, it comes up in my students' work almost as frequently as Cornell Lab's All About Birds, and here we are in Maine.

You know, at the time, you don't sometimes see the value in these projects you're working on. BirdWeb was a lot of work, and we were all really excited about it, but still we were a little skeptical that it would work online. But now I say, 'Wow, look at what we did.'

Sound to Sage was another big project of the Science Committee. It was a more comprehensive four-coun-

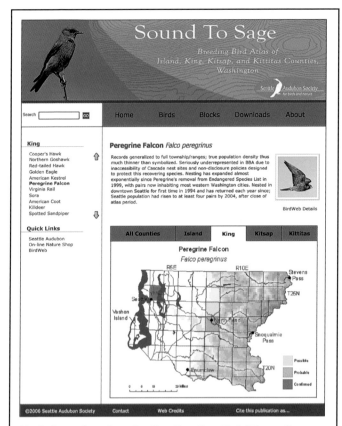

Typical page from Sound to Sage Breeding Bird Atlas, online at www.soundtosage.org. The map on this page, divided into atlas blocks, shows where Peregrine Falcons have been confirmed to breed in King County, and where else they might probably or possibly breed. There are links to the other three counties in the atlas, and a link to BirdWeb as well. (Web page courtesy of Seattle Audubon Society. Mountain Bluebird photograph © Paul Bannick. Peregrine Falcon photograph © Gregg Thompson)

ty version of the State Breeding Bird Atlas (BBA) that Phil Mattocks originally helped direct. Under his leadership, the BBA project divided the state into a grid of some 7,800 nine-square-mile 'atlas blocks.' The goal was to visit every block at least once during breeding season over the five years of the project, from 1987 to 1991, and record evidence of birds nesting. Although Phil had more than 500 volunteers out in the field and got the project extended for two more years, still only a small fraction of the atlas blocks were covered. Gene Hunn took over in 1994, and he recommended that the BBA focus on four individual counties. King County had already been well covered, and Gene began with that. By 1995, almost every atlas block in King County was visited, and Gene and Hal began to focus on Kittitas County.

At the same time, the University of Washington was going ahead with its breeding bird atlas called the Washington GAP Analysis Project. It was part of the National Biological Service's project to chart the biota of the country. Our project merged with theirs, and in 1997 a book was published by Seattle Audubon with all the data that we had collected.[20]

Meanwhile the Sound to Sage BBA work continued with observations in Kitsap County and eventually Island County. Hal, Steve Gerstle, Frances Wood, and Brenda Senturia worked really hard with volunteers to cover every block in the four counties. The data went online in 2006 as Sound to Sage, with the help of computer experts Alan Humphrey, Tom Rohrer, Josh Freedman, Sri Veena Syam Tangirala, and Gayathri Subramonian.[21]

Sound to Sage offered much more rigorous scientific information than Bird-Web, because we had to use established protocols to confirm breeding. 'Confirmation' means you must observe a bird doing certain things. We used preexisting standards that are pretty consistently used for every breeding bird atlas. Evidence for the highest level of confirmed breeding is if you see an active nest or an adult carrying food. If you see an adult with a mouthful of food, and he's not eating it, he's just flying around getting more and more food, that's confirmed evidence that the bird is breeding.

The next level after 'confirmed breeding' is 'probable breeding,' then 'possible.' If a male is singing, that indicates breeding is possible. If many males are singing in an area, that raises the level to 'probable.' I think the standard for 'probable' we used at the time was seven singing males. And then there is a level of observation where you just observe a bird but can't confirm breeding.

Sound to Sage allowed us to not so much just say that birds are in an area, but it told us whether they were breeding there, which is usually the measure for conservation. I mean, there are birds that go to downtown Seattle, but few of those inner-city areas are going to be suitable for nesting, and they aren't valu-

A Northern Pygmy-Owl fledgling perched outside its nest cavity (opposite page) and a male William-son's Sapsucker carrying food back to its young at the nest (above) both represent confirmed evidence of breeding, according to the protocols of the BBA. (Photographs © Paul Bannick)

able for conservation. Breeding habitat is a higher quality of habitat.

I loved working on Sound to Sage. It was way more fun than BirdWeb because I got to be in the field. I covered a lot of the high, remote—almost inaccessible—places up in the mountains in Kittitas County, because this was a project that had run for a long time, and most of the more accessible quads had already been covered by other birders. So I did a lot of mopping up in those more remote quads. I'll tell you, it took some doing, but it was fun, too.

For me, I have a sort of affection for volunteerism. I was really busy with a full-time job at the time, working for Woodland Park Zoo, but I still felt like I really wanted to volunteer, to give back. The Science Committee was a good fit for me. Even though I don't have a Ph.D., I keep current in science, and I thought that would be an area where I could make a contribution. Particularly in the realm of field science, if the work doesn't get done by volunteers, it often doesn't get done.

Conservation can be discouraging at times. The problems are so big. Climate change, for example, is an overwhelming problem. You look at the politics and the gridlock and you just kind of say, 'How is anything ever going to get done?'

But it really is kind of remarkable when you look at what can be done in the long process of improvement. Here in Maine, the rivers in the 1970s—we didn't even talk about them because they were so bad. They were just considered 'working' rivers, you know, where people dumped in all the pollution from the paper mills. Rivers weren't even considered natural elements. They were blocked with dams. And then when the Clean Water Act came through, people started improving water quality, trying to restore fish populations and fish runs that they barely knew about, because no one alive had ever seen them. They relied on old historic data. Now we're at the point where the Sebasticook River watershed that I live in has the largest alewife run in the world.

So I think, progress is happening. It might be hard to see it when you're in the trenches, but if you look at the long picture, more and more people do care about the environment. I see that with my students. They look at the problems in the world, and they want to do something about them. I have a lot of hope in young people."

SOUND VISION
Toby Ross: Puget Sound Seabird Survey

Toby Ross. (Photograph courtesy of Toby Ross)

Time, it is said, is the only dimension with one direction. You must go ahead. You cannot go back. Nevertheless, in all the ways that matter most, time is perhaps the most flexible of all dimensions because we perceive it with more than just our physical senses. We see time with our minds. We call it vision. Through memory, we can perceive the past and with vision, understand it. Through imagination, we can predict the future and with vision, make it come true.

Few recognize the power of vision more than do scientists, who seek to understand the world and thus help us shape its course.

Back in 2006, Seattle Audubon was blessed with several such visionaries, people who conceived the notion of documenting seabird populations along the whole of Puget Sound.

They didn't know how their survey data might be used, but they recognized the necessity of collecting it so that future generations would have baseline data on seabird species and how their populations have changed. Knowing that changes were on the way, these scientists began a project that, under the direction of Science Manager Toby Ross, continues today, growing more valuable with each passing year.[22]

"The Puget Sound Seabird Survey is a near-shore waterfowl and seabird survey conducted throughout Puget Sound, from Deception Pass in the north, down to Olympia in the south, west to Cape Flattery, and east to Seward Park.

The survey is powered by citizen science. We engage approximately 160 volunteers each season who monitor seabirds such as auklets and cormorants, grebes, and loons, and other waterfowl like ducks and geese. Volunteers conduct between 15- and 30-minute surveys at 120 sites across Puget Sound. They conduct these surveys from October through April once per month on the first Saturday of the month. Each survey must occur within two hours on either side of the daylight high tide, which maximizes the amount of seawater in the field of view at each survey location. Within that time frame, the volunteers record the bird species and the number of individuals sitting on the water.

We don't require that volunteers spend the full 30 minutes surveying at their site. If there are no birds present, the wind is howling, there's just no action, or volunteers have been able to capture everything that's going on within a 15-minute time frame, they can go home to a hot cup of tea. That's completely fine. If there are a lot of birds at the site, we ask them to survey for a maximum of 30 minutes.

We use a standard survey protocol called Distance Sampling, which is a widely used methodology for estimating bird density and abundance. It relies on the principle that birds are more difficult to detect the further they are away from

you. We then analyze the data by fitting a detection function to the bird observations to estimate how many birds were missed during the survey.[23]

After identifying the species and counting the number of individuals, our volunteers measure and record the bearing to the bird using a compass, then use a ruler held at arm's length to measure

the distance from the bird to the horizon. Only birds within 300 meters sitting on water are included in the survey. Because this is citizen science, we've boiled down the sampling protocol to the simple elements. We train all of our new volunteers every year to conduct the surveys, and they pick it up very quickly. We don't train them how to identify seabirds. The

Susan Stillman (left) and Chris Anderson conduct a survey from a site at Carkeek Park, using a protocol called Distance Sampling. (Photograph © Adam Sedgley)

majority are already competent with their identification skills. There are other projects that do train their volunteers on seabird identification. COASST (Coastal Observation and Seabird Survey Team), for example, has a long training session where they train volunteers, with the help of a comprehensive ID guide, how to identify seabirds that have washed up on the beach.

Recruitment of skilled volunteers is always difficult, but we do pretty well, at least in the Seattle area. Ours is a very well-respected project, and

word of mouth has really helped. Also, Seattle Audubon is an established and well-known organization within the Puget Sound region. If people want to get involved in citizen science, we have a strong record of engaging people in interesting projects. Of course, the project covers a very broad geographic area, and Seattle is where most of our volunteers live. I have only a finite number of sites within Seattle, so Seattle-based volunteers do end up driving a bit to do outlying surveys. Certainly when you get to the Olympic Peninsula, experienced volunteers can be harder to come by. We always need more volunteers from the locations more distant from Seattle.

Not all the volunteers are experienced at seabird IDs. I definitely accept people who are really keen to learn, but I team them up with others who are confident with their bird IDs. Hopefully over the years, as these new birders learn identification skills, they can become team leaders and train others.

It's amazing, really, how many people are willing to do this because our volun-

Two species monitored by the project are Rhinoceros Auklet (left) and Pigeon Guillemot (right). (Photographs © Doug Schurman)

teers have to be the sort of birders who really want to get out there in the winter months when it's cold and rainy and windy. We do the surveys in the winter months because that's when seabirds are here in Puget Sound. The seabirds generally come from areas further north, where they spend the summer breeding. They come to Puget Sound in winter because the Sound is full of food at that time of year, and we have a milder climate than further north, generally speaking.

But of course it's the worst weather for humans, although I suppose it depends on what you like. I personally love the tropics. I love being on islands wearing shorts and a tee-shirt. That's heaven for me. Winter in Seattle, or winter in Britain where I'm from, is not my idea of heaven at all. So I'm just so thankful for the volunteers who are willing to go out there. They stand on the coast, where it's going to be the windiest. There's going to be sideways rain. I'm amazed by the number of people I can get to go out there to do these surveys in all the terrible weathers. But they always do it with a smile on their faces. That's what amazes me the most. I thank them every day. They don't realize it perhaps, but I'm always saying how much I appreciate them. But when you say you appreciate people so much, they kind of think, 'Ah, yeah, we know, whatever.' But it's really true. This program wouldn't be anything without them.

Citizen science enables us to get a tremendous amount of data very cheaply. If the Washington Department of Fish and Wildlife (WDFW) or the Department of Ecology wanted to collect similar data, it would be prohibitively expensive. It would also be logistically very difficult, whereas with enough citizen scientists, we can do it because we have people liv-

ing—or comfortable with traveling—all over the region.

And they've been doing it for many years—the winter of 2007–2008 was the first season we collected data. That was before my time here at Seattle Audubon. My understanding is that the Science Committee got together in 2006 and made a list of all the current and active data collection projects in the Puget Sound region. This process identified one gap—seabirds. The committee decided to set up a project that focuses on seabirds, using citizen science.

My predecessor, Adam Sedgley, located the first 28 sites in 2007, with the help of an advisory committee. The PSSS Advisory Committee consists of, among others, Eric Ward of NOAA, Peter Hodum of the University of Puget Sound, Scott Pearson of the WDFW, and Jerry Joyce, who is one of Seattle Audubon's Science Advisors. The Advisory Committee helps guide the direction of the project and coordinates data analysis.

Now it is my job to find the locations of all the new survey sites. Probably over the past four years since I've been here, I've established 50 new sites. When locating sites, I want to include not just the sites that have birds, but sites that don't

have birds, so we can potentially know if seabirds are decreasing at one site, are they increasing at another?

Every year that we add another season's worth of data makes all the previous data more worthwhile. There are lots of other survey projects out there with one, two, or three years' worth of data, but we're just about to complete our ninth season.

In May 2014 we published our first scientific paper using the PSSS data. The paper was published in an online, open-source, peer-reviewed journal. It was then presented at the Salish Sea Ecosystem Conference here in Seattle. The paper is titled, "Using citizen-science data to identify local hotspots of seabird occurrence." Eric Ward was the lead author of the paper, with the rest of the Advisory Committee as co-authors.[24]

In that paper, we presented results from our study suggesting increases in probabilities of occurrence for fourteen of the eighteen species examined. However, we did find declines in occurrence in four species: White-winged Scoter, Brant, Red-necked Grebe, and Western Grebe. I am confident that major institutions such as NOAA, WDFW, University of Puget Sound, and University of Washington will use our data as it becomes more comprehensive.

I am a scientist. I love data. I love collecting it. I love how data can tell stories and help us understand what's happening with populations and threatened species. I'm not an expert on seabirds, but I've done a lot of work on endangered and threatened species. I've worked on venomous snakes, iguanas, and small lizards—geckos—all over the world, mostly in Mauritius, the Caribbean, and Southeast Asia. I also worked for five years on tree kangaroos in Papua New Guinea. I'm a conservation biologist, so anything involving threatened or endangered species is my highest interest. Monitoring populations and trying to ensure they stay healthy is of the highest importance to me.

Although very few of the species in this project are in the endangered and threatened categories, there's a chance of course that in 20, 30, or 40 years, they may be designated as such. Having all these data act as an early warning system for seabirds is really important. They are amazing sentinels for the health of Puget Sound. Puget Sound affects all of us whether or not we get our food from there. Many of us live on the coast, so making sure the Sound is healthy is really important. Seabirds can function like the canary in the coal mine. Ensuring that they are healthy will ensure that we are healthy, too.

One of the other big areas that we've been working on recently is trying to understand how our data can help in the event of a major oil spill. We have nine years of seabird population data right now during a time of little to no contaminant leakage. If and when there's a large oil spill, like the one we had off the Gulf Coast, we'll have a good amount of data to show what the seabird populations were like before the spill. We'll naturally continue our surveys after any spill, too,

Most Common Loons seen on the surveys are in drab winter plumage, but birds in breeding plumage can occasionally be seen in the spring on their way to their breeding grounds. (Photograph © Paul Bannick)

which would produce an extremely powerful dataset of before and after a spill.

We've trained a portion of our volunteers to be first responders in the event of a spill. That doesn't mean they are HAZMAT trained, but they have been equipped with information on what to do in the event that there is a spill. And because we have such a broad geographic spread of volunteers, if we are alerted to an oil spill, say out of Port Angeles, I can make a couple of phone calls and potentially get people on site within ten minutes because they live nearby. They would arrive on scene and report, 'Yes, there is lots of oil,' or, 'No, we're not seeing any oil at this survey site yet.'

We would also ask our volunteers in the region of the spill to do a seabird survey at their sites at the next high tide after a spill, so we could compare the birds that were there during the previous survey with the birds that were present directly after a spill. Sadly, we know it's really only a matter of time until there is a spill. There are massive tankers passing through the Strait of Juan de Fuca and very close to the San Juan Islands on a regular basis. Unfortunately humans are in charge of the tankers, and we're inevitably not perfect.

Even though I know an oil spill is likely, I have hope that we would do everything we could do. I have hope that nature would rebound. As a human race, we are very resourceful. We have experienced many things, and there are lots of people, like our volunteers, who care and will help out when the going gets tough.

Seabirds are beautiful. They've all just got such interesting shapes and colors and personalities. They're enigmatic and fascinating when you take the time to look at them. I don't think I really saw that many seabirds before I got involved with this project—and I say 'saw' as in, I just didn't look. But now I understand how important seabirds are, I'm looking more and learning so much. And I'm hopeful that our data will help them survive and keep their ecosystem healthy."

One of the project survey's sea-going waterfowl, a Long-tailed Duck. This one is a male in breeding plumage. (Photograph © Doug Schurman)

THE WRITTEN WORD
Richard Youel: Publications Committee Member & Past Chair

A hundred years from now, when Seattle Audubon celebrates its bicentennial, information will flow freely throughout the world at light speed. Clunky cell phones will no longer exist. People will be individually wired into a global cybernetic web. Flat screens will morph into 3D holograms, making physical travel unnecessary (though the Mercer Mess will still inexplicably be a rush-hour nightmare).

And books—ordinary, old-school volumes printed on paper, bound with thread and glue—will still be with us. Books will always be with us. Tactile, compact, visual, portable, browser friendly, books will eternally appeal to us because we take in information through our senses, and books give us information we can touch, smell, heft, see.

The Publications Committee produced its first bound publication under the Seattle Audubon imprimatur in 1924, a booklet listing the common birds of Seattle. Since then, Seattle Audubon has published 23 books and scores of booklets, pamphlets, and newsletters—all designed to give people the information they need to help connect them to nature past, present, and future.

Richard Youel. (*Photograph © Connie Youel*)

"I remember my first impressions of Seattle Audubon. I was a brand-new birder, and I was excited about finding new birds and being with people who knew birds. Someone suggested I join Seattle Audubon, one of the great Audubon chapters in the country, with intelligent, dedicated members who do a lot of important things— they even publish books. A door to a wonderful world was opening, and I was eager to enter it. I wanted to be part of that community.

I found out later that Seattle Audubon began publishing books in 1942 for people who were interested in nature. Most of the books were field guides to the identification of birds and other animals and the places where you would find them. The first book was titled *A Field Guide to the Birds of the Seattle Area*, by Earl J. Larrison.

Birding in the 1940s was really growing. In Seattle, there were many very good birders, but the field guides they were working with mainly showed East Coast birds. People used them because that's all that was available, but they were good enough birders to know the limitations of what they were working with. So they consulted among themselves: 'Who's expert enough to actually produce something for our needs?' Earl Larrison was one of those people.

Larrison graduated from the University of Washington in 1941. He wrote *A Field Guide to the Birds of the Seattle Area* when he was only 22. He donated his manuscript to Seattle Audubon, as he did all his other books. They were field guides to local and regional birds, as well as the mammals and wildflowers of Washington. His books were a great benefit to naturalists of that time.

Over the years, Seattle Audubon published more field guides covering other topics including reptiles, amphibians, water plants, shorebirds, butterflies, dragonflies, and a breeding bird atlas of Washington State. A new book would be published every few years, and so Seattle Audubon became a respected source of good books filled with high quality information related to a variety of different natural interests.[25]

The fact that they had what it takes to publish all those books said to me it was a very important organization. I didn't get involved with the Publications Committee, though, until years later. Idie Ulsh, President of Seattle Audubon then, was an excellent birder and became an expert on butterflies. Idie saw the need for an update of Bob Pyle's much earlier field guide, *Watching Washington Butter-*

flies. Bob, a Seattle Audubon member, lepidopterist, and nationally known author, agreed to write a new butterflies book, and a team was lined up. The Publications Committee at that time needed a Chair, and Idie asked me if I would fill the slot. I didn't know a thing about book publishing, but I said, 'Sure, maybe I can contribute as a manager.'

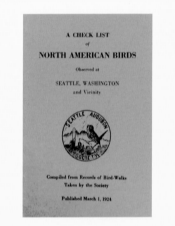

EARLY DAYS

This is the earliest-known bound publication produced by Seattle Audubon, a checklist of the birds of the Seattle area compiled from years of members' careful observations. The booklet was published in 1924. It was hoped

Coming to it as a rank amateur, not knowing how a serious book gets produced, it was a revelation to me. Bob Pyle cared not only about the words he wrote, but also about every other aspect of the book: the illustrations and photos, design, and production. He knew what it takes to produce a significant book. Bob was willing to compromise on some

that a checklist, especially of the common birds in the area, would encourage local birders to get out into nature and find all the birds they could. It was also important, according to National Audubon, to provide information and encouragement for traveling birders, who might then come to love habitats different from their own.

As National Audubon Society President Alden A. Hadley wrote in the April 1935 issue of *The Seattle Wren* (Seattle Audubon's newsletter): "Today, thousands of [people] are going afield with binoculars and camera seeking to widen their acquaintance with our native bird life, an accomplishment easily made possible by reason of the almost universal use of the automobile, by which one may travel quickly and cheaply from one part of the country to another….[Checklists] are greatly needed and would be a boon to all itinerant bird students. Therefore, any local… Audubon Society may render a distinct service by making such a contribution."[26]

things, but on questions of substance and quality, he held to the highest standard, down to the last detail. The commitment to quality on every level by every member of the team was impressive, and a great book, *The Butterflies of Cascadia*, is the result.

We've followed that tradition of high quality with all our books. That's important because our books are going to be bought by people who really want to use them. They're not books that will just be a nice addition to the library. The words are going to be read. The photographs and illustrations are going to be studied. The maps are going to be followed. Our readers depend on the information we provide, so we must be sure everything is as accurate as we can make it.

I'm really proud that our books deliver that level of quality, especially because many of them are not books that other publishers wanted to publish. Mainstream publishers have a potential problem with books that might not sell in huge numbers, that might be too regional or specialized to appeal to a broad market. So a commercial publisher might just say, 'No, I don't think such a book is going to be profitable for us. We'll pass on that.'

But Seattle Audubon would say, 'We believe this is an important book that needs to be published. It supports our mission.' With lower production costs, because our staff are volunteers, we can produce a book with smaller sales potential and make sure the information gets in the hands of people who want and need it. And as it turned out, often our books did sell well. In fact, the Publications Committee's budget was refilled each time we produced a new book.

More important, though, our books had the effect of getting people out into the field to look at and study nature. Certainly, Eugene Hunn's book, *Birding in Seattle and King County*, did that when we published it in 1982. Gene wrote a unique book that told people where to find birds in King County, what birds were here in each season, and how common or rare they were. People who didn't know anything about birds in King County were given a way to get started. Gene says he's heard from many people over the years who say that his guide book was instrumental in getting them into birding.

Gradually, though, his book became outdated. Development in the county changed the habitat for birds. Gene had been working on an update, and we published his revised edition in 2012.

It's interesting to have the original book and the new one to compare. Of course, changes to the environment are happening everywhere, but I think that again, it is a credit to Seattle Audubon that we do recognize these changes and stay on top of them. It's not archaic information. It's good information that began in the early 1940s and then just keeps updating to the present day.

Knowing the past guides us, because we see changes that are oftentimes not good. I think the birds in some way for me and maybe for a lot of people are an indicator of how things change. We see what used to be and what we have now, and then think, 'Oh, what's it going to be like in the future? What are our grandchildren going to have?'

Having snapshots of earlier times lets you see trends. You can see what price we paid for development, and what it might cost in the future. Working for what we believe the future should be

Seattle Audubon's publications have long benefited from the generosity of local artists and photographers, who often donate their work. This Pileated Woodpecker by the talented photographer Gregg Thompson, for example, appeared in Eugene Hunn's revised book, Birding in Seattle and King County, *published in 2012.*

is important because there will be a lot of pressure to alter the environment in directions we think might not be good for nature—or for us.

Nature, for most of us, is a wonderful, unfolding mystery. When you actually get into it, you find everything is interrelated. Your understanding of nature expands, and you see what a complex and miraculous world this is. Discovering something so awesome can be life-changing—and even move us to action.

Of course, *we* are also related to everything else in nature and ultimately depend on a healthy environment to survive. We can encourage people living in an urban environment like ours—where it's not always easy to see the interrelatedness of nature—to discover this fact. That's where I think Seattle Audubon's publications have played an important role. They have provided access to nature for a broad community well beyond the limits of our membership.

Our books have shown a real commitment to involving people in nature, to educating them about the importance of preserving nature, and to step up, as our predecessors have done, and work for solutions that leave a better future for those who come after us."

BOOKS PUBLISHED BY SEATTLE AUDUBON

1942 *A Field Guide to the Birds of the Seattle Area*, by Earl J. Larrison

1947 *Field Guide to the Birds of King County Washington*, by Earl J. Larrison; illustrated by Elizabeth L. Curtis

1952 *Field Guide to Birds of Puget Sound*, by Earl J. Larrison;
      illustrated by Elizabeth L. Curtis, Lucy Wells Heald, and Marjorie W. Wells

1962 *Field Guide to the Birds of Washington State*, by E.J. Larrison and E.N. Francq; illustrated by Zella M. Schultz

1968 *Washington Birds—Their Location and Identification*, by Earl J. Larrison and Klaus G. Sonnenberg;
      illustrated by Zella M. Schultz

1970 *Washington Mammals—Their Habits, Identification and Distribution*, by Earl J. Larrison;
      illustrated by Bonnie L. Lustig

1974 *Washington Wildflowers*, by Earl J. Larrison, Grace W. Patrick, William H. Baker, and James A. Yaich;
      reprinted in 1977

1974 *Watching Washington Butterflies*, by Robert Michael Pyle

1976 *Mammals of the Northwest—Washington, Oregon, Idaho and British Columbia*, by Earl J. Larrison;
      illustrated by Amy C. Fisher

1982 *Birding in Seattle and King County—Site Guide and Annotated List*, by Eugene S. Hunn;
      revised and reprinted in 2012

1986 *Natural History of the Wenas, Washington Area*, by Earl J. Larrison; illustrated by Gregory A. Pole

1993 *Shorebirds of the Pacific Northwest*, by Dennis Paulson; published jointly with University of Washington Press

1993 *Amphibians of Washington and Oregon*, by William P. Leonard, Herbert A. Brown, Lawrence L.C. Jones, Kelly R.
      McAllister, and Robert M. Storm; reprinted in 1996 and 2000

1995 *Reptiles of Washington and Oregon*, by Herbert A. Brown, R. Bruce Bury, David M. Darda, Lowell V. Diller, Charles
      R. Peterson, and Robert M. Storm; coordinating editors Robert M. Storm and William P. Leonard; reprinted in 2000
      and 2006

1997 *A Field Guide to the Common Wetland Plants of Western Washington and Northwestern Oregon*, edited by Sarah
      Spear Cooke; reprinted in 2007

1997 *Breeding Birds of Washington State—Location Data and Predicted Distributions Including Breeding Bird Atlas
      Data & Habitat Associations*, by Michael R. Smith, Philip W. Mattocks, Jr., and Kelly M. Cassidy

1999 *Dragonflies of Washington*, by Dennis Paulson; reprinted in 1999 and 2007

2002 *The Butterflies of Cascadia, A Field Guide to All the Species of Washington, Oregon, and Surrounding Territories*,
      by Robert Michael Pyle; revised and reprinted in 2007

2003 *Gardening for Life—An Inspirational Guide to Creating Healthy Habitat*, by many contributors;
      joint venture with National Audubon Society and funded by award assistance from the EPA;
      since then Seattle Audubon funded a reprint

2005 *Amphibians of the Pacific Northwest*, edited by Lawrence L.C. Jones, William P. Leonard, and Deanna H. Olson

2016 *Birds of the Pacific Northwest: A Photographic Guide*, by Tom Aversa, Richard Cannings, and Hal Opperman;
      published jointly with University of Washington Press; Canadian edition co-published with Heritage House Publishing Co. Ltd. in Canada under the title, *Birds of British Columbia and the Pacific Northwest: A Complete Guide*

2016 *Caring for Birds & Nature: 100 Years of Seattle Audubon*, edited by Constance Sidles

TO APPEAR *Pacific Northwest Insects*, by Merrill A. Peterson

"TUNE IN" TO THE LIVES OF BIRDS
Christina Peterson: BirdNote

Christina Peterson. (Photograph © Jennifer Leach and BirdNote)

It's two minutes to nine. Across the region, thousands of people stop what they're doing and reach for their radios. They twirl the dial, listening for the lilt of an oboe and ocarina, gradually blended with the sounds of birds. "This is BirdNote," says a warm voice, and we are transported. For a brief moment, we leave behind our everyday world and enter the wild, where nature rules and birds fly, carrying us away to the places we yearn to go in spirit and imagination.

BirdNote® is the brainchild of Chris Peterson, the Executive Director of Seattle Audubon from 1995 to 2005. With the help of committed volunteers within Audubon, she launched BirdNote on February 21, 2005. The first show, about the Bald Eagle as our national symbol, aired on Washington's public radio station KPLU. Today, BirdNote's daily two-minute shows reach more than a million and a half listeners, both online and on 200 radio stations across the country, delighting us with stories about birds and the people who love them.

"The intention of BirdNote was to invite listeners into the intriguing lives of birds. I wanted people to feel connected to birds and to nature. The lives and needs of birds are invisible to most of us. Yet there are people who are curious about birds and willing to take action on their behalf. Stories that inspire can generate the interest and create the empathy that are necessary for action. Birds need places to hide, things to eat, places to rest—these are all within our power to provide. I believed the power of story-telling could be a force for conservation.

Being the Executive Director for Seattle Audubon for close to ten years put me in the milieu of many hundreds of volunteers who were keen about birds. We also had a staff of fifteen people working for conservation, education, science, nature sales, or the bird-watching activities of Seattle Audubon. Yet I could see that for all our hard work, good intentions, and terrific energy, our reach was still quite local. Meanwhile, too many bird species were declining throughout the flyways.

I was looking for a way to reach more people. As our human population continues to grow, our footprint keeps expanding. We are overriding and oftentimes overwhelming the needs of other species for the resources that we share. I thought we needed to do more to address this issue.

In 2002 my husband Todd and I were driving across the Cascades when the idea for BirdNote grabbed me: Why don't we create a show like *StarDate* but do it for birds?

StarDate is a two-minute program about the heavens. Tell me, here in the Northwest—where it's cloudy and we don't actually see the stars very often— why are we so thrilled by that show? It's because it draws you in. It gives you a moment of respite from the human conflict that's always on the news. It invites you to feel a part of systems that are larger and more beautiful and important than you are.

I began to keep a notebook. For the next year and a half, anytime anybody came into my office, after we had conducted our business I would ask, 'If you could hear a program about birds on the radio that resonated with you, what qualities would it have? What kinds of stories would interest you enough to tune in again?'

I got a wealth of information from people. In addition, I found two or three producers in other parts of the country who conveyed a lot of know-how, even though they would always start with, 'Hey, just skip it. It's hard to create and sustain a radio program. Save yourself the trouble.'

But I'm kind of a bulldog. Once I get onto an idea and I can see that it has merit, I'll stick with it. This idea had merit, and it started to attract talent. I began to assemble a team. That's where Seattle Audubon was so instrumental, because it provided a network. I had access to eminent scientists such as Dennis

Paulson and Gordon Orians, and a truly exceptional birding-by-ear individual named Bob Sundstrom, who, after Frances Wood, became our lead writer. Along with Adam Sedgley, John Kessler, our producer, and Ellen Blackstone, our web manager, they became our foundation.

We had a small, tight team working together on stories. Bob, Dennis, Ellen, Frances, Gordon, Adam, John, Idie Ulsh, Todd Peterson, Victor Scheffer, and I convened quarterly to outline potential stories. You can't just start with one! You have to have a lot in the pipeline. When we were ready to create a 'demo,' Nancy Rumbel and John Kessler composed and recorded the theme music.

With the help of business-oriented Seattle Audubon Board members, the business plan came together. Donors began to step forward. Ardell Kuchenbecker, Nancy Nordhoff, and Harriet Bullitt took the lead. Intellectual property contracts were signed, trademarks applied for, and a partnership with the Cornell Lab of Ornithology (for use of the bird sounds) was established. Chris Altwegg and Ellen Blackstone began fashioning what became a huge database to catalog the stories, while Adam Sedgley vetted and cataloged the sound database.

The original BirdNote crew gathered each quarter to discuss ideas for new shows. Left to right: Ellen Blackstone, Bob Sundstrom, Chris Peterson, Idie Ulsh, Dennis Paulson, Gordon Orians, and Todd Peterson. (Photograph © Chris Peterson)

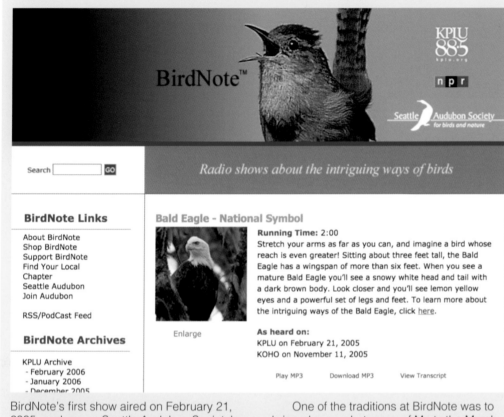

BirdNote™

Search [____] GO

Radio shows about the intriguing ways of birds

BirdNote Links

About BirdNote
Shop BirdNote
Support BirdNote
Find Your Local
Chapter
Seattle Audubon
Join Audubon

RSS/PodCast Feed

BirdNote Archives

KPLU Archive
- February 2006
- January 2006
- December 2005

Bald Eagle - National Symbol

Enlarge

Running Time: 2:00
Stretch your arms as far as you can, and imagine a bird whose reach is even greater! Sitting about three feet tall, the Bald Eagle has a wingspan of more than six feet. When you see a mature Bald Eagle you'll see a snowy white head and tail with a dark brown body. Look closer and you'll see lemon yellow eyes and a powerful set of legs and feet. To learn more about the intriguing ways of the Bald Eagle, click here.

As heard on:
KPLU on February 21, 2005
KOHO on November 11, 2005

Play MP3   Download MP3   View Transcript

BirdNote's first show aired on February 21, 2005, and ran on Seattle Audubon Society's website with a link to the show. The webpage included a photograph of a Bald Eagle, contributed by renowned photographer Paul Bannick. On the banner was a photograph of a singing Marsh Wren, contributed by former Seattle Audubon President Idie Ulsh. Ulsh called her photo "Marty the Marsh Wren."

One of the traditions at BirdNote was to bring along a photocopy of Marty the Marsh Wren on trips and then take a photograph of it next to the entry sign of a Natural Area, Wildlife Refuge, or National Park. It was BirdNote's version of Flat Stanley, a children's book character who was inadvertently flattened and could then mail himself all over the world.

Writing for radio is different from writing for print. For one thing, we were going to have only two minutes for each broadcast. That meant about one minute and 35 seconds for the actual narrative. We had to make every word count. Unlike print, where the reader can go back and reread a story, a radio story must convey its message in the one time the listener has to hear it. I don't mean you need to make everything simple, but the sentences need to be ten words or fewer. And even though it's short, the narrative needs to convey complex topics clearly.

John Kessler opened the door to Joey Cohn, KPLU's program director at the time. After listening to our demo, Joey decided to take a chance on BirdNote. Our inaugural show aired on KPLU on February 21, 2005—that was 21 months after I first had the idea. Then in 2006, Seattle Audubon fledged BirdNote to become its own nonprofit organization. Given that it was a media program, the geographic reach for BirdNote had become much bigger than the audience for Seattle Audubon.

In starting BirdNote, I believed naively that by putting a message on the air every day, we could build membership in Seattle Audubon. We could attract people who were now thinking about birds and were willing to improve conditions for them. But a savvy friend told me,'You know, Chris, you're a fool if you think people are going to listen to a few shows on the radio and change their behaviors. There's a huge gulf between hearing something and making a change. You are asking people to jump over a really big gulf.'

I realized then that the role of BirdNote is to pique people's curiosity about nature and birds. To further engage and enlist them in conservation is the role of organizations like the Audubon chapters. As partners, we can move conservation forward.

I worry, though, that we won't in time find a respectful way to live with nature. We need a way to live so that all species that depend on the same resources have the access they need for their livelihoods. I worry that the constituency for conservation is not growing at the pace required to resolve our environmental issues.

Still, that doesn't mean we should stop creating or telling stories about the lives of birds. These stories invite us all to feel we are a part of systems in nature that are much larger and more important than we are. For as Stephen Jay Gould, the scientist, once said, 'We cannot win this battle to save species and environments without forging an emotional bond between ourselves and nature as well, for we will not fight to save what we do not love.'[27]

Surveys of our listeners tell us that people are changing their behaviors as a result of listening to BirdNote. They're using fewer pesticides, planting native plants, drinking shade-grown coffee, joining organizations like Audubon. They're tuning in to the lives of birds. That brings me a lot of hope. Though birds are the ones to sing, we can all be a voice for them."

BirdNote airs episodes describing the lives of birds, but it also produces shows about the people who care for them. And that can include all of us, as this shade-grown coffee episode illustrates.

(Photographs: The screen shot of BirdNote is courtesy of BirdNote; the Western Tanager is courtesy of Dave Herr; the Scarlet Tanager © Daniella Théorêt; the background sand dune and grass © Gerrit Vyn)

Opposite page: Dunlins in flight. (Photograph © Stephanie Colony)

PARTICIPATION:
BUILDING COMMUNITY

WELCOMING THE WORLD
Russ Steele: The Nature Shop

Russ Steele in his office at the Nature Shop. (Photograph courtesy Constance Sidles)

Seattle Audubon's Nature Shop is not your typical store. You realize this the moment you walk through the door. With the silvery tones of the bell overhead still quivering in the air, a volunteer steps up with a conspiratorial smile and says, "Our hummingbird just laid her second egg. Would you like to see?" He leads you to a window overlooking a rhododendron bush. "Look where the leaves bend down over three little branches," he whispers. "She's on the nest right now." And so the wonder begins.

The Nature Shop is the face of our Society. For many people, it is the first contact they have with Seattle Audubon. But the shop is far more. It is the living heart of the Audubon community. Whether you're a birder, a conservation activist, or just a nature lover who wants to feed a few backyard birds, you feel the minute you come in that you are in the presence of like-minded people, folks who are eager to share their passion for birds and nature. And you know you are home.

"I started managing the Nature Shop in September 1998. I had sold my bicycle shop because our daughter was entering first grade and I wanted to be an at-home father. I was working for a magazine downtown when I saw an advertisement for part-time retail manager here in Wedgwood, where I live. I thought, 'Wow, I can do that.' I applied and got the job, and managed the shop for seventeen years. Now I'm Seattle Audubon's Finance and Operations Director.[1]

At the time, Seattle Audubon had a marvelous volunteer, George Johnson, who had been working as the Merchandise Manager of our retail sales for fifteen years. He had a background in business, and after he retired, he came to Seattle Audubon to volunteer.[2]

In those days, Audubon didn't do much with retail sales, except for the books we published ourselves. Our first major outside product was the 1983 edition of National Geographic's *Field Guide to the Birds of North America*. Back then, the National Geographic Society wasn't the sophisticated publisher they are today, which is to say, they didn't know how to distribute their book. So they offered it to nonprofit organizations first. Somehow they found Seattle Audubon.

It was just at the time George was retiring. The Board said to George, 'Here's a product, and here you are. Maybe we can put the two of you together and have you march forward.'

From there, George saw a need amongst the membership for bird supplies—mostly feeders and seed. So he started cobbling together a product line. We didn't have our own building then. We rented offices in the Joshua Green Building downtown, but there wasn't any room there for sales. So George initiated a series of seed depots, he called them. I think he had six around the city. George would have a big load of seed delivered to his house in Bellevue, and then he would distribute it himself, driving it around to all the different depots. Volunteers would sell feeders and seed at the depots and give the money back to the organization.

When Seattle Audubon moved its offices in March 1990 to Wedgwood at 8028 35th Avenue NE, we had the space for more product offerings. Once we had a storefront, the seed depots started drifting off, because there was a place where customers could get to easily and park. But George was still putting in probably 30- to 40-hour weeks, and even when

he'd go on vacation, he'd still call in to be sure the volunteers were doing what they needed to do. Finally, he wrote a letter to the Board in 1991 saying they really needed to hire somebody to do this.

It took the Board seven years more to come to the conclusion that George was right, and they needed to hire someone part-time. It was a really big decision for the Board to make. Not only did they have to decide whether the new position was going to be salaried, hourly, or on commission, they also had to get clear on what the purpose of a nature store might be and what products we ought to stock.

In the end, I was hired part-time to manage the store and later did part-time bookkeeping too. The advertising budget I had when I started was a total of $600, but half of that had been spent on advertising for the position, so I had very little marketing money to work with at the start. But the bar was not set very high for success. The gross revenues for the shop were about $160,000.

Retail is very simple. You have stuff. You buy it for X. You sell it for Y. You have somebody in the shop to sell. You unlock your doors. You let people in. They buy. You lock your doors. You count your money.

George Johnson. (Photograph courtesy of Seattle Audubon Society)

But our retail operation is not really that simple. It's grown since I started. Now we're in our own building, and the store has a full-time manager. We stock more than 2,000 items, and we use a big pool of volunteers to do the labor. There's a core of about 40 volunteers. We're open from 10:00 a.m. to 5:00 p.m. Monday through Saturday. The volunteers work in two shifts, and there are two volunteers per shift. A big part of the manager's job is supporting those volunteers. Many of them come in to work on a regular basis. For example, generally there are a steady two people who work every Monday morning, and another two people who work every Monday afternoon. That's typical for every day of the week. But people get sick, they have friends visiting, they travel. So there is

a second group of subs who fill in. It's a great group of people. They appreciate the flexibility. They don't need a regular shift. It's a nice blend.

Mainly volunteers do the clerking. But they have other responsibilities too, and those responsibilities are at a high level. Volunteers register people for classes and field trips. They need to be literate about all our products, including optics (which is about half our business) and non-optics. They need to know how to register people to become members of Seattle Audubon. They must welcome all the visitors who come into the shop, no matter how busy we are. On a Saturday in December, for example, we'll have 100 to 200 customers during the day. And then the phone is going to ring, and somebody is going to say, 'There's a person about to chop a tree down across the street. How do I stop this, because I know birds nest in it?' Or, 'A hawk has been stuck in my chimney for the last two days and won't come out. I've been putting Cheerios in the grate, but the hawk doesn't seem to like them. What

Shop volunteers Virginia Bound (far left) and Marilyn Busher (far right) help customer John Sidles select just the right birdhouse for his backyard. (Photograph courtesy of Constance Sidles)

should I do?' Or, the most common, 'There's this bird I saw. Can you tell me what it is?'

All these interactions, including sales, are termed 'transactions.' Last December we had 2,300 transactions for the month. Although we hold firm to the priority to create positive net revenue for the organization—we need to make money— the Nature Shop has other goals. We could sell things people don't need. We have those skills. But that's not our job here. We aren't here to push sales up. Our job is to find out what people need and then try to make sure they get it. For example, a customer might come in and say, 'I already have a feeder and I want to buy another one just like it.' Our volunteers are trained to find out why that customer wants another feeder. Sometimes, it's because a customer wants to attract different birds than the ones already coming. So we would say, 'We probably need to talk about a different feeding strategy. Do you have a suet feeder? A hummingbird feeder?' We try to learn what a customer's needs are so we can fulfill those needs.

At the same time, because of who we are, we have an obligation to not be purely profit-driven. We don't stock

BUILDING HISTORY AND A HOME

Real estate agents know all about location. A great location can boost business, a bad one can spell doom. On the other hand, when you're just starting out, you can't always be too choosy. You take what you can get. Such was the case with Seattle Audubon. When a few teachers, scientists, and philanthropists in town decided to get together to discuss the formation of a new Audubon society on April 17, 1916, they asked the Seattle Chamber of Commerce if they could use the Chamber's meeting room in the Central Building downtown. The Chamber was happy to agree, and the Society held its first two organizing meetings there.[3]

In May, however, the Chamber signed a lease to move its offices to the Arctic Building, where there was more room for its commerce museum. Seattle Audubon followed. When the Chamber built its own building in 1924, Seattle Audubon moved again.

But a meeting room is not a real center. Other groups can claim it when they need to meet. There's no phone service in a meeting room, and nowhere to keep records. For years, the President, Mrs. Charles Crickmore, kept the Society's papers in her home. Eventually, everyone agreed Seattle Audubon needed our own office, and money was raised to rent a small room in the Joshua Green Building on Fourth Avenue downtown. There the Society stayed until George Johnson arrived on the scene in 1984.

Johnson had been a traveling salesman and a retired business manager. His decision to join Seattle Audubon coincided with National Geographic's offer to let Seattle Audubon sell its first bird field guide exclusively in Washington and Oregon. Unfortunately, no one at Seattle Audubon knew how to market the book. We had published books since 1942, but press runs were small and sales were made mostly to members during meetings.

Johnson stepped in to fill the need. As he noted later, "I retired and was looking for another job!"[4] He broadened the market, expanded the inventory, and created a dependable revenue stream that provided a substantial part of the money used for the Society's operations for many years. He did it despite the fact that the quarters in the Joshua Green Building could not support sales. Instead, Johnson established depots around the city, staffed by volunteers. The depots sold mostly birdseed and feeders.

Realizing that sales and revenue could rise only if Seattle Audubon had its own storefront, Johnson began lobbying for a new location. In December 1989, the Board agreed to lease the building at 8028 35th Avenue NE to house offices and a store.[5] The Nature Shop opened on April 2, 1990.

In 1996, Seattle Audubon purchased its own building a few steps north on 35th. Two years later, Russ Steele took over to manage store operations, and Johnson "retired" to help with inventory and deliveries. In recognition of his many years of service as Merchandise Manager and then as shop volunteer, in 2007 the Nature Shop was renamed the George Johnson Birding Resource Center. Johnson died on December 29, 2014, but his spirit lives on in the hearts of the many volunteers who continue his tradition of sales and service, welcoming all who enter our doors.

The Central Building, site of Seattle Audubon's first meeting on April 17, 1916. (Photograph courtesy of Museum of History and Industry, PEMCO Webster & Stevens Collection, 1983.10.8045)

some products because we don't believe they're the right choice for the birds. For example, we don't carry any desiccants for seed feeders. Those are chemicals that absorb moisture so the seed doesn't go bad in the feeder. While one of our scientists tells me desiccants are probably harmless to the birds, to stock them sends the wrong message to our customers. It sends the message that you don't have to clean your feeder.

Feeder hygiene is a very important message for us to give people because it's more than just the seed going bad that can be harmful to birds. It's also the birds' fecal matter that's a vector to spreading disease. So we want people to clean their feeders. When we sell them seed, we have an opportunity to educate them about best practices.

We are doing about half a million dollars worth of business now, so we've trebled the revenue since I was hired. Our customer satisfaction rate is around 97 percent. The volunteers have enjoyed the ride. They've enjoyed the growth. They feel part of it, and they should feel part of it. They really are the face of the organization.

They volunteer for the Nature Shop because they care about birds. That's why they came to Seattle Audubon. They want to apply their passion and be evangelists for birds. They would never use that word, but I certainly would because that's what they're doing. They're sharing their passion.

Left: A female Anna's Hummingbird snags a spider for her young. (Photograph © Gregg Thompson) Right: The two eggs have hatched in the nest built by the Anna's Hummingbird outside the Nature Shop. While the mother is away fetching food, the two-week-old babies nestle quietly in the nest. (Photograph © Toby Ross)

One day we had a little boy come in with his dad. He was a quiet little guy, maybe seven or eight years old. He had a jar of money in his hands, and he said, 'I want to give this for the birds.'

That's when our volunteers showed how great they really are, and how much they get what we're all about. They got down to his level and helped him count the money. We asked his name, but he said he wanted to be 'anonymous.' So he had been coached by his dad, obviously, but we could see he wanted to help the birds himself. And he did.

That's really why we're here."

MULTIPLES OF ONE
Hazel Wolf: Organizing Audubon

After retiring as a legal secretary, Hazel Wolf joined Seattle Audubon in 1964—but not because she was interested in birds. Mostly, she said, it was because a friend kept pestering her to join. To shut her up, Wolf paid the Society one dollar and became a member.

Wolf, however, was never one to sit on the sidelines. Born in 1898 in the slums of Victoria, she grew up in great poverty among prostitutes and pimps. She emigrated to Seattle in 1923, a single mother trying to escape the Great Depression that had settled into the Canadian economy long before it hit America. She didn't have great luck. Jobs were scarce here for women and became even scarcer during our Great Depression. That's when Wolf joined the Communist Party. She liked what the Communists said about workers' rights and unemployment security, and she admired how willing they were to organize against oppression. Political ideology was never her interest, though, and gradually she moved away from the Party to pursue other causes: civil rights, labor unions,

anti-McCarthyism, and immigrants' rights (a personal fight, as the federal government tried for years to deport her).

Soon after joining Seattle Audubon, Wolf became Board Secretary, a position she held for the next 35 years. She liked being a secretary, she always said. It put her in the center of things. There, she could push for new causes she believed in: banning DDT, protecting ancient forests, fighting for clean air and pure water, standing up for Native American fishing rights, lobbying for a freeze on nuclear power.

Above all, Wolf was an organizer. She carried Seattle Audubon membership applications with her wherever she went and signed up more new members than anyone else ever has. She also prodded people to start their own Audubon chapters separate from Seattle. Helen Engle remembered that when Hazel finagled her to become President of the newly started Tahoma Audubon, two Board members of Seattle Audubon went down to Tacoma to try to prevent the new chapter

Hazel Wolf in the field. (Photograph courtesy of Seattle Audubon Society)

from splitting off, claiming that Tahoma would diminish Seattle Audubon by taking away its South Sound members. Engle replied that far from diminishing anyone, the new chapter would increase total membership, thereby increasing the clout of Audubon. That vision—multiplying one to become many—was pure Hazel.

"The environmental movement thinks it's big, but it isn't. We're a very small percentage of the population. Organized and committed as it is, the movement does not have enough political clout to put through the program of preserving the planet. We have to reach out to the rest of the community, especially to people of color and poor people, to find out what their concerns are. It means getting together to see what we have in common.

I think the turning point for the Seattle Audubon Society and my role in it was when we agreed to host the sixty-fifth annual National Audubon Society convention in May 1970, only a few weeks after the first Earth Day, April 22, 1970. The Seattle Board was afraid to take it on. I said, 'Okay, I'll be chairman.' It was two years' work getting that thing going, lining it all up. A thousand people had to be taken care of—housing, programs, banquets, and speakers. I reserved the Opera House, the entire suite of rooms at the Seattle Center, and five hundred rooms at the Washington Plaza Hotel—which had not yet been built! I had committees in charge of decorations, hospitality, publicity, and finances, and a chairman for each one.

We got tremendous publicity because I went to see the editor of the *Seattle Times* and the AP and UPI news services and chatted with them one on one. The *Times* ran a front-page spread in color of bird cartoons, and all kinds of bird stories throughout the paper. I visited the Seattle Art Museum, and they put up their famous Japanese work called *Crows* [from the Edo period, ca 1650], as well as bird paintings by Kenneth Callahan and other Northwest artists. They had special days and special shows just for Audubon. I also got the National Park Service to install a premier exhibit at Seattle Center of black-and-white photographs taken in parks all over the nation. We got articles in all of the neighborhood papers. Governor Evans declared May, the month of the convention, Washington State Bird Month, and he held a ceremony in Olympia, to which we all went trooping down.

It was the most beautiful convention that had ever taken place—everybody said that. After the convention, our membership jumped up to eighteen hundred in no time, and we cleared thirteen thousand dollars from our two post-convention field trips into Canada and into Alaska. It was quite a transformation. Boise Cascade gave every person at that convention a cellophane bag with a fir seedling, little roots and everything.

Note: This story is excerpted from a book: Starbuck, Susan. Hazel Wolf: Fighting the Establishment © 2002. Reprinted with permission of the University of Washington Press.

AUDUBON CHAPTERS CATALYZED BY HAZEL

- Admiralty Audubon Society
- Black Hills Audubon Society
- The Gorge Audubon Society
- Grays Harbor Audubon Society
- Kitsap Audubon Society
- Kittitas Audubon Society
- North Cascades Audubon Society
- North Central Washington Audubon Society
- Olympic Peninsula Audubon Society
- Pilchuck Audubon Society
- Rain Forest Audubon Society
- Rainier Audubon Society
- San Juan Islands Audubon Society
- Skagit Audubon Society
- Tahoma Audubon Society
- Vancouver Audubon Society (BC)
- Vancouver Audubon Society (WA)
- Vashon-Maury Island Audubon Society
- Victoria Audubon Society (BC)
- Whidbey Audubon Society
- Willapa Hills Audubon Society
- Yakima Valley Audubon Society[6]

Now they're planted all over the United States—in Florida, Texas, and Tennessee. People still come up to me at National Audubon conventions to tell me, 'My Washington State tree is growing.' I found out later that those treelets came from Pennsylvania, but Boise Cascade got a lot of PR out of it. Of course, that didn't stop us from suing them and testifying against them at hearings whenever we needed to. No hard feelings. If they do something that is laudable, we give them credit. And if they do something that's not so good, we tell them about that, too. You never know in this rickety old world when you're going to need an ally. You don't want to alienate

HAZEL AT WORK

Skagit Audubon members Grace and Jack Hubbard remember the day Hazel Wolf showed up to help start a local Audubon chapter. "She was small and very old," says Grace Hubbard, "wobbly but full of fire. She persuaded us that political action was as essential as bird-watching." Hubbard says Wolf proceeded to make up a "volunteer" board by pointing at people, including a number of women, and saying, "You and you and you. I like the women doing it."[7]

She was, Hubbard says, "unforgettable, miraculous. A tiny giant. What an inspiration."

somebody just because you're having a big fight with them. I remember sitting down at a banquet next to the Boise vice president and saying, "Oh, hi, John. How are you coming along with the destruction of our National Forests?"

So [after the convention] I got to organizing. Of twenty-six Audubon chapters in Washington State, I helped start twenty-one. We turned a bunch of bird-watchers into an effective environmental lobby. We went from a couple of hundred to five thousand members in Seattle, and somewhere around eighteen thousand in the state. In 1975, I founded the annual meeting of the Washington State Council of Audubon Chapters so all these new groups could get together. On my way home from a speech at a school or community center, I might stop at what looks like the main bar or restaurant in town, start talking with the owners and the clientele, and find out who the birders are. When I get home I write to them, call a meeting, get the gang going. Organize, organize, organize.

Nature is everything—the stars, you and me, mice and everything, including the big bang. A little over a hundred years ago, Frederick Engels wrote that we don't rule nature like a conqueror over foreign people, but with flesh, blood, and brain, we belong to nature and exist in its midst. We have the advantage over other living things by being able to understand nature's laws. Otherwise, we're just one of the species. Through the countless centuries of evolution, our species, *Homo sapiens*, has had a tough row to hoe to survive. We don't have much going for us. We have very little hair, and this is mostly in patches, and some lose a lot from the top of their heads rather soon in life. We have almost nothing to protect us from the rain, snow, or sun—no feathers, scales, wool, fur, or even fuzz. In fact, we're almost naked. And we are physically handicapped compared to other animals. For example, we can't run very fast to overtake something to eat other than plants. We can't see very well nor for great distances as eagles, owls, hawks, and many mammals can, nor are we able to see on both sides at once, gnat-eyed, like horses and frogs. We have hardly any sense of smell. Our hearing is defective. We cannot climb trees, like monkeys. We cannot slither along gracefully, like snakes. We are indifferent swimmers, and we cannot fly, of course. So, in summation, we are a sorry species.

And how was it possible for humans to hunt the abundantly endowed and superior animals? The answer is simple—we ganged up on them....'Gregarious' is the term used to describe this trait.... It comes in the gene package. One human couldn't kill a lion or overtake a deer, but many humans hunting together could.

In human beings, 'gregariousness' is another word for 'brotherhood.' I'm sorry to have to use such a sexist word, but 'sisterhood' is just as sexist if used in a general sense. The only word I can think of is 'siblinghood,' which should be kept restricted by law for use only by sociologists. So I am back to the warm, fuzzy word of 'brotherhood.'

No species in the whole living world has ever destroyed its habitat knowingly, willfully. They might do it unwittingly, or as a consequence of being unable to adapt, but not deliberately. I think this is a law that holds good for all of creation, including humans. This need for brotherhood, for keeping together and working together, is in our genes, and it's in our culture,

Wolf was an athlete all her life and an outdoorswoman when that was not common for women. Kayaking was one of her favorite sports. (Photograph © Fred Felleman)

and I think that these two things will come together to save our habitat. It will be a long and stormy road and I don't know how we're going to do it. I can't see that far into the future. I just go along from day to day. But I see the awareness growing in people in all walks of life.

Now, this gregariousness is not going to save us just because it's in our genes. We have to activate it. And that means get out to meetings. As a child, I thought meetings were so romantic, exciting, and important. I wondered if I would ever go to one when I grew up. I must have had a premonition that I was going to spend the latter half of my life in meetings. I still like them.

Here's [a] question—do we have an evolution that's based on randomness, or is it planned and designed? I feel that it is random, there's no design, and there's no justice. And I don't care. I just don't care! So what! You live here. Whether or not the universe is random doesn't alter anything. My job is to introduce some justice where I can in my small way. It's the job of all people to introduce peace despite all this random business, or lack of it, because we are thinking and feeling beings who can judge and plan for the future. We're part of the web, but we're a qualitative leap above the rest of the animal kingdom because we have in us this gift, a certain freedom of will.

It's partly conscious and partly unconscious. We don't have absolute control because, after all, we're basically victims of our environment and our culture, but we do have some control, and we have some responsibility. A two-edged sword—we can plan destruction, or we can plan the other way. That's our challenge.

People invent God to explain this human difference, this strange leap. It's natural to invent answers to things we don't understand....It's a system of crutches to deal with the basic randomness that is too much for people to bear. [But] see, I've lived without [crutches] all my life, so to me it's old hat.

Well, yes, I do have a crutch. It's my faith in human beings and it's never been knocked out from under me. I can read all the crime columns in the world and I'm not going to let go of that crutch. I have that faith that human beings are headed toward brotherhood."

WONDERFUL WENAS

In an article she wrote for Earthcare Northwest's *September 1984 issue, Hazel Wolf described the beginnings of the now-famous annual Audubon Memorial Day Campout at Wenas. The Campout is another example of her genius for community.*

What is it that induces hundreds of families to drive on a dirt road full of ruts and rocks, to spend two days in a campground that has no potable water, no picnic benches and has dilapidated pit toilets? What, then has Wenas got going for it? It has, for one thing, over 200 species of birds oberved over the past 20 years. In addition there is an abundance of wildflowers, trees and shrubs, many insects (none of which bite, such as mosquitos), but most importantly there are the Auduboners from all over the state who love to get together to renew friendships and make new ones, and who like to sing around a campfire and listen to the talk, and watch the children toast marshmallows.

In 1963 Bea Buzzetti, Ruth Anderson, Ruth Boyle and I, looking for a camp spot, wandered into the place a few days prior to Memorial Day when we were to meet Seattle Audubon members and join them on the field trip. We persuaded them to give up their plans and instead return with us to Wenas. The lovely spot and unusual birdlife inspired us to make this an annual event for Memorial Day. The field trips fan out in a radius of five miles through the Wenas Valley, to Wenas Lake, two state wildlife refuges and up onto the high dry ridges. It is the variety of habitat that gives the campout its great drawing power.

We wrote to Boise Cascade asking them to put up signs to protect the wildlife of the large campground, and received a warm response from Don Caldwell, an official of the company and a dedicated bird-watcher, who said they would prepare a sign, which they did. The following year we invited Don and his family and other Boise people to join us, and thus started a most happy relationship with Boise Cascade.

For the first few years only Seattle Audubon and a few from the Oregon society came to Wenas, but as the chapters increased, so did wider participation....There have been as many as 300 men, women, and children at some of the campouts. [Sometimes it snows] and it frequently rains. But nothing seems to discourage the hundreds of people who turn out for the Audubon Memorial Day Campout at Wenas, because the birds always return and so do the wildflowers, the trees, shrubs, the insects, bugs and butterflies.[8]

Lupine in full bloom, one of the many wildflowers that bloom in the Wenas area in time for the Campout, and one that Hazel especially loved. (Photograph © Rob Sandelin)

SHARING THE WONDER
Neil Zimmerman: Outreach Coordinator

Neil Zimmerman. (Photograph © Carleen Ormbrek Zimmerman)

Nature belongs to no one but itself. You cannot own the sky or the Killdeer's cry. Nature is home to all life, a world of infinite mystery and everlasting beauty. Perhaps that is why Seattle Audubon members take such delight in sharing our passion for birds with anyone who will listen, in the hope that other people will come to love and hence value the wild as much as we do.

This has always been so. The first official field activity of the Seattle Audubon Society was a neighborhood bird walk held on May 13, 1916. The public was invited to take the Lake Burien streetcar to the end of the line, there to meet up with Audubon members to bird around the lake. "Lunches and field glasses or strong opera glasses should be taken along," said the announcement.[9]

Since then, Seattle Audubon members have led thousands of such walks in every neighborhood of our city. Countless speakers have given talks and slide shows to garden clubs, school groups, business clubs, and fairs. In the 1950s, 1960s, and 1970s audiences numbering more than a thousand at a time attended the presentation of dozens of nature films sponsored by Seattle Audubon. Audubon volunteers mentored hundreds of kids in Boy Scouts and Girl Scouts, helping them get their bird and naturalist badges. In the 1990s, Seattle Audubon partnered with National Audubon and nature groups to produce a booklet titled Gardening for Life,[10] *a free handout giving gardeners tips on how to create havens for birds in their backyards.*

Nowadays, a team of volunteers, led by Seattle Audubon Master Birder Neil Zimmerman, continues to take our message on the road, reaching out to a growing circle of birders old and young, beginners and experts, inviting them to share the wonder and fall in love with birds—as we have.

"I always thought that everything I've done for Seattle Audubon from the start has been about outreach and environmental education. The neighborhood walks, the gardening for wildlife talks, the science nights, the bird fests and community fairs—to me they all tie into environmental education. I always hope if I can get people interested in the birds in their backyard, one step at a time, pretty soon they'll be interested in the birds in the park, and then maybe they'll want to get more interested and involved in conservation as a whole.

Outreach is the face and voice of Seattle Audubon to people who don't know us. We reach out to people at our events so they become familiar with Seattle Audubon, associate us with birds, and associate birds with being part of the environment. I always tell my volunteers, I want people to go away knowing we are the bird people, we're friendly, and we've got smiling faces. The next time people see us, or read about a bird walk in their neighborhood, maybe they'll join Seattle Audubon.

But I'm always looking at the bigger picture, too. Seattle Audubon is a kind of tool to accomplish goals I have for the world. Maybe I'm naive, but I believe we can make the world better. I cannot save the world by myself. But I *can* take little steps to help. I can make some of my day-to-day decisions more mindfully. I can think about what I put down the drain, how much I drive my car, whether I put pesticides on my lawn. You know, the average homeowner per acre puts more pesticides into the water system than any farmer ever would.

Zimmerman often uses his own yard to show people how to landscape with native plants that are low maintenance and that attract birds. (Photograph © Carleen Ormbrek Zimmerman)

A lot of people think it takes time to get involved in conservation or to do something for nature. But I landscaped my yard with native plants to attract birds, and I'm not mowing my lawn anymore. I'd like people to start thinking about the little things like that they could do to make a difference. If everybody did that, maybe overall together, we could help the Earth.

And I think maybe we already have. I've had people come up to me at a booth and say, 'I heard you talking before, and I went home and put in a water feature. I planted snags. I got these great woodpeckers.' Those are little things people can add to their yards to increase habitat, help birds, and help the environment. Small steps, but I figure I've got to work in small steps. I can't change the world in one fell swoop.

When I first got started doing this about 15 or 20 years ago, it was oftentimes pretty much just me. Somebody

would call Seattle Audubon, and people there would ask me if I could go out and do a science night at a school, or talk to a garden group, or set up a booth at a show. But now I have a team of 15 to 25 volunteers who are really into it. When a request for a speaker comes in, I put the word out, and some of the volunteers respond so fast, no one else even gets a chance! They love going out to events,

but they especially love going to science nights at schools.

We take along gardening literature to promote backyard habitat for birds, Nature Camp brochures to promote our summer school programs, and little cards that tell people about BirdWeb (our online encyclopedia about the natural history of Washington birds) and Sound to Sage (our online Breeding Bird Atlas). I want people to have at least one thing to take away with them.

But our primary display is a collection of bird study skins. When I first asked about taking skins around to events, the staff were a little protective. They didn't want anything to hurt the specimens. But I said, 'The skins aren't doing any good in the drawer. Let's get them out.' So now we put them out for people to look at and touch.

I cannot overstate how much of a draw these bird skins are. I had one woman tell me she can walk right past a booth with a thousand brochures on the table, but she could not walk by five bird

Left: Neil and Carleen Zimmerman staffing the Seattle Audubon outreach booth. (Photograph by Kathy Paul, © Seattle Audubon Society) Right: Northern Flicker. (Photograph © Larry Hubbell)

skins. Kids come up, and they simply can't get enough of touching and feeling. They don't get to touch birds very often. Our birds are dead, of course, but they're *real*. They're close up. So the kids pick them up, turn them over, and ask, 'What's this bird? What's that bird?'

I remember we were doing a science night at Lake Forest Park Elementary. There was a little boy who got to our booth early, and he asked me what each bird skin was. I have talking points for every bird, so I told him about each one. Half an hour later, he came back with some of his friends. He picked up a flicker and he said, 'Now, this is the bird that hammers on your chimney cap in the spring every year because flickers don't sing to attract mates. They drum.'

He was like a little tape recorder. He had picked up every talking point I had. I said to myself, 'This kid is a natural. He's teaching his friends, word for word!' So that night, I reached a kid who was so interested he brought his buddies over to teach them.

That level of interest happens with adults sometimes, too. My wife Carleen and I do the bird walks at Discovery Park in the fall and spring. (Some of our other volunteers do walks in the other

parks.) Most of our walks are geared toward beginners. They're a great introduction for people to get started in birding because each walk takes only two hours. You don't have to sign up ahead of time. You just show up. It's free.

For me the neighborhood walks are fun because I don't have to come up with a rare bird to get people excited. If I can show them a hummingbird or a flicker through my spotting scope, they come away enthusiastic. A couple of years ago, I found a hummingbird nest on one of our walks. I got 20 people in line to look at that nest through the scope. I think only one person had ever seen a hummingbird on a nest before. People got so excited. To me, success is people enjoying themselves. A positive experience like that is what I'm looking for because I can build on that. I tell people they can go to our web site and find out which field trips are coming up, or which classes they can sign up for. I try to funnel people's enjoyment to the next level.

I really am energized by all the people who get interested in birds and nature. They're not just pooh-poohing what I try to show them. It makes me want to do even more. That positive feedback keeps us going, with the hope that we can accomplish something important. It's fun.

Sometimes it's not just fun—it's inspiring. One year we were doing outreach in Shoreline, and a woman came up with her little girl, who must have been about three, I think. She said her daughter was blind and asked if she could feel our birds.

'Sure,' I said, 'no problem.'

So I gave the girl a Northern Flicker to hold. She began to stroke the bird skin, running her fingers over the feathers. As she did, I heard her quietly say, 'Wikka, wikka, wikka.'

I gave her a Steller's Jay, and she imitated that one, too. She knew her bird calls. Then I gave her a Barn Owl, and she said, 'Oh, it feels like my blankie,' because the owl's feathers are so soft.

This was a little girl who will probably never see birds, may never feel live birds, but she had a chance to feel these skins and make a connection between the sounds she heard and the bird she was feeling. I will never forget her face as she was stroking those birds."

A PACKED HOUSE:
AUDUBON SCREEN TOURS

Nowadays, Google Earth can fly you anywhere on the planet to see distant, exotic places for free. But in the past, if you wanted to explore the faraway, you had to hire a travel agent and spend a fortune on airfare. Or, you could ride the bus to the Olympic Room at the Seattle Center, pay $1.50, and let Seattle Audubon take you on a visual tour of the wilds of Northern California, or the alpine meadows of the Rockies, where you might meet the occasional grizzly.

These nature shows, called Audubon Screen Tours, were silent movies filmed in color and produced by some of the nation's finest photographers. The idea for a film tour originated in the 1930s when St. Louis Bird Club's President Wayne Short put on silent shows narrated by naturalists. The general public flocked to see the them. During World War II, when birding was curtailed due to the U.S. Army's suspicions of people who liked to wander around observing things using high-powered binoculars, Short offered his idea to National Audubon, suggesting that a nation-wide tour of these films could be sponsored through local Audubon chapters.[11] Seattle was one of the earliest chapters to try it out.

Our first foray into this terra incognita of public outreach occurred on November 12, 1945, in the Woman's Century Club Theatre.[12] *Our Heritage in the Rockies* by naturalist Karl Maslowski was shown, narrated by his wife Edna. The film was about Yellowstone, and attendance was restricted to sustaining members only. By 1956, Seattle Audubon recognized the films could reach a much

larger audience, as they had in other cities. Seattle Audubon President Emily Haig proposed the Society show five films in the coming season. Her proposal was hotly debated. National Audubon required cash upfront to lease the films. Other expenses included rent for the theater, pay for the projectionist, and money for publicity. Members worried Seattle Audubon might lose a lot of money we could ill afford.

But it must have been very hard to say no to Mrs. Haig, for not only did she carry the day, but one month later, the Screen Tours Committee consisted of 26 members—this at a time when total membership numbered fewer than 400 and monthly meeting attendance ran to a tenth or less of that.

Volunteers sold tickets, twisted relatives' arms to buy ticket blocks, designed and printed posters, bought ads in local newspapers, wrote press releases, mailed flyers, were interviewed on the radio, found theater space, housed the traveling narrator, and ushered theater-goers to their seats.[13]

Audiences began to grow. During the late 1950s and early 1960s, viewers often numbered more than 1,000 per show. Seattle Audubon made a good profit until audiences began to fade in the 1970s with the advent of nature shows on color television. The Society ended the program in 1976.

Although Seattle Audubon made a profit in the heyday of Screen Tours, even when a show lost money (as one did in 1953, plunging $5.40 into the red), the most important concern of the members was to educate the public about the value of nature. As one member said during the early debates, "in order to help make the public more conservation-minded, these pictures are essential."

Flyer advertising Seattle Audubon's 1955-1956 Screen Tours season, showing Northern Flickers photographed by Allan Cruikshank. National Audubon supplied the templates for these flyers to local chapters to use for promotion.[14]

IN THE NEWS
Frances Wood: Newsletter Editor

We humans are an odd species—highly individualistic, yet completely dependent on each other. Perhaps because we lack fangs and talons, we have always had to band together to survive. The need to join a group, to be a part of something larger and more powerful than ourselves, seems encoded in our DNA.

In 1916, a small group of birders felt the need to start a Seattle-based organization of like-minded people. The purpose was mostly to have fun with others who shared a passion for birds. But gradually, as people met together each month to talk about the birds they had seen and the places they had been, the group began to make use of their numbers to promote the preservation of birds.

They took advantage of their regular meetings to sign postcards and write letters. They formed committees to boost membership. They gave talks in schools and led walks all over the region. They began to shape themselves into an entity that had its own identity separate from the individuals who belonged to it.

That entity eventually demanded a voice, a way of expressing itself, both inwardly to members and outwardly to others. In the latter half of 1933, seventeen years after its first meeting, Seattle Audubon published its first newsletter: The Seattle Wren.[15]

It was a quirky little quarterly filled with whatever the editor, L. Roy Hastings, seemingly took into his head to print. Sometimes it would carry a story about a conservation fight or a piece about natural history. Sometimes it would report on the travels of a member or the results of the latest Christmas Bird Count. New members were welcomed and older ones encouraged to pay their dues. Now and then a poem would appear. In one issue, a full-page story told readers how to pronounce difficult bird names such as guillemot.[16] There were no regular features or columns. Yet despite its quirks, it was an utterly charming publication.

Unfortunately, it ended in 1941, due to lack of money. There followed years of on-again, off-again bulletins, newspapers, and newsletters, each one speaking strongly for a while, then fading out or morphing into something else because of the expense.[17] But like a joke candle that you can never completely extinguish, the spark remained. That

Frances Wood. (Photograph © Michael Stadler, Stadler Studio Photography)

spark was our need to share our passion for birds with each other and with the world.

Finally in 1995, Frances Wood, a professional writer and editor, was hired to help retool the entire approach. Seattle Audubon's voice was to be recast as a nine-issue-a-year educational brochure. Its mission? To build a sense of community, boost awareness of environmental issues, showcase the breadth and

THE FIRST NEWSLETTER

The Publishing Committee, chaired by L. Roy Hastings, created Seattle Audubon's first newsletter in the fall of 1933. It was titled *The Seattle Wren* in honor of our local Seattle Wren, which was an accepted subspecies of the Bewick's Wren in those days. The newsletter was professionally typeset and printed, issued as a four-page quarterly. The lead story was written by T. Gilbert Pearson, President of National Audubon, who laid out the goals of Audubon.

depth of our expertise, and have fun. Since then, Earthcare Northwest *has continued to evolve. It is now a combination of online newsletter (focusing more on announcements) and quarterly printed publication (focusing more on education). But though the form has changed, the message has not. We speak for the birds.*

"It was in 1992 that I left an intensive corporate job at GTE. I decided my life needed to be less stressful and high powered. I wanted time to follow my passion of writing about and painting birds. So I went into freelance writing and editing. One of my first opportunities to edit was with *Earthcare Northwest*. Seattle Audubon brought me in at a time when they wanted to do a complete change of the look and content of their newsletter.

Before I arrived on the scene, *Earthcare Northwest* was published in a newspaper format that came out nine times a year. As a newspaper, it was great. In 1989, it won first place in the Washington Press Association's contest in the category of non-daily newspapers with a circulation under 15,000. Two years before that, it won National Audubon Society's

grand prize for best newsletter of chapters with more than 900 members.

But the Board wanted the newsletter to move away from a home-grown look. They wanted it to be less like a newspaper and more of an educational tool. The Board wanted readers to be able to learn about birds, habitat, and ecology. They tasked me and Ellen Blackstone, the publisher, with the job of providing significant content, written by some of the wonderful ornithologists in our area such as Dennis Paulson, Bob Sundstrom, Bob Pyle, and Gordon Orians, people who really knew about birds and nature.

Ellen and I got together with Sandy Welch, our designer, and started to toss around ideas. Instead of the newspaper format, we decided the newsletter should be a kind of booklet, 8-1/2 x 11 inches. We designed a template for it so it would have the same look from month to month. There was always an interesting article on the first page, and then holes we had to fill each month. On the bottom of the front page we announced the monthly meeting program. We always tried to write the program description to make it inviting but also to tie it to the Seattle Audubon mission. We had a President's blurb; a department we called 'Chapter Chat,' describing what was happening within our chapter; and a column by Dennis Paulson, answering a question from a reader about birds. There was always something on conservation, and a report on bird sightings. Before the annual meeting, we published any bylaws changes the Board was proposing and also the nominees for officers. Toward the back, we described the upcoming field trips and classes.

We had to do all that because the newsletter was the only venue we had to get that information to the members. We didn't have a website.

Now we have so many ways to get the word out, and a lot of it is electronic. I do see the benefits and cost effectiveness of going electronic. For nonprofit organizations, it makes a lot of sense because of the savings. When I was editing *Earthcare* we had several thousand members. The newsletter was expensive to print and mail. It became a line item in the annual budget, but Ellen and I also solicited ads to help pay for it. I think the ads provided a service to the readers, but the money we got helped the budget.

So I understand the appeal of online media. But I think something is lost as we move away from print. Think about

The Label Ladies working to get out another newsletter (from left): Esther Bailey, Genevieve Reckamp, Martha Wood, Lise Larsen, and Oralee Richter. Not shown: Frances Applegate, Elizabeth Bryer, Sheri DuCette, and Sandy Lindsey. (Photograph by Linda Murray, courtesy of Seattle Audubon Society)[18]

Earthcare Northwest sitting on somebody's kitchen counter. People can pick it up when they're having their morning coffee. They can set it down on the coffee table and pick it up again in the evening. There is a presence to it. I think it is better read and more remembered, whereas when something comes to me online, if I'm busy, sometimes I just delete it because I've got to move on with my day.

The other thing about people getting their information online is that they have to take more responsibility for what they read and hear, especially if they get their news from social media. A lot of what comes out in social media is more about the person's bias, the person's feeling of joy or anger at the moment. Our newsletter was different. It was written by experts and edited professionally.

I was reminded of this when I was interviewed recently for the local paper. I had taken an Audubon group out for Earth Day. This fresh-faced young reporter just out of the University of Washington interviewed me for a story about that. He knew nothing about birds, and I was nervous about him getting all the species correctly written, because he was quoting me. I suggested to him that I could review his story, just to find any mistakes so nobody would have egg on their faces. He said, 'Well, you know it's not our policy.' I did understand that, but he was so new—I just wanted to help him get it all right.

That article came out, and it was flawless. The reporter had paid attention. He knew what he was doing. He quoted me correctly. All the bird species were correct. It reminded me how important trained reporters are. They're in the profession. Even if they're new and are feeling their way, they have pride in what they're writing. It's about the story, not about them.

With social media, it's different. People can write anything. I get so jaded reading unprofessionally written news. I don't pay as much attention to it anymore because I'm just not convinced it's valuable enough for me to try to get information from it.

Print newsletters serve another purpose, too. They preserve our institutional memory. Online venues can also do that, but somehow, they don't seem to. Things disappear. But our newsletters were the only regularly printed record of what we were doing in the past. That's important, because what was done in the past guides the future. So much of what we can do now is possible because of what people did before us.

There were big movers and shakers in Seattle Audubon throughout its history, and we need to remember them. I mean, think of Hazel Wolf and all she did, starting all these Audubon chapters around the State, just hammering home conservation issues. I will always hold her up as a mentor and model for the way a person, particularly a woman, can act and get good work done without all the money and all the prestige that some people get to start with. Or Gene Hunn—he could have kept his whole life busy with his career, teaching at the UW and working in the state of Oaxaca, but he taught bird classes, too. I also think of Dennis Paulson and the commitment he made to teaching Master Birder classes. These people spent a huge amount of time and effort spreading the good word about birds and habitat conservation. They are a part of our history.

The newsletter to me was also a way to build community. It was the voice for Seattle Audubon. And it was such fun to put together. I was excited to do this work, and I loved all of it. I was not flying across the country to go to a meeting with GTE and having long days of stressful, corporate work. Of course there were late nights when Ellen and I would be on the phone trying to sort out the last cutting of this or that, deciding what was going to go in this month or saved till next month. Those times got busy and stressful, but it was such a lovely group of people to work with that I can't say I ever had a bad time.

After I would send the stories and ads over to Sandy and she had thrown them together to make a draft, we would turn it over to Ellen. She was the content approval person. Right before the newsletter was ready to go to press, Hanna Atkins, our proofreader, would proof everything. She was amazing—always so quick.

When the newsletters came back from the printer, we would have the Label Ladies come in and put on all the address labels. Then George Johnson would haul the newsletters to the post office. Everybody stepped forward to do their particular task to make this all happen. They did it because they loved the newsletter and they loved birds. They thought the newsletter was an important part of protecting birds and getting the word out about enjoying nature.

I know we can't put the genie back in the bottle. As a broader community, we have to figure out how best to work with all this new media. I attend a lot of meetings electronically. The technology allows people to get to meetings they wouldn't otherwise be able to attend. I think, too, about how often a question will come up in conversation, and somebody will pull up a smart phone and get the answer. That allows the conversation to move forward so we can talk about something deeper. We're not confused about when something happened or who was involved. It's all fascinating.

But we have to realize that online venues are not the same as being together. There's an energy that goes on when people physically come together or hold something. We're going to have to learn that a lot of our lives will happen online, but then we also have to remember that the really important interactions still have to happen, through print media or meeting each other face to face. We are going to have to rethink how best to communicate, get the word out, and still find out how we can share the joy in what we love about birds and birding."

THE POWER OF THE PRESS

Throughout its history, *The Seattle Wren* served a wider purpose than just informing its members about the latest happenings. When Seatte Audubon wanted to lobby for a particular conservation issue, the press run was increased, sometimes more than doubled, so that copies could be sent to politicians, clubs, organizations, and the general public. It was the old-school form of an Action Alert, making Audubon's position clear and giving activists the information they needed to write letters and send telegrams to the movers and shakers of the day.

In January 1939, Seattle Audubon member Ellsworth D. Lumley wrote a scathing article excoriating Ducks Unlimited's opposition to National Wildlife Refuges. According to Lumley, Ducks Unlimited didn't like the idea of Wildlife Refuges in the United States because such Refuges would restrict hunting by limiting open seasons and imposing bag limits.

Ducks Unlimited advocated instead that Refuges be established in Canada, where many duck species were known to breed. Here in the States, they contended, no Refuges were needed because there were plenty of ducks.

Lumley reported that the U.S. Biological Survey had assessed duck populations and found the number of breeding birds low, despite the fact that Canadian habitat was good. Scientists attributed the absence of breeding waterfowl to overhunting, yet Ducks Unlimited was calling for more hunting.

Lumley concluded, "Our ducks are limited, and it will take more than the improvement in breeding areas in three Canadian provinces combined with more killing to make them unlimited."[19]

The newsletter proved so popular among environmental groups that Seattle Audubon had to reprint the issue, the only time in our recorded history when this happened.[20]

Green-winged Teal. (Photograph © Gregg Thompson)

WALK WITH ME
Phyllis Moss: Bird Walks & Field Trips

In the mundane world of 9:00 to 5:00, Wahkiakum Lane on the western side of the Center for Urban Horticulture at the edge of Montlake Fill is little more than a through-way for pedestrians and cyclists on their way to the University of Washington. But in the early morning, before the office rush begins, before the cross-country team thunders past, Wahkiakum Lane is a pathway to magic.

To find it, you must ease past the towhee who is always on guard at the serviceberry bush. If he sings his burry song to you, you may creep by, step across the little stone bridge on your left, and enter a world of song and swift wing. Humans do not rule here. We must come quietly, patiently awaiting an invitation from the wild. Perhaps it will be given by the Anna's Hummingbird who hovers overhead, his wings beating a tattoo of tiny thunder. Or maybe it will be the Bushtits busily fetching moss and lichen to build their hanging nest. In the bushes lurks a female Ring-necked Pheasant. She will not

Phyllis Moss. (Photograph © David Moss)

welcome you. She is much too suspicious of your motives, coming as she does from a long line of ancestors who appeared mainly on our tables, stuffed. But if you stand still, she will resume her hunt for seeds. After all, you are now a part of wild nature too, for you are on a very special journey: a bird walk.

Bird walks and field trips have been a part of Seattle Audubon's history from the very first. In fact, you could say our first official act after organizing the Society was a bird walk to Lake Burien in May of 1916.[21] Since then, Audubon members have taken thousands of such walks into the field, both here in the Seattle area,[22] and to distant realms as far away as the Pribilofs in the north and the cloud forests of Costa Rica in the south.[23]

Master Birder Phyllis Moss has led many such walks for birders and wannabes. She does it for love, to invite others to see the wonder, and to help preserve nature for generations to come. For Moss, Seattle Audubon is not just about birds. It's about people too.

A Hairy Woodpecker, common in coniferous forests, might not get experienced birders too excited, but when seen through the eyes of beginners, it is a spectacular bird. (Photograph © Paul Bannick)

"I lead local Neighborhood Bird Walks, guided bird walks, and field trips outside the greater Seattle area for people who range in skill level from beginners to Master Birders. Neighborhood Bird Walks are a specific program designed by Seattle Audubon as outreach. The walks are open to the public and welcoming to anybody who's interested in spending a couple of hours investigating a local Seattle park. People can come without having to register or even plan in advance. All they need to do is show up at a given park at a designated time.[24] Neighborhood Bird Walks tend to draw people who are new to bird-watching and who think, 'Maybe this could be an interesting hobby for me or something I'd like to learn more about.' They also draw people who are new to Seattle, who may already have an interest in bird-watching and want to get to know the bird life in the local area and maybe some other birders as well.

Neighborhood Bird Walks also draw families with children. To me, that's one of the really fun parts about leading bird walks. I love introducing children to nature. They're very spontaneous about getting engaged to help look for the birds, and they don't think they have

to know the names of anything. You can tune them into listening for a bird, or looking for whether a bird is present. You don't have to see the whole bird to tell if one is near. Maybe all you see is a tail or a movement among the leaves. Kids will point out everything, where adults will often withhold judgment. 'Something's moving there,' kids will say. 'Is it a bird? No, it's brown. Wait! It is a bird.' I love that part because kids really jump right in.

Kids make me hopeful, too. I want them to love nature and support it when they grow up. I think the more they are aware of nature all around them, the more likely they are to become involved in preservation of habitat in our local parks. One day, they're going to be building homes and planting trees and making decisions about what to plant in their backyards. I'd like to see bird-friendly habitat all over the city. And some of these children are going to become leaders. It's important they have a love of nature.

The other thing is, kids are funny. They observe things I might have missed, and ask questions that make me more aware. I learn something new every time I take a child bird-watching because kids bring into focus how well birds can be adapted to living the way they do. Why do they have that kind of a bill? It's to help them forage for food. Why did that Great Blue Heron drop that stick in the water? He was trying to attract a fish, and that's how he makes his living, by developing a fishing strategy.

I've always loved the complexity of nature, and having kids around makes me think about that. Even sometimes the simplest action is part of a complex chain of events that allows a bird to survive. It's the interactions I find fascinating, the reactions that fit together as part of our natural world. Sometimes it takes a kid to remind me of that.

Field trips are different. They always require people to sign up in advance. They are geared more toward people who are already interested in bird-watching. Field trips often go outside the metropolitan area and require driving. They also tend to focus on a specific area, such as Eastern Washington, or they might have a focus on a season, like breeding season or migration. There is, I think, more of an expectation from participants. If you get an experienced group—they can get on the birds quickly, they already know a lot about the life history of birds—you have to move along faster because people are going to have special targets. They often know what they want to see in a given habitat.

Of course, if you want to lead a trip like this for advanced birders, then you need to say so when you advertise the trip. You should let people know it's going to be fast-paced and you'll be looking for target species. How you pitch the trip determines how people are going to respond, whether they join you or not. It's important to be clear about that.

With Neighborhood Bird Walks, I have favorite parks I like to go to, parks I know well and often walk. With field trips, I will often choose a place I don't know very well, or at all. I decide where to go based on a number of factors that come into play. I like to bird throughout the year, but there are certain favorite times. I love spring migration. I like witnessing courtship among birds. So I might lead a trip to Eastern Washington

(From left): Miss Lois Davis, Mrs. Neal Harvey, A. Kenneth Benedict, and Neal Harvey record bird species seen on a bird walk around Green Lake in 1963, probably in mid-January when the lake had frozen over. Other members of the group continue to observe gulls. Green Lake was a popular destination for Seattle Audubon bird walks, partly because the Society had long been interested in establishing a bird sanctuary at Duck Island on the northwest side of the lake. In the end, Seattle Audubon's efforts were thwarted by officials of the Seattle Department of Health,[25] who believed more ducks on the lake would be unsanitary. (Photograph by Paul Thomas, © Seattle Times; reprinted with permission)

in spring so I can see courtship behavior.

I always scout before I go. I want to make sure I know the area, because there are lots of things other than just the birds I have to look out for when I'm taking a group. I have to know that I can give specific directions to everyone about how to get there if we're taking multiple vehicles, and that people understand how to carpool together in a safe manner. I have to know where the restroom stops are and where there's a possible lunch stop. I have to know where there are safe places for parking more than one car along the roadside or in a parking lot. I have to think about parking permits. There are lots of different small things that go into shaping a field trip.

But for me, part of what I want is a trip that builds along the way. I think of it as kind of a crescendo. I don't want to wear people out too early in the day, so I try to time the trip in terms of the physical exertion that's involved. But I also want to have a highlight, if I can. I can't control birds. That's the thing. They fly. So what I always try to do is, around midday, I try to make sure I have two or three stops that are kind of close together, where we're likely to see some interesting, different species. It perks

people up a little bit. And then toward the end of the day I make sure to have a highlight stop—save something for last, if I can. But you know, all this is within the parameters of a simple fact: What might have been there the week before, when I was casing the trip, might not be there the following week.

This happened. A friend and I had advertised a two-day overnight trip to Eastern Washington to see Greater Sage-Grouse. We knew the people who signed up for the trip were putting in resources, both time and money. So we scouted the trip a week ahead of time. We went to the place where we expected to see the grouse, where they had been reported previously that season. We pulled the car up, walked over the hill, lifted our binoculars—and there were no birds. We had that feeling of, 'Wow, what are we going to do now? What if we have 20 Seattle Audubon people with us and we can't find the birds?'

Luckily on the actual trip, we found the grouse, but we were reminded that you have to have a backup strategy in your pocket. If you can't find the birds you intended, you need to know where there are some of the local resident birds that you can find. Or maybe you look at

the wildflowers, or the trees, or you go and have a cup of coffee, depending on the weather. If it's rainy and cold, you definitely go have a cup of coffee. You don't stay out there and freeze to death.

It's also important to have a trip narrative. When you can't find the birds you were hoping for, that's part of bird-watching. You should be prepared to have stories about why the birds aren't there. Where could they be? What might it mean that they are absent? Why can't you control everything? I think that's a very important lesson. And always know where the good pastry shops are.

In the larger scheme of things, people who go on the field trips I lead are Seattle Audubon members. It's a great benefit of membership that field trips offer you the opportunity to explore a new place. They offer the opportunity to learn more about the bird life in that place. If you're like me and enjoy the social aspects of bird-watching, it's an outing with a fun group of like-minded people. They come from a variety of backgrounds and have different viewpoints. Sometimes they'll disagree about a bird we're all seeing. I like the idea that people respect one another and can have a discussion about that. In the end, we join together to solve a problem. I like that process, working together.

Field trips also make the public aware of us, that there are people who do value the bird life of a community. I think about that every day I walk in the local parks with my binoculars on. People will often stop me to ask about the birds. It gives me an opportunity to educate them a little about what's going on in our local community. It creates awareness, not only for the people who come with me on the field trips or walks, but also about the need to keep going out there, to

make sure that others know we are really interested.

The thing about enjoying a quiet pursuit is that it doesn't make noise. There's no applause, no cheering. You can see a soccer team playing in a local park, and everyone's yelling if their team is winning. It gets them involved. But they're totally unaware of the birds that live among us on the edge of that soccer field. If they see bird-watchers, though, counting birds as part of the Neighborhood Bird Project or just a single bird-watcher enjoying the wildlife, people might think a little bit more about supporting the natural, quiet part of the park. Maybe they won't feel like everything has to be a groomed area for sports or other activities.

I didn't plan to become a bird-watcher, you know, although I did grow up loving nature. My special time with my father was foraging for mushrooms in the woods or identifying leaves and flowers. He loved the woods. So from childhood I had him as a model. But

Greater Sage-Grouse male, displaying at a lek. Leks are open areas in sage habitat where males can show off for females. (Photograph courtesy of Pacific Southwest Region, U.S. Fish and Wildlife Service)

bird-watching caught me by surprise about ten years ago when I was on a trip to Arizona with my husband. We went to Portal, Arizona. It was spring, the height of the migration season, though we didn't know it. We were sitting outside our cabin in the evening, just relaxing, and all of a sudden, people came tearing out of their cabins like there was some kind of national emergency. Into their cars, and off they went in a cloud of dust. We were left sitting there, saying, 'That's very funny. What are they doing?'

Well, somebody had spotted an Elegant Trogon in the area, a big rarity. I got curious. I had to find out what it was that drew people into such craziness at a time when they should have been winding down in the evening, and here they were, carrying on. So I went to find the bird the next day. People were very helpful. Some birders with their spotting scope took me to show me the bird. They told about the bird's life history. Wow. I had no idea that there could be such an amazing, beautiful bird in the world.

On that same trip to Arizona, we went along with the birders we had met to a place with hummingbird feeders in Ramsey Canyon. It was actually the only part of bird-watching that my husband liked because we all sat around in a circle with the feeders and talked about where we were from, where we were going on our next trip, movies we liked, books. People from all over the United States were there, and some Europeans too. All of a sudden, a bird would fly in, and the conversation would stop, with no 'please excuse me.' It just stopped. People looked at the bird, studied it, discussed it, and when the bird flew away, the old conversation started again from exactly the point where it had been interrupted.

There was something very appealing to me about that. As a group, we all understood that when a bird showed up, it was a special moment. We didn't know how long it would stay. Maybe it would come back, maybe not. So we had to focus on this now, share the moment now.

My father was a hunter, so I learned early on about the habits of wildlife. It was always like a treasure hunt. You have to know about the bird's habits, what habitat it prefers, what it eats. You have to know the season when it's going to be there and what it's going to look like in that season in order to make an accurate identification. At the end, then you have your treasure. Bird-watching is like that, too."[26]

UNFORGETTABLE CLASS PROVES ANYTHING CAN HAPPEN ON A FIELD TRIP

In June 1980, Seattle Audubon Notes *published an account of an unusual field trip taken by Ann Mahnke and a friend. The two friends had met up with Dennis Paulson in Eastern Washington for a class about shorebirds and gulls on May 16. When the class returned to Seattle, Ann and her friend decided to drive to a campground near the Yakima Firing Center and camp out for one night. At 8:30 the next morning, they heard a tremendous explosion but thought it was just the U.S. Army firing practice rounds. It was not:*

"By midmorning, 'storm clouds' and thunder and lightning were slowly approaching us. We continued to bird-watch, but when the flashes grew very frequent and the skies dark gray, we adjourned to our car.... The cloud as it approached looked very dark; something about it made me think of tornado clouds in the Midwest. The lowest layer was boiling and puffing and re-forming again and again. The dark gray of the sky deepened and contrasted sharply with the sun at its edges. As the surroundings reached a charcoal gray color, my friend and I finally put our heads out the window. [We realized we were witnessing an eruption, the eruption of Mount St. Helens.] The sky continued to blacken until the lights of a farmhouse a quarter-mile away could not be seen. Eventually, we could not even see each other!

Through 24 pitch-black hours of alternate radio-listening (wanting more information, never getting enough) and puzzling for ourselves what to do, we concluded that to try to travel was crazy. It was lucky for us that the rather airtight car admitted little dust, although the interior became very hot and stuffy. It was likewise fortunate that among the supplies we brought for the weekend we had food, bedding, clothing and materials for a makeshift 'chamber pot'—with which we could survive with only moderate discomfort for quite a while.

One full day [later] we left the parking lot. We found in the three inches of ash, tracks of confused beetles and other insects, tiny mice and voles—and even a few live beetles, moving in slow circles. A few birds were calling and flying about, landing here and there on dusty fences and bushes. Coots were sitting on the ponds into which the ash had fallen.

Driving was unpleasant. Even with masks over noses and mouths, we found breathing [difficult]. Seeing where the car was going was another serious problem The movement of our car and of those which passed us threw up clouds which remained suspended for a long time.

As we aimed for George, I remembered that a nearby friend had several times invited me to drop by. Little did she know how I would 'drop by,' for 48 hours. Our hostess, investigating the damage done to crops, found that her 20 acres of alfalfa—which had been just ready to harvest—were crushed beneath ash covering the landscape at 55 tons per acre.

[As we finally left the George area, faces masked again], we saw an abundance of warblers and thrushes visiting the cottonwoods, which had been cleared of ash by our friend's sprinkler. Travel was again uncomfortable and visibility sometimes nearly zero until we reached Wenatchee, then the air seemed clear of ash. We did find a light film of ash on leaves in Leavenworth. As we came over the mountains, I felt that our familiar rain had never looked so good, nor the green of Western Washington so welcome!"[27]

WE BELONG
Marina Skumanich: A Community of Members

Marina Skumanich. (Photograph by Jennifer Leach, courtesy of Seattle Audubon Society)

What does it mean to be a member of Seattle Audubon Society? In 1916, the answer was simple. It meant that you belonged to a women's club. It meant that most, if not all, your Board members and officers were women. It meant that your meetings and doings were reported in the society pages of the daily newspapers, right alongside the news of debutantes and society matrons, not to mention hat ads.[28]

But it also meant something more, for in the era before women could vote, one of the few ways they could exert political influence was through the men in their lives. Rich men, prominent men, the men who moved and shook the world had prominent wives, sisters, and daughters, and these women ruled society. In their way, they were just as powerful. Politicians, especially local politicians, listened when they spoke.

That's not to say all members of Seattle Audubon initially were women. As a reporter for the Seattle Daily Times rather sheepishly tried to explain, "The Seattle Audubon Society, although not altogether a women's club, having admitted a few men into its midst, nevertheless includes in its membership many of the most prominent clubwomen in the city."[29] In fact, the male charter members of the Society numbered about as many as the women. They brought a special expertise with them, for many were professors at the University of Washington.

Members came together to observe and help birds, gather valuable data about them, teach others, and share the enjoyment of nature. A century later, these four streams of interest, established so early in Seattle Audubon's history, continue to flow through the Society today.

Few people are more aware of this history than Marina Skumanich. Skumanich is a past President of Seattle Audubon (2006-2008). She has been interim Executive Director, served on the Board as a member and as Treasurer, and represented state chapters on the National Audubon Board. She belongs to many environmental organizations but keeps a special place in her heart for Audubon.

"I always am struck by how thoughtful, creative, determined, kick-ass those people from the old days were. We like to think they were just puttering along in their Ford Model T's, and we're the innovative ones. It's just incredible the energy, the zest that they brought to their work for birds and the environment.

Times were different then, and so were the challenges, but to me there are some things that have stayed the same. One that I believe is a fundamental value and orientation of Seattle Audubon—and I would say the Audubon world in general—is the focus on community. I don't know when 'community' became a word that's in the Seattle Audubon mission statement, which is: 'Seattle Audubon leads a local community in appreciating, understanding, and protecting birds and their natural habitats.' But my feeling is that it is a cornerstone of the organization and reflects our commitment to how we relate to the world.

What I mean by that is, it's one thing to say, 'We want to accomplish this conservation goal—protecting birds, for example—and we're going to do it by creating a membership program that brings people in to help.' It's another thing to say, 'We want to build a community. This is where we sit in the world. These are the people we want to share everything with. We want to share science and all the technical details about birds. We want to share going out and observing them. We want to share activism and making sure birds are protected. And we want to share the fun of creative times together.'

Many environmental organizations are very 'other centered'—'other' in terms of the world and the resources, the conservation objectives. Seattle Audubon and Audubon in general are very 'we centered,' in the sense that we humans and the birds are in the natural environment together. That creates the kind of place where people do stay for their whole lives. They might come at one point because they have kids, perhaps, and think it would be fun to have them do Nature Camp. Then they see how much fun their kids are having and they think they'll take a class, too. Then before you know it, they're donating. They're giving their time and working in the Nature Shop when they retire. Seattle Audubon really is a home for people. It's a home that reflects basic values, and that's a thread that has run through the organization from the beginning.

Since 1962, Seattle Audubon has been a branch (or chapter) of National Audubon. In terms of our relationship with National, I sometimes think about it like a family. Families squabble. There are expressions of anger and boundaries and things to be resolved. But fundamentally there's a commitment to each other. Families go through periods where people don't talk to each other, and Seattle Audubon has sometimes said to National, 'We don't want to be a part of you. We're going to walk away from this family.' But we've always come back.[30]

We started out forming an Audubon Society of our own in April 1916. In August of that year, T. Gilbert Pearson, the Secretary of National Audubon Society, came out West on a fact-finding mission to learn about local game birds and laws. During his visit, he gave a talk to Seattle Audubon about bird life and the preservation of game birds. That contact led to Seattle Audubon joining National as an affiliate, with a kind of on-again, off-again relationship. We didn't become an actual chapter until 1962, and that was a big internal struggle for Seattle Audubon. Many members were reluctant to join National because they didn't like the idea of letting a New York-based organization set the agenda for us.

For awhile, we did have issues with that. National Audubon didn't seem to pay much attention to how a given decision at the national level might affect members locally. They also didn't think very much about what the chapters might be able to add to an issue.

I was on the National Board from 2009 to 2014. There are nine members on a 30-person Board that are elected by chapters and regions. I was one of those regional representatives. Like the other regional representatives, I came to the Board with a strong grounding in the chapter perspective. Over my six years on the Board, there was an incredible evolution, a broad recognition among people at National who never were involved with chapters that chapters truly are the lifeblood of the organization.

Another reflection of this commitment is the local nodes or sanctuaries that National supports. We have one of those in Seattle, the Seward Park Audubon Center, which provides a place for bird and nature activities and education

YIPPEE! ANOTHER MEETING

Nowadays Seattle Audubon meets only quarterly, partly because people have become too overwhelmed with work, family, and the daily stresses of modern life to want or need meetings more often. We tend to stay connected to each other and to the world electronically, through social media. Also, Seattle Audubon volunteers have many chances to form mini-communities focused on particular activities, such as citizen science, school programs, or conservation activism. Such things often take up so much time and are so enveloping that people don't necessarily feel the need for frequent gatherings of the entire Society.

But for many years, the Society did hold a meeting every month. The meetings were not just for members to touch base with one another and exchange bird stories, although that part was eagerly anticipated. The meetings also were Action Alerts, so members could learn about the issues of the day and take appropriate action. For example, at the March 12, 1918, meeting, a U.S. Marine Corps representative talked to Seattle Audubon members about the needs of the Marines for field glasses, which Seattle Audubon later donated.[31]

Above all, meetings were educational opportunities, where experts from within our own community as well as from outside could share their knowledge. Subjects were wide-ranging. Sometimes the presentation would be on a particular bird species, as it was for the March 1989 meeting, when Don Norman gave a talk on "How Many Great Blue Herons Do We have in Puget Sound?"[32]

Often the talks would be about conservation issues that the Society needed to address. Such a talk was given in May 1961 by Carsten Lien, who at that time was just beginning his research into the history of the fight to establish Olympic National Park. Lien had been a seasonal ranger in the Park when he learned about serious logging going on within Park boundaries, encouraged by the Park Service itself. He soon found out that the Park Service had opposed the Park from the beginning, and was still doing its best to make it possible for timber companies to clear cut as much old growth as they could.[33]

Occasionally speakers would describe their travels to birding hotspots, as Neil Hayward did at the October 2014 meeting. His description of travels to places as far apart as Adak Island, the Dry Tortugas, and Newfoundland as he tried to set a North American Big Year record were calculated to whet the appetites of all the avid listers in the audience.[34]

Not all the talks were about birds. At the November 1988 meeting, for example, Dr. James W. Foster gave a talk on the Mountain Gorillas of Rwanda. The December 1989 meeting hosted Dr. Douglas Fenner for a talk titled, "Ecology of Tropical Coral Reefs."[35]

Perhaps the two quirkiest talks ever given in our long history occurred in 1917 and 1951. At the March 1917 meeting, Ronald E. Chapman gave a talk about his family's pet Sandhill Crane, a bird that saved the family from being burgled one night by scaring the bejeezus out of an unsuspecting robber. After that, "David the Crane" could do no wrong, even when he ate the neighbor's tulip bulbs. Unfortunately, some years later, he broke a leg when it got caught in a sidewalk crack. It had to be amputated. Rather than euthanize the bird, Mrs. Chapman had a carpenter make David a wooden leg, which worked fine.[36]

The second quirkiest talk was given by Frank G. Lowman at the January 1951 meeting: "Birds of Bikini and the Effects of the Atom Bomb." This was at a time when people were becoming concerned about the effects of radiation on living things. It was thought that radiation might accelerate the rate of mutation and lead to all kinds of horrors. Ants, for example, might mutate into something only the U.S. military could stop with flamethrowers. No doubt Lowman's talk was a little less over the top than Hollywood screenwriters' presentations.[37]

in one of Seattle's most special parks, located in one of the most ethnically diverse neighborhoods in the country. It's a little confusing for people who don't know us, perhaps, but Seward Park Audubon Center is actually run by the Washington State office of National Audubon. Although we're all the same family, and we really work on things together, it's important to recognize that we are formally different organizations. We have different Boards, different fiduciary requirements, different bylaws, etc., even though we are completely aligned in values and largely in activities. The State Office of National Audubon is also located now in Seward Park, coterminous with the Audubon Center there. The State Office used to be in Olympia to be a voice for Audubon's issues in the State government. Its mission was and still is to pull the challenges and issues from the various chapters together so that we can be effective with legislation and administration at the State level.

We were invited to be a part of the Seward Park Audubon Center when it was being formed. As I recall, we decided it would be better for us to have a little bit of distance from the Seward Park Audubon Center because we want-ed to allow ourselves to continue to be watchdogs with the City and their parks' activities. Seward Park Audubon Center is on City of Seattle parkland, so there's a certain cooperation between them.

As far as I'm concerned, that's a perfect answer. National Audubon through the Seward Park Audubon Center works very closely with the Parks Department as partners, and we can be a little bit on the outside saying, 'Wait a minute, you could do an even better job keeping the birds safe in the parks.' [38]

I'm very grateful that we have a healthy relationship with National now. The reason I say that is because, again, we're a family with the same objectives. Just like any family, different parts bring different strengths. National's reach, their resources, the ability to do ground-breaking science research on climate effects on birds or other issues such as toxins in the water, is something we can rely on. And they, of course, rely on us for on-the-ground action. In its best form, it's a completely symbiotic relationship, where the whole is so much more than the parts.

Seattle Audubon has joined with other environmental organizations, too. One of the most wonderful is ACOW

A MILESTONE IN MEMBERSHIP

The 1,000th member joined Seattle Audubon in December 1968: Alki Elementary. The membership was the gift of teacher Ruth Heinzinger. In acknowledgment, the school received prizes: a copy of Earl Larrison's *Washington Birds*, a hawk chart, and a wildflower chart. The principal, Anna Overheat, invited Audubon to present a conservation program to an all-school assembly. Eleanor Stopps and Zella Schultz did so.

The principal told Seattle Audubon that Alki Elementary had 407 students from kindergarten through sixth grade. Did that mean that Seattle Audubon Society now had 1,407 members? "Well," said the report in the newsletter, "maybe not right now, but hopefully they will all join us when they grow up."[39]

Seabirds in Summer, *crayon on paper by Nathan S.*

(Audubon Council of Washington). Once a year, all the Audubon chapters in the State gather to share lessons learned, to bring issues forward that can be agreed on as joint projects in the State, and to share good times.

Another part of the Audubon family we belong to is WSACC (Washington State Audubon Conservation Committee). WSACC is a committee of the Conservation Chairs of the different chapters, along with Audubon Washington's conservation team. They hold regular meetings by phone and meet once a year at ACOW. They are a very effective group. They've made quite a difference in terms of advocacy work at the State level. For example, with WSACC's help, we were able to ensure that renewable energy standards address impacts on birds. WSACC and Audubon Washington also helped get a new State law passed that recognizes Important Bird Areas— habitat that deserves protection because it's critical for birds.[40]

That spirit of collaborating has not been confined to working only with like-minded groups. It has expanded across divides as well. For example, the early 2000s saw the founding of the Cats Indoors Coalition, which was at the time an unusual coalition between bird-lovers and cat-lovers focused on keeping cats indoors to protect both birds and cats. As another example, since the 1999 World Trade Organization (WTO) protests in Seattle, Seattle Audubon has worked in close partnership with labor unions, faith groups, and social justice groups on trade policy reform to ensure that international trade agreements include protections for both workers and the environment. These types of issues show that often there is much more that unites us than divides us.

Although Seattle Audubon's role in conservation work is huge in the State, it's not the only thing we do. We offer members access to classes and field trips. We have quarterly meetings where people can get together and hear presentations. If they're interested in education, there are volunteer opportunities with our elementary school program (Finding Urban Nature), or our youth bird-watching club (Young Birders). There are really dedicated volunteers who do citizen science with our monthly Puget Sound Seabird Survey or the Neighborhood Bird Project, counting birds and recording observations for later analysis. Once a year, we sponsor the Christmas Bird Count, where volunteers try to count every bird in a fifteen-mile-radius circle.

We're a large organization with almost 3,000 members. Part of the openness of our community is that it has so many different activities. You can find an affinity in activities close to your own interests. People sometimes say we are a mile wide and an inch deep. I don't see that as a criticism. I think we *want* to be a mile wide. That reflects my value system. The world is complicated. We humans are complicated. To say we should focus on only one thing or a few things seems limiting to me. Yes, we are going to have to manage the tension of being many different things to people. We are going to squabble with each other sometimes about what's going to be a priority. But when I think about the range of all we do, that's one of our strengths.

That's really why I joined Seattle Audubon. You can act on your own, but if you join Seattle Audubon, you can work in concert with other people. You can leverage your power to be more effective. So when an issue comes up, you can write a letter to your representatives, but Seattle Audubon is writing a letter too on behalf of its 3,000 members. That is a really powerful force for change.

By joining Seattle Audubon, you can add your voice to the community. More than that—you're part of *creating* that community. I don't want to strut and crow, but one of the things that seems to me to be unique about our community is the sense of loving people as well as the environment. We understand that love for nature should extend to the people as well as to the birds. Many environmental groups keep those two things separate, but I love the fact that Seattle Audubon doesn't see a split here. We see it all together. That feeling is important to me. Very important to me."

HOST TO THE NATION

Only eight years after Seattle Audubon joined the National Audubon Society, we offered to host the 65th Annual National Convention. We had two years to prepare. Hazel Wolf took charge of the whole thing and began to organize. She reserved the Opera House for the meetings and festivities and reserved 500 rooms for the delegates at the Washington Plaza Hotel, which at the time had not been built yet. In fact, the Orpheum Theatre, which stood on the site of the new hotel, had not even been demolished. The "Historical Vignette" below was written by Hazel and appeared in the May 1981 issue of Seattle Audubon Notes.[41]

Organization of the convention was handled by nine committees through which more than 200 volunteers were involved. This spoke well for the enthusiasm of the 1,500 members making up the membership in the spring of 1970. Volunteers came from outside Seattle Audubon as well. The committees and those heading them were: National Field Trips, Ruth Anderson, Aileen Robinson, Bob and Elsie Boggs; Local Society Field Trips, Loretta Slater; Finance and Accounting, Ruth Kephart and Ruth Boyle; Hospitality, Olga Gull; Book Sales, Leonard Steiner; Decorations, Emily Haig; Publicity, Katherine Wensburg; Entertainment, Sylvia Epstein; and Local Artists' Exhibit, Elizabeth Anderson and Bettina Bailey.

The convention had exceptional support in the media. The *Seattle Times* in its Sunday magazine ran a series of political "bird" cartoons by Alan Pratt featuring the "Cantankerous Crop Duster or Spraying Cuckoo," the "Short-sighted Roadrunner," the "Surf-side Slicker or Oily Bird," and other "Birds to Watch." Both metropolitan dailies ran frequent special articles and news releases.

The Seattle Art Museum exhibited "Birds in Art" in honor of the convention. This included important works, ancient and contemporary from major cultures throughout the world; it was arranged by the late Betty Bowen. The University of Washington's *Arboretum Bulletin* devoted an issue to articles on birds (one by Dorothy Siewers, now Editor of the *Seattle Audubon Notes*) and a special editorial of welcome to the delegates. Governor Dan Evans declared the week of the convention "Environmental Quality Week."

Farwest/Acme Press donated an elegant program with color photos contributed by Ruth Kirk and Johsel Namkung. Art students at the Florence Crittenton Home prepared table centerpieces for the banquet, and the North End Garden Club brought carloads of flowers for Emily Haig's beautiful arrangements throughout the conference area. A Girl Scout Troop acted as ushers. The National Park Service, the Seattle Center, and Weyerhaeuser co-hosted a pre-banquet social hour in the Flag Pavilion against a background of National Park Service paintings and photographs. (This was the first showing of the National Park Service's "Artists in the Parks" exhibit.)

Harold Kephart, President of Seattle Audubon, welcomed the 1,000 registered delegates, and Dr. Elvis Stahr, newly elected National President, made the keynote address. The theme: "A Question for America: What Is Progress?" was part of all speeches and discussions throughout the program. Panels addressed the various aspects of analysis and redirection of "Progress." One workshop on "Outdoor Education for the Classroom and Urban Environment" attracted many teachers.

City notables and representatives of government agencies attended the concluding banquet held in Exhibition Hall. U.S. Representative Paul McCloskey of California, co-sponsor of Earth Day, was the main speaker. Emily Haig was honored with a National Audubon Citation, and the National Society accepted a deed from Seattle Audubon making it owner of a muddy little lot in the Nisqually delta so it would have standing in court if needed in a future lawsuit.[42]

Three trips were organized for delegates by Loretta Slater: east of the Cascades; around the Olympic Peninsula; and Vancouver Island and the San Juans and north to Alaska. Delegates were given ample opportunity to discover the Pacific Northwest.

After deducting all expenses of the convention, Seattle Audubon found itself richer by some $13,000. In the days that followed about 300 new members were added to the rolls as a direct result of the convention and its publicity in metropolitan and neighborhood papers, on radio and TV programs. It was a turning point in the history of Seattle Audubon.[43]

NOW IS THE TIME
Carleen Ormbrek Zimmerman: The Art of Nature

There is a trail that winds through Montlake Fill, one of Seattle's premier birding spots. It starts from a small parking lot on the west end of the Center for Urban Horticulture on the UW campus. From there it flows gently west, through groves of shady trees, past a rolling prairie that skirts the Youth Farm, where inner city kids tend their crops. Eventually it crosses University Slough, where ducks dabble and rails breed, and comes out at the Husky Stadium parking lot: Wahkiakum Lane, a little piece of paradise.

Hundreds of people walk this trail every day on their way to work. When football is in season, thousands trek through on their way to the stadium. Most people enjoy the walk outdoors, but "being" outdoors and "being in" nature are two very different things. To "be in" nature, you have to stop awhile, look, and listen. You can't be on a deadline or in a rush. You have to take your time. Use your senses. Fit yourself into the place.

No one knows this better than Carleen Ormbrek Zimmerman. Zimmerman is an artist and teacher who offers classes to Seattle Audubon adults and children. She specializes in the art of the moment. She does so by journaling and sketching, using art to focus her senses and connect her spirit to the wild. Wherever she goes, she takes her sketchbook with her. Sometimes in quick studies, sometimes in extended meditations, she paints and writes. Through her art, she enters the world of now, where there is no past, no future, only the moment. It is there she finds peace.

"I was an art major my first three years of undergraduate school. I also did a lot of creative writing, and I liked to paint with acrylics. But for me, art classes became too much of a formality of academia: drawing and painting and then having a class critique. So I didn't pursue that major very long. Instead, I ended up getting my bachelor's and master's degrees in Norwegian language and literature. Art became a kind of a latent interest that just sat there for awhile.

Then I met Neil, my future husband, when I went to Fargo, North Dakota, for a year to teach. Neil had just got hooked on birding after a trip to Corkscrew Swamp in Florida. One of our first dates was to Fargo's sewage treatment plant. I didn't know the difference between a duck and a goose, but I liked to go out into nature with Neil.

After we moved here in 1986, we took a trip to Malheur with some of Neil's Master Birder friends, and I got overwhelmed with everything I didn't know. I was tiring of always asking, 'What was that bird you said I just saw?' I decided

I needed a timeout. So I sat down on a stool and did a blind contour ink drawing of a thistle.

Blind contour is an art technique where you keep your eyes on the object you're drawing, and you don't look at the paper. You keep your pencil or pen on the paper the whole time and focus on letting your eyes see the detail that your brain sometimes dismisses. Your drawing usually comes out pretty wonky looking, but the idea is to represent the gist of something. Birders would call it the 'jizz.'

I was doing that technique just as an exercise because I wanted to do something different from trying to see a bird in my binoculars. Sketching that thistle made me concentrate more on the multi-sensory experience of being in nature. I can remember to this day what the lighting was like, the weather, the sky. I can remember what I was hearing and what it felt like to be in that habitat.

Sketching became my hook and a reason to be outside birding. I've since taken Dennis Paulson's Master Birder classes, so I know more about birds than I used to. But even now, stopping, listening, and field sketching often become more important to me than birding. I'm not chasing a bird. I am being in the habitat where I know the bird is.

In a way, I blame it all on Lyanda Lynn Haupt. Hers was the first nature book I ever read—*Rare Encounters with Ordinary Birds*.[44] She made me see that the ordinary can be extraordinary if you stop, look, and listen. That's always been the premise behind my sketches. Whether you're a geologist or a plant person or a naturalist or a birder wannabe, just being in the moment—looking and listening, and trying to use all your senses—connects you to the natural world.

That's important. Sketching nature brings me back to baseline. I worked at Harborview and Children's Hospital for 28 years before I retired. I was in medical records, reading horror stories in people's charts every day. For me, sketching

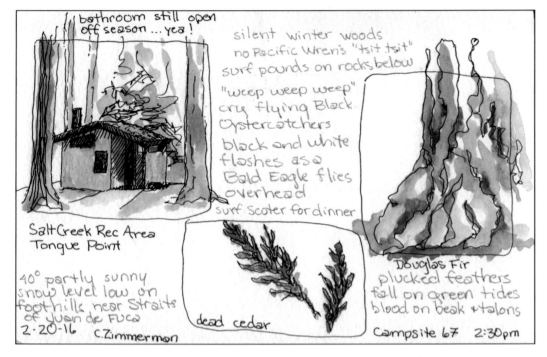

bathroom still open off season ... yea!

Salt Creek Rec Area
Tongue Point

40° partly sunny
snow level low on
foothills near Straits
of Juan de Fuca
2-20-16   C. Zimmerman

silent winter woods
no Pacific Wren's "tsit tsit"
surf pounds on rocks below

"weep weep weep"
cry flying Black
Oystercatchers
black and white
flashes as a
Bald Eagle flies
overhead
surf scoter for dinner

dead cedar

Douglas Fir
plucked feathers
fall on green tides
blood on beak + talons

Campsite 67   2:30pm

POETRY ON THE WING

Seattle Audubon has always understood that birds can be a bridge into nature for many people. But there are other bridges, and the Society has embraced them, too, knowing that what matters is the connection itself, not the connecting mechanism. Art is the bridge for some people. Science is the bridge for others. Participation draws many others to nature, for the fun of sharing experiences with like-minded friends. Even poetry can be the path that connects a soul with the wild, as it did for Seattle Audubon member Adelaide Lowry Pollock, author of this poem published in The Seattle Wren, *July 1935. It was written in the depths of the Great Depression, with Adolf Hitler and the Nazis on the horizon:*[45]

The Western Martin Calls

Far up in the air above our heads
A voice swells out where wings outspread.
'Tis the martin's call so free and gay
As he wheels about in airy play.
Flying back to us year after year
Bringing a message from far and near.
He wheels and shouts above the street,
Where we plod along on weary feet.
He gives a greeting which few of us hear
Since most of our minds are stunned with fear.
Still his calls ring out with their merry sound
As he goes whirling around and round.
Yet those who hear as he speeds along
Their souls call with him his wild, clear song.

was a way to get out of that, lower my blood pressure, and just connect to a different way in life.

Part of my approach to field sketching, what I call multisensory, might be because I have synesthesia. Sounds to me have texture. Letters of the alphabet and numbers have colors in my mind— shades of yellow and gray and silver, like looking at water when it comes out of a faucet and it's a translucent color. I don't hear things in color, but when I'm sitting outside sketching I am very aware of the sounds all around me, and they might have a shape, like dots. At Wenas Campground, where I've taught field sketch-ing classes for years, there are Ponderosa Pines in the valley, and when you hear the wind, it's high in the treetops, way above where you are. Down below is the creek rushing by. You're surrounded by the habitat because you're seeing it, hearing it, smelling it. That's the experience that comes with field sketching.

Everything I create is loose and kind of unrestricted. I don't paint just what I see because I'm not that disciplined of an artist. I paint the jizz of what I see, a fleeting impression of something that's flying by. I'd rather have a loose, quick sketch of a duck in motion and let it be, than go back and try to perfect it and make it look like a scientific illustration. That's why I sketch in pen usually—it's so I can't go back and erase and perfect.

The purpose of my sketching is not to create art but to use art and language to record my observations. Nothing more. I don't think I would ever have my sketch-es published. I don't think anybody would want to look at them. They're intensely personal. Things I want to re-member. One time Neil and I were near Mount Shasta and we stopped to use the restroom. The sun was just coming up and the sky was sherbet. But there were a bunch of semis blocking my view. I thought, 'I'll go use the restroom, and when I come out, maybe the trucks will be gone.' Well, the trucks had gone but so had the light. So sometimes now I'll just do splashes of color as fast as I can with no drawing. Just because that mo-ment is going to go, and I want to paint it before it does.

I don't limit the medium to just wa-tercolor, pen, or pencil. I write, too. For example, I might write the date and time where I am, maybe what the weather is like. I'll list the birds I see and hear. In some of the art classes I was taking, the teachers would tell me, 'You should choose. Either write or paint. You could publish if you wanted.'

I thought, 'Why? These sketches are me. They're my personal journey of where I've gone.' I didn't realize until I found books by Clare Walker Leslie that what I was doing was nature journaling, combining writing with other media.

I realized that Seattle Audubon might be interested in a class like that because most people have never heard that it's okay to write and draw at the same time. It was a big jump for me to go from something so personal and to say in-stead, 'Hey this is what I do and maybe you'd like to do it too.' But now I've taught classes to birders at Wenas Camp-ground and to all kinds of people at Seat-tle Audubon, from kids to adults. I think my calling is to teach people to become naturalists and just observe—anything. It doesn't have to be nature, though that's usually the setting I'm in. Just be aware of the natural world around us because it's fragile.

That's ultimately how I made the transition from doing art as a personal journey to showing more people how to do what I'm doing. My hope is that by teaching kids about the natural world, there will be somebody who will devel-op a passion for what he or she is ob-serving and writing about or sketching. And maybe that person will be able to do something that I can't do to insure that there is always some protection for wildlife. That's the ultimate hope I have for the world."

Carleen Zimmerman (far left, behind the scope) with Seattle University students from Trileigh Tucker's "Natural History" class. Tucker's students walked around Montlake Fill with Carleen and Neil Zimmerman, observing the birds of spring, examining their dependence on the restored habitat there, and sketching and journaling. The students reportedly loved every minute. (Photograph © Leland Sutton)

THE ART OF THE POSSIBLE

Many artists have contributed their work to Seattle Audubon over the years. One of the most multitalented and generous of these was Zella M. Schultz, who created all the paintings used in *Field Guide to the Birds of Washington State* by Larrison and Francq, and *Washington Birds— Their Location and Identification* by Larrison and Sonnenberg.[46] These two important field guides drew many people into the wild to find birds and fall in love with nature.

Schultz was a self-taught artist who began painting as a child growing up on a chicken ranch in Everson, Washington. She used road-killed birds as her models, making her own brushes out of chicken feathers and her own paints out of berries and food coloring. Her first subject was a Gray Partridge.

As her interest in nature developed, Schultz learned how to make study skins out of the dead birds she found, but she also learned the value of observing birds in the field. When it was time for her to go to college, she decided to major in biolo-gy, later receiving a master's degree in zoology. Schultz's thesis was on gulls, a lifelong interest. She spent many hours on Protection Island banding seabirds, especially gulls. In 1951 and 1952, Schultz published the results of her 30-year scientific study of gulls. It was a definitive work, providing the basis for much of what is known about these birds today.[47]

Barbara Williams, a dear friend of Zella's, remembers some of those banding trips. "I met Zella for the first time on a bird-banding trip to Protection Island. We had bands around our necks, our pincers, hard hats, and raincoats. The raincoats weren't for rain. We wore them because the gulls used natural ammunition on us. We would form a line and move across the island, banding nestlings. By the time we got back to the boat, we were all covered with natural ammunition. When we got into town, we took off our raincoats and went into a coffee shop, without realizing the aroma had followed us. The other people in the shop started turning their heads in the other direction and moving away. Oh, we laughed so hard about that. Zella was fun to be with. She did her research and her art from the heart, I think. She understood birds from the scientific end, but she also knew them from the artist's point of view."

After Schultz died, her friend Eleanor Stopps decided Protection Island should be forever set aside as critical bird habitat. It is the nesting ground for 65 percent of the marine birds of the Puget Sound Basin, including Tufted Puffins, Rhinoceros Auklets, and thousands of gulls.[48] Saving the island was no easy task—Protection Island was privately owned by a series of people who tried to develop it over the years as farmland, a game range, and a retirement community, even though the island has no potable water, electricity, sewage, or fire protection. The last attempt to develop the island was perhaps the strangest. A group of investors bulldozed the island for an airstrip, roads, and 1,100 house lots, making empty promises to buyers about a future assured water supply. Many alcid nests were destroyed.

Stopps was appalled. She began a nine-year effort to save the remaining nests, selling Schultz's paintings and prints to raise money to buy up house lots, contacting environmental groups and politicians, and raising awareness about the importance of the island for seabirds. Eventually she persuaded the Nature Conservancy to buy 48 acres of auklet nesting grounds on the western end of the island. In 1974, the Conservancy resold the land to the State Game Department, and eventually it became the Department's first nongame sanctuary, the Zella M. Schultz Seabird Sanctuary.

But much of the island was still at risk of development. Stopps and her allies at Seattle Audubon—notably Lorna Campion Smith, Chair of the Conservation Committee—continued their fight to save it. In 1982, they won. U.S. Representative Don Bonker managed to push a bill through Congress to make the entire island a sanctuary. Homeowners were offered a fair price for their property, or they could elect to live out their lives on the island. The entire island is now the Protection Island National Wildlife Refuge.

What is the legacy we leave behind? Zella Schultz left behind a body of scientific data that has informed our understanding of gulls for the past 40 years. She created paintings of such surpassing beauty they are treasured by all who see them. She taught hundreds of people about birds on countless field trips and banding expeditions. She was a wife and mother of three children. A savior of injured birds.[49] A conservationist who catalyzed the permanent protection of one of the most important seabird nesting sites in Washington. A humble woman who did not think she was anything out of the ordinary. Yet she accomplished the extraordinary. And that perhaps is her greatest legacy of all: the example of what one person with love in her heart for nature and for humanity can do to save the planet.

Right: A Schultz painting, reprinted from Washington Birds—Their Location and Identification, *Plate VI. (Courtesy of Seattle Audubon Society) Opposite page: Great Blue Heron. (Photograph © Alex MacKenzie)*

BACK MATTER:
APPENDICES, ENDNOTES, INDEX

APPENDIX 1: SEATTLE AUDUBON PRESIDENTS

1916-1919 Mrs. Charles C.
(Minnie) Crickmore
1919-1923 Mrs. C. N. (Mary) Compton
1923-1927 Julia Shourek
1927-1929 Cecil M. Baskett
1929-1931 Kate Thompson
1931-1933 George Fahey
1933-1935 Harry W. Higman
1935-1936 Walter Hagenstein
1936-1938 L. Roy Hastings
1938-1940 Mrs. Albert
(Lillian) Forsman
1940-1941 Earl J. Larrison
1941-1942 Edwin J. Johnson
1942-1945 Mrs. James G. (Florence) Grove
1945-1950 Ellsworth D. Lumley
1950-1952 Mrs. Earl (Mabel) Larrison
1952-1956 Mrs. Neil (Emily) Haig
1956-1959 Alban B. Fiedler
1959-1962 Dr. Claude C. Heckman
1962-1964 Theron Strange
1964-1965 Elizabeth (Betsy)
Heitman Anderson
1965-1967 Harold Kephart
1967-1968 Emile Grahlfs
1968-1969 Aileen Robinson
1969-1971 Harold Kephart
1971-1972 Anne Mack

1972-1973 Dr. Earl J. Bell
1973-1974 Thomas O. Wimmer
1974-1975 Wendell Hoag
1975-1976 Clifford Imsland
1976-1978 Fayette Krause
1978-1980 John Huskinson
1980-1982 David Galvin
1982-1984 Wilma K. Anderson
1984-1986 Robert Y. Grant
1986-1988 Richard (Dick) Butler
1988-1990 Eugene (Gene) S. Hunn
1990-1992 Gerry Adams
1992-1994 Bob Sieh
1994-1996 Steve Hallstrom
1996-1998 Idie Ulsh
1998-2000 Richard Youel
2000-2002 Charles Kahle
2002-2004 Tom Riley
2004-2006 Jane Hedberg
2006-2008 Marina Skumanich
2008-2010 Randy Robinson
2010-2012 Cathy Jaramillo
2012-2014 Charles Kahle
2014-2016 Cynthia Wang
2016-present Rod Brown

Mountain Bluebird. (Photograph © Doug Schurman)

APPENDIX 2: A CENTURY OF SEATTLE AUDUBON AT WORK

Compiled by Alex MacKenzie & Constance Sidles

Here are the highlights of events, projects, successes, and failures of the last 100 years—and here's to 100 years more:

1910s

- Seattle Audubon founded on April 17, 1916
- Took over statewide responsibility for Junior Audubon Clubs (from 1916 to 1955)
- Mentored Boy Scouts to earn merit badges; later included Girl Scouts and Camp Fire
- Began leading bird walks and field trips (first one: May 1916)
- Pressed City of Seattle to create a bird sanctuary in Seward Park (sanctuary established in 1919)
- Sponsored monthly lectures about birds and nature
- Taught adult education classes (first one November 4, 1917)
- Held first group count of Christmas Bird Count (1919; annual counts ever since)

1920s

- Helped stop feather trade from Mexico (1924)
- Lobbied and campaigned to save raptors, owls, and other birds not protected by the Migratory Bird Treaty Act of 1918 (raptors and owls ultimately protected, some in 1961, others in 1972)
- Published our first bound publication (a checklist of North American birds in 1924)

1930s

- Published *The Seattle Wren*, our first newsletter
- *The Wren* published a checklist of Seattle birds and sold more than 1,000 copies (1935)
- Lobbied strongly (with many others) for the creation of Olympic National Park (the Park was created in 1938)
- Lobbied with others to increase size of Olympic National Park (the Park was enlarged in 1940)

1940s

- Published our first book, *A Field Guide to the Birds of the Seattle Area,* by Earl J. Larrison (1942; 23 books published to date)
- Suspended Christmas Bird Counts due to WWII
- Began showing Audubon Screen Tour nature films to big audiences in downtown theaters (1945)
- Lobbied with others to keep boundaries of Olympic National Park secure (succeeded in 1954)
- Opposed the construction of a stadium in Woodland Park (no stadium was built)

1950s

- Launched Junior Audubon Society (1955)
- Lobbied to pass the Wilderness Act (the bill passed in 1964, with help from many other groups)
- Established Ellsworth D. Lumley shelf at Seattle Public Library, dedicated to nature books
- Worked to remove Mourning Dove from game bird list (ultimately failed)
- Worked to remove Mountain Goat from game list (ultimately failed)
- Launched a birdhouse-building project for Western Bluebirds with some initial success
- Lobbied with others to protect marine mammals (Marine Mammal Protection Act passed in 1972)

1960s

- Rented office space in Joshua Green Building downtown (1962)
- Joined National Audubon Society as a branch (now called a chapter, 1962)
- Lobbied hard against the 520 Bridge placement through the Arboretum and Foster Island (ultimately failed; bridge opened in 1963)
- Hazel Wolf joined Seattle Audubon (1964)
- Started Wenas Campout (1964)

- Fought against underground nuclear bomb tests at Amchitka Island, part of the Aleutian Islands Reservation set aside by President William Taft in 1913 (failed; three nuclear bombs were set off in 1965, 1969, and 1971; further tests were not conducted)
- Lobbied in favor of Wild and Scenic Rivers Act (passed in 1968, with help from many others)
- Campaigned with many others to create North Cascades National Park (Park established in 1968)
- Lobbied for years to ban DDT (it was banned in 1972)
- Lobbied in favor of a clean air bill and a stronger water pollution bill (Clean Water Act passed in 1972; Clean Air Act passed in 1973, with wide support)
- Lobbied against allowing ski lifts and other "rides" in National Parks (campaign succeeded)
- Lobbied to make Fort Lawton a City of Seattle Park (most of it became Discovery Park in 1973) instead of an Anti-Ballistic Missile base, as the military wanted
- Lobbied to protect Montlake Fill (now Union Bay Natural Area)
- Gave major support to efforts to turn the Nisqually delta into a National Wildlife Refuge; went on to defend its integrity by insisting that the surrounding habitat be protected, too (Nisqually National Wildlife Refuge established in 1974)

1970s

- Hosted the 65th annual meeting of National Audubon (1970)
- Lobbied to pass a bill that placed all wildlife (not just game) under the protection of the State Game Department (bill passed in 1970)
- Opposed a bill that would have allowed hunting in National Parks (bill failed)
- Opposed dam on Middle Fork Snoqualmie River (no dam was built)

- Collected signatures in record time for an initiative to protect shorelines (Washington's Shoreline Management Act passed in 1972)
- Opposed (as did other groups) siting of Seattle Aquarium at Golden Gardens Park in favor of a central waterfront location (the Aquarium was built on the waterfront in 1977)
- Lobbied to set aside Alpine Lakes area as a wilderness (Alpine Lakes Wilderness was designated in 1976, with help from many others)
- Lobbied to make Conboy Lake a refuge (Conboy Lake National Wildlife Refuge established in 1979)

1980s
- Held our first Birdathon, which raised $2,400 (1980)
- Launched Nature Camp for kids in first through ninth grades (1982)
- Protection Island National Wildlife Refuge becomes a reality, after years of effort (1982)
- Purchased Carnation Marsh, our bird sanctuary (1984)
- Insisted that National Audubon include the chapters' representation on its Board (1987)
- Began Master Birders, a program to educate highly skilled adult learners (1988)
- Established Martin Miller Fund (1988)
- Began FUN (Finding Urban Nature), an in-school program for elementary ages (1989)
- Began decades-long efforts with other environmental groups to protect ancient forests to save Northern Spotted Owl and Marbled Murrelet (the Northwest Forest Plan went into effect in 1993, achieving success with habitat protection, though owl and murrelet populations continue to decline)
- Pushed to get Northern Spotted Owl federally listed (listed as threatened in 1990) and state listed (listed as endangered in 1988)
- Pushed to get Marbled Murrelet federally listed (listed as threatened in 1992)
- Began major effort, with others, to get Elwha dams removed (dams finally removed in 2012)

1990s
- Opened Nature Shop (1990)
- Sued U.S. Forest Service over Spotted Owl habitat; won an injunction to stop logging federal lands until owl viability was ensured (1991)
- Began Neighborhood Bird Project (1994)
- Purchased our own building (1996)
- Launched Northwest Shade Coffee Campaign (1996)
- Started BirdWatch (now Young Birders) for teens (1997)
- Promoted FSC-certified wood products, including paper, and pushed DNR to get on board (DNR's South Puget Habitat Conservation Plan Planning Unit certified FSC, 2001)

2000s
- Sued U.S. Army Corps of Engineers to protect Caspian Terns in Columbia River (suit was settled in 2002 and tern colony was moved to East Sand Island)
- Lobbied the Clinton Administration to leave a significant environmental legacy, resulting in the Roadless Rule that protects more than 58 million acres of forest (2001)
- Started Science Committee (2002)
- Launched BirdWeb (2002)
- Graduated first class of Master Advocates (2003)
- Intervened to protect Snowy Plover habitat (2003)
- After years of effort to conserve Great Blue Herons, produced a comprehensive map of critical habitat (2006) and helped persuade the City Council to adopt the Great Blue Heron as the official bird of the City of Seattle (2003)
- Published *Gardening for Life*, our outreach effort to encourage bird-friendly urban landscaping (2003)
- BirdNote aired its first broadcast (2005)
- Launched Sound to Sage (2006)
- Started Puget Sound Seabird Survey (2006)
- Worked with coalitions and agencies to control invasive aquatic species (ongoing)
- Worked with state and local agencies to develop a response plan for a potential Puget Sound oil spill (ongoing)

2010s
- Formed Save Our Swifts with other chapters and persuaded the State Legislature to fund an earthquake retrofit of the chimney of Frank Wagner Elementary in Monroe, where tens of thousands of Vaux's Swifts roost at night during migration (2010)
- Started Canopy Connections (2010)
- Opposed wind power farm on Radar Ridge (project cancelled in 2011)
- Opposed (as did others) leasing of Port of Seattle terminal space to oil industry (Shell Oil Company ceased Arctic drilling operations in October 2015)
- Continued work on Northwest Forest Plan to protect Northern Spotted Owls (revision in process)
- Lobbied for conservation of Marbled Murrelet habitat on Washington State DNR lands (Long-term Conservation Strategy pending)
- Continued to work hard on Puget Sound issues, including cleanup of the Sound, protection of forage fish, and attempts to prevent further pollution (ongoing)
- Continued (with others) to work to protect open space, green space, and natural areas within City of Seattle (ongoing)
- Worked to restore shorebird migration to Puget Trough, especially at Montlake Fill (failed but haven't given up)
- Worked to protect Double-crested Cormorants from getting shot on East Sand Island (ongoing)
- Supported American Alps Legacy Project, a push to expand North Cascades National Park (ongoing)
- Helped secure Urban Bird Treaty City designation for City of Seattle (2016)

Opposite page: Mount Rainier as seen from Naches Peak Loop Trail. (Photograph © Doug Schurman)

APPENDIX 3: HELPING THE WILD
Compiled by Alex MacKenzie

Over the past century Seattle Audubon has helped establish or preserve natural areas throughout North America in many ways: legislative outreach, letter campaigns, meetings, petitions, constituent education, legal action, and financial aid.

The list below includes parks, refuges, wilderness, rivers, wetlands, and other natural habitats that Seattle Audubon has helped, in partnership with other environmental groups. This work is never finished.

Washington State

Alpine Lakes Wilderness
Arboretum (Washington Park Arboretum)
Bainbridge Island Wildlife Corridor
Bald Eagle Natural Area (Upper Skagit River)
Barnaby Slough (Skagit River)
Barney Lake Conservation Area
Bear Creek headwaters
Bergquist Conservation Easement
Big Soos Creek

Black River Heronry
Bowerman Basin
Burke-Gilman Trail
Carnation Marsh
Christensen Creek watershed
Columbia River Gorge
Commodore Park
Conboy Lake National Wildlife Refuge
Copper Creek
Cougar Mountain Regional Wildland Park
Crockett Lake
Cypress Island
Deer Lagoon
Denny Creek
Discovery Park (Fort Lawton)
Dosewallips River
Dumas Bay Park and Wildlife Sanctuary
Dungeness National Wildlife Refuge
    (Dungeness Spit Migratory Bird Refuge)
Ebey's Landing National Historical Reserve
Elwha River
Foster Island
Franklin Falls
Gifford Pinchot National Forest

Glacier Peak Wilderness Area
Goat Rocks Wilderness Area
Golden Gardens Park
Green Lake
Grovers Creek Preserve
Guemes Island
Hines Marsh
Juanita Bay Park
Kellogg Island
Kent-Renton wetlands
Keystone Spit
Lake Quinault
Lake Sammamish State Park
Leadbetter Point
Long Beach Peninsula
Long Island cedar grove
Loomis State Forest
Magnuson Park
Marymoor Park
McNeil Island
Mercer Slough Nature Park
Middle Fork Snoqualmie River
Mima Mounds Natural Area Preserve
Montlake Fill (Union Bay Natural Area)
Moses Coulee
Mount Baker-Snoqualmie National Forest
Mount Rainier National Park
Myers Parcels
Nisqually National Wildlife Refuge (now,
    Billy Frank Jr. Nisqually National Wildlife
    Refuge)
Normandy Beach Park
North Cascades National Park
North Fork Nooksack River
North Fork Skykomish River
Okanogan-Wenatchee National Forest
Olympic National Forest
Olympic National Park
Otto Preserve (Lummi Island)
Padilla Bay
Pioneer Park
Protection Island
Puget Sound
Ravenna Creek
Reardon Ponds
Ruby Creek
San Juan Island National Historic Park
Sauk River
Seward Park
Shi Shi Beach

Snoqualmie Falls
Swan Creek Recreation Area
Tarboo Creek watershed
Thornton Creek
Turnbull National Wildlife Refuge
Upper Elochoman Salmon Conservation
    Project
Vashon-Maury Island Heronry
Whispering Firs Bog
White Creek (Sauk River tributary)
Willapa National Wildlife Refuge
William O. Douglas Wilderness Area
Woodland Park
Yakima Greenway
Yakima River Wildlife Corridor

Beyond Washington State

Arctic National Wildlife Refuge (AK)
Beaver Marsh-McKenzie River (OR)
Dinosaur National Monument (UT/CO)
Don Edwards San Francisco Bay National
    Wildlife Refuge (CA)
Eagle Cap Wilderness (OR)
Echo Park (CO)
Everglades National Park (FL)
Grand Canyon National Park (AZ)
Hells Canyon/Snake River (ID)
Horsepasture Mountain (Willamette National
    Forest, OR)
Jack Miner Bird Sanctuary (ON)
Kings Canyon National Park (CA)
Malheur National Wildlife Refuge (OR)
Rainbow Bridge National Monument (AZ)
Redwood National Park (CA)
River of No Return Wilderness (now,
    Frank Church–River of No Return Wil-
    derness, ID)
San Rafael Wilderness (CA)
Sequoia National Park (CA)
Snake River Birds of Prey National Conserva-
    tion Area (ID)
Three Sisters Wilderness (OR)
Upper Flint River (GA)
Voyageurs National Park (MN)
Walden Pond State Reservation (MA)
Wichita Mountains National Wildlife Refuge
    (OK)
Yellowstone National Park (WY)

ENDNOTES

SECTION 1: CONSERVATION

1. "General Notes: Cotton Mather's manuscript references to the Passenger Pigeon," *The Auk* 62:2 (1945), pp. 306-307.

2. Frank Graham, Jr., "1900s: The Age of Extermination," in *The National Audubon Society: Speaking for Nature, a Century of Conservation*, edited by Les Line (National Audubon Society, 1999), pp. 22-39.

3. University of Washington Libraries, Special Collections, Seattle Audubon Society Records, Accession #1171-001, Box 1, Folders 9, 10, 11, and 12. It should be noted that the correspondence with Alcaraz did not begin with Seattle Audubon's request that Mexico stop the feather trade. Alcaraz sent a letter the previous year, dated September 12, 1923, to President Julia Shourek announcing that he was undertaking a study of Mexico's game laws and would like Shourek to send him all of Seattle Audubon's relevant publications on hunting regulations so that his government could adapt them to Mexican conditions. Seattle Audubon did so and later received a letter of thanks. Why Alcaraz singled out Seattle Audubon for this request is unknown.

4. The slogan: "Sufragio efectivo. No reelección" refers to supporters of the Mexican Revolution, an armed struggle that lasted from 1910 to 1920. The Revolution was in reaction to dictator Porfirio Díaz, who fixed elections so he could serve as perpetual President. He served seven terms, although the Constitution allowed only one six-year term. When he refused to give up power to his legitimately elected rival, Francisco Madero, civil war broke out. After several assassinations, General Alvaro Obregón emerged as President. He served from 1920 to 1924, giving Mexico its first stable government in a decade. Obregón was noted for his educational, land, environmental, and labor reforms. Alcaraz served in Obregón's government.

5. *Wickard v. Filburn* [317 U.S. 111 (1942)].

6. The Lacey Act of 1900 [31 Stat. 187].

7. For a fuller exposition of the Treaty and its enabling legislation, see "No More Bad Birds; Victor Scheffer: Changing Perceptions," pp. 8, 12, above in the Conservation Section.

8. *Missouri v. Holland* [252 U.S. 416 (1920)].

9. The Migratory Bird Treaty was signed by Great Britain (on behalf of Canada) and the United States in 1916. Other countries signed on to the Treaty later: Mexico in 1936, Japan in 1972, and the Soviet Union in 1976. For the full text of the Migratory Bird Treaty of 1916, consult "Convention Between the United States and Great Britain for the Protection of Migratory Birds." *The American Journal of International Law,* Vol. 11, No. 2 (1917), pp. 62-66. For the text of the Migratory Bird Treaty Act of 1918, consult the Congressional Record for the Sixty-fifth Congress, Sess. II, Chap. 128, 1918. Both sources are available online on many websites.

10. Victor B. Scheffer, *The Shaping of Environmentalism in America* (University of Washington Press, 1991), pp. 43-44.

11. U.S. Department of Agriculture Office of the Secretary, press release (December 8, 1922). Available online at: http://www.fws.gov/news/Historic/NewsReleases/1922/19221208.pdf. [Downloaded March 24, 2016.]

12. University of Washington Libraries, Special Collections, Emily Haig Papers, Accession #1898-001, Box 16, Folder 2. Letter dated February 3, 1957.

13. University of Washington Libraries, Special Collections, Emily Haig Papers, Accession #1898-001, Box 16, Folder 2. Letter dated February 9, 1955.

14. University of Washington Libraries, Special Collections, Seattle Audubon Society Records, Accession #1171-001, Box 1, Folder 11.

15. Wilderness Act of 1964 [78 Stat. 890].

16. Lynda V. Mapes, "Killing cormorants to save salmon: 11,000 in crosshairs of controversial program," *Seattle Times* (September 18, 2015). Available online at: http://www.seattletimes.com/. [Downloaded March 22, 2016.]

17. George Catlin was a painter who traveled the West in the early 1830s, painting portraits and scenes of idealized Native American life. Other painters of the Hudson River School, who painted romantic scenes of pristine nature, showed us the beauty of our own wilderness areas, untouched by what we today call "development." It was a viewpoint totally at odds with the idea that nature exists to be tamed.

How much influence these artists had on the American mind is difficult to determine. However, they did contribute to the conversation Americans were having about issues surrounding the ownership and use of public lands, a conversation spurred by the realization that human activity was having adverse effects on wildlife and wildlife habitat. Boundless wilderness was not so boundless after all.

18. George Wuerthner, "Conflicts: Local Interests and Conservation History," available online at the Conservation Land Trust website: http://www.theconservationlandtrust.org/. [Downloaded May 31, 2016.]

19. "First Publication Of Detailed Statement By Majority Of Governor's Olympic National Park Advisory Body, Minority Report," in *Port Angeles Evening News* (January 26, 1955). This was a story that told the insiders' view of how the original majority report and later the minority report were released to the public by the *Port Angeles Evening News* on April 13, 1954. The story reprints in full both reports, as well as Governor Langlie's reaction. Reprinted with permission of the current owner of the *Port Angeles Evening News,* the *Peninsula Daily News;* story © 1955, Sound Publishing, Inc.

20. Niilo A. Anderson, "Mountain Goat Study Progress Report," *Washington State Game Commission Biological Bulletin No. 2* (June 1940).

21. University of Washington Libraries, Special Collections, Emily Haig Papers, Accession #1898-001, Box 16, Folder 2.

Seattle Audubon has never shied away from advocacy, using many avenues to educate our members about environmental issues and encouraging people to take action. One such effort was our Master Advocate program, the brainchild of Board member Lauren Braden in 2003. For ten weeks, students would learn about grassroots organizing, lobbying, testifying, and working with the media. They graduated from the program better able to advocate for the issues they cared about. The program was high powered but short lived, ending only three years after it began.

And still the spark lives on, the urge to speak up to help nature. The modern version of Emily Haig's weekly letter-writing sessions evolved in the early 2000s into email Action Alerts, a means whereby Seattle Audubon's Conservation Committee would periodically send out Alerts to a listserv of people who had signed up to be part of a response team on Audubon's conservation issues. At its height, Action Alerts went out to more than 200 volunteers. The premise of the Alerts was that people did not have to be experts on the issues, but given a little background information, could be empowered to speak with their own voice on behalf of birds and nature. Alerts would suggest specific actions to take, such as sending emails and letters to public officials, or attending a hearing. Because of the strong affiliation that Seattle Audubon members have for our conservation efforts, the Action Alerts consistently generated high response rates.

From these humble beginnings, Seattle Audubon has now moved into the social media age, using Facebook, Twitter, and Instagram to share our messages and Alerts.

22. "26 Stat. 1095" and other such citations in this book refer to the United States Statutes at Large, the official record of laws passed by Congress. They include the proclamations issued by Presidents as well. They are searchable online at many websites.

23. Arthur Dodwell and Theodore F. Rixon, *Forest Conditions in the Olympic Forest Reserve, Washington, Professional Paper No. 7, Series H, Forestry, 4,* Department of the Interior United

States Geological Survey (Washington: Government Printing Office, 1902), pp. 14–18.

24. Much of the information for this timeline was culled from one of the most comprehensive books ever written about the history of Olympic National Park: *Olympic Battleground: The Power Politics of Timber Preservation,* by Carsten Lien (The Mountaineers Books, 2000). Also very helpful was *Extraordinary Women Conservationists of Washington: Mothers of Nature,* by Dee Arntz (Charleston, SC: The History Press, 2015). Online sources were also consulted, among which was Olympic Park Associates' website at http://olympicparkassociates.org/. [Downloaded May 31, 2016.]

It should be noted that this timeline covers only the highlights of the battles over the status, boundaries, and administration of the ancient forests of the Olympic Peninsula. The story is complex, long standing, and ongoing. It is, more than anything else, a story about our values, not just what we value but who decides. It is also a story that continues to play out in many other parts of the country, both in National Parks and, most especially, in other federally owned areas such as National Forests. State-owned lands are also battlegrounds over similar issues.

At times, we as a society have decided that forests should be used as a source of wood products, jobs, and profits. At other times, our values have favored preservation of forests for recreational or ecological purposes. Sometimes we have tried to favor both extraction and preservation by implementing so-called sustainable forestry practices intended to cut down trees without impacting the functionality of the forest as an ecosystem. Depending on how "functionality" is defined and assessed (more societal values, these loosely based on science), sustainable forest practices have either worked well or have proved to be inadequate to maintain targeted species.

25. One of the most prescient of these scientists is Eric Forsman, who began studying Spotted Owls as a graduate student. For the story of how Forsman discovered Spotted Owls in ancient forests and then went on to become a nationally respected expert on them, see "Northern spotted owl marks 20 years on endangered species list," by Scott Learn, *The Oregonian* (June 25, 2010). Available online at: http://www.oregonlive.com/. [Downloaded July 8, 2016.]

26. Rachel Carson, *Silent Spring* (Houghton Mifflin, 1962).

27. Paul R. Ehrlich, *The Population Bomb: Population Control or Race to Oblivion?* (Sierra Club/Ballantine Books, 1968).

28. One of the most famous photographs ever taken by astronauts is the so-called *Earthrise* photograph taken by William Anders in 1968, during the Apollo 8 mission. It shows the desolate moon in the foreground, bare of any life, with Earth—alive with water and clouds—floating in velvet black space, alone in our solar system. Photograph available online at many sources.

29. "The History of Earth Day," online at Earth Day's website: http://www.earthday.org/. [Downloaded June 30, 2016.]

30. For the text of these laws, consult two sources: the U.S. Statutes at Large citations provide the text of the original laws; the U.S. Code citations provide the text of each law as it actually exists today, complete with amendments and rescissions. Clean Air Act of 1963 [77 Stat. 392; 42 U.S.C. §7401 *et seq.*]; Wilderness Act of 1964 [78 Stat. 890; 16 U.S.C. §1131 *et seq.*]; National Environmental Policy Act of 1969 (NEPA) [83 Stat. 852; 42 U.S.C. §4321 *et seq.*]; executive order that established the EPA in 1970 [84 Stat. 2086]; executive order that established NOAA in 1970 [84 Stat. 2090-93]; Clean Water Act of 1972 [86 Stat. 816; 33 U.S.C. §1251 *et seq.*]; Marine Mammal Protection Act of 1972 [86 Stat. 1027]; Endangered Species Act of 1973 [87 Stat. 884; 16 U.S.C. §1531 *et seq.*]; National Forest Management Act of 1976 (NFMA) [88 Stat. 476; 16 U.S.C. §1600 *et seq.*]. All these citations are available online at many sources. For a history of the regulatory and legal battles that resulted in the ban of DDT, consult the EPA's website at: https://www.epa.gov/. [Downloaded July 1, 2016.]

31. For the story of how the first MAMU nest was discovered, see "Marbled Murrelet" on the National Park Service's website at: https://www.nps.gov/. [Downloaded June 21, 2016.]

32. Maria Mudd Ruth, *Rare Bird: Pursuing the Mystery of the Marbled Murrelet* (The Mountaineers Books, 2005, reissued 2013), pp. 86-95.

33. Personal email from Kara Whittaker, Senior Scientist and Policy Analyst, Washington Forest Law Center, June 29, 2016. Also see a draft report by the Regional Ecosystem Office (REO, the inter-agency group responsible for monitoring the Northwest Forest Plan), which notes that in Washington the annual change in MAMU population showed between a 3.9 to 6.7 percent decline per year. Such declines cannot be sustained. If they continue, the species will be extirpated here. The draft report can be accessed online at: http://reo.gov/monitoring/reports/. [Downloaded June 21, 2016.]

34. For more information, including a complete document of the Habitat Conservation Plan, consult DNR's website at: http://www.dnr.wa.gov. [Downloaded June 23, 2016.]

35. The Encumbered Lands Act of 2012 [2012 Wash. Sess. Laws Reg. Sess. Ch. 166] allows small counties that are highly dependent on State timber revenues to replace encumbered State forest lands with unencumbered State forest lands that could keep the timber revenue stream going. Those counties that are too small to have enough unencumbered lands to replace trust lands are allowed to use revenue from such lands in other counties. For more information, see DNR's website, "Replacing Encumbered State Forest Lands," accessible online at: http://file.dnr.wa.gov. [Downloaded July 1, 2016.]

36. The Marbled Murrelet Science Team: M. G. Raphael, S. K. Nelson, P. Swedeen, M. Ostwald, K. Flotlin, S. Desimone, S. Horton, P. Harrison, D. Prenzlow Escene, and W. Jaross, *Recommendations and Supporting Analysis of Conservation Opportunities for the Marbled Murrelet Long-Term Conservation Strategy* (Olympia: Washington State Department of Natural Resources, 2008). Available online at DNR's website: http://www.dnr.wa.gov. [Downloaded July 10, 2016.]

37. From a widely reported statement Goldmark made at the time the sale was released. Available online at many sources, including Oregon Public Broadcasting's website at: http://www.opb.org/. [Downloaded June 30, 2016.]

38. Web Hutchins, "Stop funding school construction with clear cuts," *Crosscut* (Cascade Public Media: January 13, 2014). Available online at Crosscut's website: http://crosscut.com.

39. The Roadless Area Conservation Rule (informally, the Roadless Rule) was promulgated by the Forest Service in the Clinton Administration on January 12, 2001. It forbade the construction of new roads through various public lands, including National Parks and National Forests. One effect has been to preserve more than 58 million acres of federal lands from logging, since without access to roads, timber companies cannot log. The incoming Bush Administration fought the Rule for years, as did litigants. In every Federal Circuit Court of Appeals that has ruled on the merits of the Roadless Rule, the Rule has been upheld. The issue is still alive in the District Court for the District of Columbia. For a concise history of some of the legal wrangling over the Roadless Rule, see the most recent Court of Appeals decision from July 29, 2015, again upholding the Rule: *Organized Village of Kake v. U.S. Dept. of Agriculture,* 795 F.3d 956 (9th Cir. 2015).

40. In 1909, a member of The Mountaineers—George E. Wright—asked President Theodore Roosevelt to proclaim the Olympic Peninsula a National Monument, thereby saving it from logging. (See: "Olympic National Park and The Mountaineers," on The Mountaineers' website, at: https://www.mountaineers.org/; downloaded June 21, 2016.) On March 2, 1909, Roosevelt did so. For more details about the struggle to save old growth on the Peninsula, see "Olympic National Park Timeline: A 125-Year Battle Over Who Owns the Forests," in "You Shall Not Cut; Emily Haig: Helping to Save Olympic National Park," p. 26 above in the Conservation section.

41. The decision to list the Northern Spotted Owl as a State-level endangered species was made in January 1988. It became effective on February 12, 1988, when the decision was published in the Washington State Register at WSR 88-05-032.

42. See "Record of Decision for Amendments to Forest Service and Bureau of Land Management Planning Documents Within the Range of the Northern Spotted Owl," April 13, 1994. Available online at: http://www.reo.gov/. [Downloaded June 21, 2016.]

Properly speaking, the Northwest Forest Plan and the Record of Decision are agency actions, not Presidential ones. This matters because agencies need to comply with the federal Administrative Procedure Act [5 U.S.C. §500 et seq.], but Presidents don't. Within the scope of their power, Presidents can act arbitrarily and without any evidence or reasoning. Agencies, even when acting within the scope of their power, may not act arbitrarily or without any evidence or reasoning. Presidents have only the powers delegated to them by the Constitution, whereas agencies have the powers delegated to them by Congress. This is why, for example, President George W. Bush could not get rid of the Roadless Rule no matter how much he wanted to—the Roadless Rule didn't come from any President; it came from an agency. This dynamic is fundamental to our system of government.

43. The draft report, "Status and Trends of Northern Spotted Owl Habitats," can be accessed online at: http://reo.gov/monitoring/reports/. [Downloaded June 21, 2016.]

44. This report, "Northwest Forest Plan: The First 15 Years (1994-2008), Status and Trends of Northern Spotted Owl Populations and Habitats," can be accessed online at: http://reo.gov/monitoring/reports/. [Downloaded June 21, 2016.]

45. Op. cit., Endnote 5 above.

46. SOHAs are referenced in a document published in 1990. See "A Conservation Strategy for the Northern Spotted Owl, Report of the Interagency Scientific Committee to Address the Conservation of the Northern Spotted Owl," (May 1990), pp. 52 ff. (See Endnote 49 below.)

47. This ruling, ordering U.S. Fish and Wildlife to reexamine the status of the Spotted Owl is known as Northern Spotted Owl v. Hodel. [716 F. Supp. 479 (W.D. Wash. 1988)] When Fish and Wildlife did the reexamination based on science, it became clear that the Northern Spotted Owl must be listed.

48. This Record of Decision was published as, "Final Supplement to the Environmental Impact Statement for an Amendment to the Pacific Northwest Regional Guide—Spotted Owl Guidelines." Available online. [Downloaded June 27, 2016.]

49. "A Conservation Strategy for the Northern Spotted Owl,

Report of the Interagency Scientific Committee to Address the Conservation of the Northern Spotted Owl," (May 1990). Available online at: https://www.fws.gov/. [Downloaded June 27, 2016.] This report is sometimes referred to as the ISC report (for Interagency Scientific Committee), and sometimes as the Jack Ward Thomas report, as he was Chair of the ISC.

50. Op. cit., Endnote 39 above.

51. "Order Granting in Part and Denying in Part Plaintiff's Motion for Preliminary Injunction, Seattle Audubon Society v. Sutherland," No. C06-1608MJP (W.D. Wash. Aug. 1, 2007). To read about the Policy Working Group, see Washington Forest Law Center's website at: http://wflc.org/cases/NSO/NSOworkinggroup. [Downloaded July 1, 2016.]

52. See "Recommendations and Supporting Analysis of Conservation Opportunities for the Marbled Murrelet Long-Term Conservation Strategy," accessed online at: http://file.dnr.wa.gov. [Downloaded June 28, 2016.]

53. "Final Report to Forest Practices Board, Including November 10, 2009 Report; December 31, 2009 Report," by Northern Spotted Owl Policy Working Group, 2009. Available online at DNR's website: http://file.dnr.wa.gov. [Downloaded July 1, 2016.]

54. Lynda V. Mapes, "The Niagara of the Pacific" in Elwha: A River Reborn (The Mountaineers Books and the Seattle Times, 2013), pp. 51 ff.

55. In 1983 WPPSS defaulted on $2.25 billion in bonds that had been sold to pay for the nuclear power plants. One plant had been built; the others were cancelled. At the time, it was the biggest bond default in U.S. history. See: Charles P. Alexander, "Whoops! A $2 Billion Blunder: Washington Public Power Supply System," in Time magazine (August 8, 1983). Available online. Also see "Washington Public Power Supply System (WPPSS)" online at HistoryLink's website: www.historylink.org. [Downloaded July 26, 2016.]

56. Public Utility Regulatory Policies Act of 1978. [92 Stat. 3117]

57. Federal Power Act of 1920. [41 Stat. 1063]

58. The Federal Power Act of 1920 was not the only law at the time that applied to hydropower. Critically important was the act of March 3, 1921, to amend the Federal Water Power Act. [41 Stat. 1353; 16 U.S. Code, §797(a) (PL 66-369)] Specifically, this amendment says that on and after March 3, 1921, no permit, license, lease, or authorization for dams, conduits, reservoirs, powerhouses, transmission lines, or other works for storage or carriage of water, or for the development, transmission, or utilization of power within the limits as constituted, March 3, 1921, of any National Park or National

Monument shall be granted or made without specific authority of Congress.

59. An Act to Establish the Olympic National Park. [52 Stat. 1241] Glines Canyon Dam was within the new Park's boundaries.

60. Confederated Tribes and Bands of the Yakima Indian Nation v. Federal Energy Regulatory Commission. [746 F.2d 466] (9th Cir., October 30, 1984) (Note: The Yakima Indian Nation is now the Yakama Nation.) Among the findings in this case were:

•Relicensing involves a new, irreversible and irretrievable commitment of a public resource and in that sense is akin to an original licensing for which an EIS is obviously required.

• Congress limited the maximum term of any license issued by the Federal Power Commission to 50 years and thereby preserved for the Nation, acting through subsequent Congresses, a full opportunity to reevaluate the best use of each project upon expiration of the license.

• Relicensing, then, is "more akin to an irreversible and irretrievable commitment of a public resource than a mere continuation of the status quo.... Simply because the same resource had been committed in the past does not make relicensing a phase in a continuous activity." Relicensing involves a new commitment of the resource, which in this case is to last for a 40-year period.

61. Armed with court victories (the "Boldt" and "Orrick" decisions) at the federal level that upheld their treaty fishing rights, and with recognition by Washington State of Tribal co-management responsibilities, the Tribes began to play a major role in federal development and licensing issues. Agencies such as FERC initially resisted this but were dealt stinging defeats, such as in Yakima v. FERC (see Endnote 60 above) and Tulalip Tribes of Washington et al. v. Federal Energy Regulatory Commission [732 F.2d 1451] (9th Cir. 1984). By 1983–84, FERC was leery of having further setbacks and unwanted attention, and was according the Tribes a quasi-institutional role in proceedings. In the case of the Elwha, the Tribe's interest was so strong that any attempt to keep it out of the licensing proceedings would have been doomed.

The "Boldt" and "Orrick" decisions (known for the judges who heard the cases), constitute Phases I and II of United States v. Washington. [384 F. Supp. 312] (W.D. Wash. 1974), aff'd, 520 F.2d 676 (9th Cir. 1975), certiorari denied by 423 U.S. 1086 (1976); and 506 F Supp. 187 (1980) 506 F. Supp. 187, 191 (W.D. Wash. 1980), aff'd in part, rev'd in part by 694 F.2d 1374 (9th Cir. 1983)

In the 1800s, Tribes in what would become the State of Washington signed treaties with the federal government. In these treaties the Tribes retained the right to continue to fish in their usual, off-reservation locations. But by the 1950s and

'60s, State fish and game officers would regularly confiscate Indian fishing boats and gear, and arrest or physically assault Tribal members who were fishing. In 1970, after ten years of effort by the Tribes, federal officials announced they would file a lawsuit against the State of Washington to protect treaty fishing rights.

In Phase I, after three years of review, Judge George Boldt ruled in 1974 that treaty Tribes had been systematically denied their rights to fish off their reservations, and that the Tribes were entitled to catch half of the harvestable salmon and steelhead returning to the traditional off-reservation fishing grounds. The State appealed to the Ninth Circuit and then the U.S. Supreme Court, which upheld Judge Boldt's decision against the State of Washington.

Phase II was heard initially by Judge William Orrick, who ruled in 1980 that hatchery-bred fish were included in the Tribal share. The majority of his opinion dealt with habitat issues. He ruled that the Tribes' fishing rights included the right to have treaty fish protected from environmental degradation. While the case was affirmed in part and reversed in part, Phase II has left the Tribes with treaty-based environmental rights that have made them participants in natural resource and environmental decision-making in the State of Washington.

But while Washington State was losing all of the court battles, the victories were not yielding increased fish for the Tribes. Over time, both parties moved toward co-management of the salmon and steelhead resource, in which the State acknowledged the Tribes' right and ability to co-manage and regulate their fisheries. Importantly, the Tribes asserted their right to co-manage not only fisheries harvests, but also habitat protection and enhancement.

62. David Ortman of Friends of the Earth, Polly Dyer and Harry Lydiard of Olympic Park Associates, and Jim Blomquist of the Sierra Club were very supportive in the effort to enlist their organizations in the Elwha fight.

63. Friends of the Earth provided major staff coordination and assistance for our effort by assigning several Northwest Rivers Project Coordinators (Michael Rossotto, Jim Baker, Shawn Cantrell) to assist. The conservation groups provided very able legal assistance by Ron Wilson (counsel to the Sierra Club Legal Defense Fund) and locally by Len Barson of Keller Rohrback, with review by John Lundin of Seattle Audubon, Seattle attorney and conservationist Norm Winn, and Eric Broman of Sierra Club. Russ Busch and Toby Thaler at the Evergreen Legal Services, Native American Project, provided legal assistance to the Lower Elwha Klallam Tribe, and also provided extensive assistance and discussion of various legal points and interpretation of the FERC regulations during

the preparation of the intervention for the original four conservation groups. The Lower Elwha Klallam Tribe strongly supported removal of the dams as the appropriate remedy.

64. Pacific Northwest Electric Power Planning and Conservation Act. [94 Stat. 2697]

65. Elwha River Ecosystem and Fisheries Restoration Act of 1992. [106 Stat. 3173](PL 102-495)

66. Shawn Cantrell of Friends of the Earth (and eventual Executive Director of Seattle Audubon) coordinated the long effort to acquire and accumulate the necessary money. A final serious threat to the removal was engineered by Senator Slade Gorton, who had never liked the idea of removing the dams. He attempted to block the removal by giving support to a group in the Port Angeles area that generally opposed environmental protection measures. Tacoma City Light (also the backer of the odious Elkhorn project on the Dosewallips River, against which Rutz wrote an intervention and Seattle Audubon was a party, and which eventually was argued successfully before the U.S. Supreme Court) provided money under the table to the group, in order to try to head off possible problems for the relicensing of their Cushman project (because the dam's pool, when filled to high levels, intruded unauthorized into Olympic National Park). Bill Robinson from Trout Unlimited, Joe Mentor, and Harry Lydiard worked with the community, and eventually persuaded it that dam removal is in its best interests. With the loss of local support from the community, Gorton gave up the fight; subsequently he was defeated for re-election. The last major threat, other than actually getting the funding appropriated, had been thwarted.

67. The American Recovery and Reinvestment Act of 2009. [123 Stat. 115]

68. While the critical role of the public in this fight seems obvious, it is in fact an important insight that has been missed by most of the reporting and writing concerning the removal of the dams. See Chapter 6 and especially the Epilogue in *Elwha: A River Reborn*. (See Endnote 54, above.)

69. For details of Seattle Audubon's commitment to bird sanctuaries, and particularly to Carnation Marsh, see "Carnation Marsh and the Sanctuary Story," p. 48 above.

70. Board minutes, April 4, 1985, in *SAS History*, Vol. 2. This looseleaf binder is currently in the Seattle Audubon archives.

71. "Carnation," *Seattle Times* (September 7, 1987), p. C2.

72. Martin Miller's papers were left to Seattle Audubon in Miller's will. The papers are currently in the Martin Miller Collection in the Seattle Audubon Society archives.

73. The Martin Miller Committee's records, including

selection criteria and lists of acquisitions, are currently in the Martin Miller Collection in Seattle Audubon Society archives.

74. Google Ngrams (http://books.google.com/ngrams/) is an online application that searches all published books for key word usage. It's a rough but useful way to identify and estimate the level of interest on issues that Americans have cared about over time. In this case, a key word search for "wildlife refuge" showed a first appearance in 1896, a peak in 1944, and another peak in 2000. "Bird sanctuary" first appeared in 1880, with a peak in 1919 and another peak in 1940. "Wildlife reservation" made its first appearance in 1919 and had a peak in 1920, followed by a complete falloff until 1937, when it began to rise again. [Downloaded May 26, 2016.]

75. "History of the National Wildlife Refuge System," Wikipedia. [Downloaded May 26, 2016.]

76. Originally printed in *The Seattle Wren* 6:3 (July 1938), pp. 2 and 4, under the title, "Conservation of Bird Life." A copy of this issue can be found in University of Washington Libraries, Special Collections, Seattle Audubon Society Records, Accession #1171-001, Box 12, Folder 18.

77. "Wildlife and the Land: A Story of Regeneration," a report prepared by Bureau of Biological Survey for the Special Committee on Conservation of Wildlife Resources (pursuant to Senate Resolution 246, 71st Congress), U.S. Government Printing Office, 1937. Available online at many sources.

78. "Seward Park History," on City of Seattle's website at: http://www.seattle.gov/. [Downloaded May 28, 2016.]

79. "Audubon Society Takes Lead in Providing Refuge for Feathered Denizens," *Seattle Daily Times* (January 5, 1919), p. 164.

80. Edwin J. Johnson, "Bird-Feeding in the Arboretum," *The Seattle Wren* 8:1 (April 1940), p. 4. This issue can be found in University of Washington Libraries, Special Collections, Seattle Audubon Society Records, Accession #1171-001, Box 12, Folder 20.

81. On August 18, 1918, an ordinance to require cat owners to buy licenses for their pets was introduced by the Seattle City Council, at the request of Seattle Audubon. The ordinance received widespread support from the City Council, but at the committee hearing convened prior to the vote, Homer W. Hill, Secretary of the Taxpayers' Association, showed up to object. He contended that cats were not responsible for most songbirds' deaths and that cats ate only birds that were already dead. Responded City Councilman T. H. Bolton, "Sure, they're dead when the cat eats them." The ordinance passed. ["Hill Sole Opponent of Licensing Cats," *Seattle Daily Times* (August 26, 1918,) p. 12.] Since those early

days, Seattle Audubon has continued to educate the public about the danger free-roaming cats present to birds. Our current efforts center around promoting the idea that all cats should be indoor pets.

82. A copy of this letter can be found in University of Washington Libraries, Special Collections, Seattle Audubon Society Records, Accession #1171-001, Box 1, Folder 12.

83. Cecil M. Baskett, "Inspirational," *The Seattle Wren* 2:1 (October 1934), p. 1. A copy of this issue can be found in University of Washington Libraries, Special Collections, Seattle Audubon Society Records, Accession #1171-001, Box 12, Folder 15.

84. For a description of the Board's application for branch membership in National Audubon and the process whereby Seattle Audubon finally joined (including William Goodall's visit), see the annual summary of events from May 1962 to May 1963 in *SAS History,* Vol. 1. This looseleaf binder is currently in the Seattle Audubon archives.

85. *Ibid.,* May 1964 to May 1966.

86. Minutes of a special Board meeting, March 17, 1965: copy of the question and answer session after William Goodall's talk about National's policies and goals. Goodall made it clear that while National encouraged local branches to acquire land for nature reserves, National had no funds to help either with acquisition or maintenance. All such projects would have to be funded completely from local sources. ("Special Board Meeting of the Seattle Audubon Society Board—March 17, 1965," in *SAS History,* Vol. 1, following the annual summary of May 1964 to May 1965.) This looseleaf binder is currently in the Seattle Audubon archives.

87. For the ups and downs of the Sanctuary Fund, see: Treasurer's report, March 15, 1965, in annual summary, *SAS History,* Vol. 1, May 1964 to May 1965. See also the bequest of $2,000 from the estate of Michael and Francis Affonin, noted in the annual summary, *SAS History,* Vol. 1, May 1968 to May 1969. See also Board minutes, September 14, 1970, in *SAS History,* Vol. 1; and Board minutes, February 12, 1976, in *SAS History,* Vol. 1. For the Jelliffe bequest, see Board minutes, September 11, 1980, in *SAS History,* Vol. 1. *SAS History,* Vols. 1 and 2 can be found in Seattle Audubon archives.

88. "Audubon Society considering N.W. sanctuary," *Seattle Times* (November 30, 1980), p. 46. See also "History," on the Portland Audubon Society website, http://audubonportland.org/ [downloaded May 30, 2016]; and "Silverwood Wildlife Sanctuary," Wikipedia, https://en.wikipedia.org/wiki/Silverwood_Wildlife_Sanctuary. [Downloaded May 30, 2016.]

89. Lyda Held, "SAS Proud Owners of Carnation Marsh,"

Earthcare Northwest 24:5 (February 1984), p. 1.

90. Terra Prodan, "Seattle Audubon Hopes to Buy Carnation Marsh," *Earthcare Northwest* 23:9 (June-August 1983), p. 1. Prodan was very involved in the acquisition of Carnation Marsh and in efforts to turn it into a viable sanctuary. Among other visionaries who pushed hard for an active, education-based sanctuary were Gene Hunn, Dick Butler, Gerry Adams, Tom Campion, and Steve Hallstrom, as well as the other Sanctuary Committee members already mentioned. At the time of its acquisition, Carnation Marsh lay within Seattle Audubon's official territory, as delineated by National Audubon. Now it lies within the territory of Eastside Audubon.

91. By the time the Board was done buying parcels of Carnation Marsh lands, Seattle Audubon owned 99.25 acres, making up the northern part of Carnation Marsh. (Dick Butler, personal note, June 22, 2016.) Meanwhile, King County, using aquatic enhancement funds, purchased 83 acres of the southern part of the Marsh. Seattle Audubon and King County entered into an agreement whereby Audubon would manage both the north and south sections of the Marsh.

Over the years, Seattle Audubon acquired several other significant, though small, tracts of habitat in King County, which we sought to preserve from development. They included, among others, the McIlraith Wildlife Preserve in Kirkland, which is part of the Swamp Creek watershed and basin; the Harris Creek headwaters in Duvall; and property at Hanstead Creek north of Harris Creek.

92. Having preserved from development the properties acquired through our sanctuary efforts over the decades, Seattle Audubon is now in the process of finding "good homes" for them, meaning, entities that can continue to preserve and in some cases even increase habitat for wildlife.

93. For a view of the parcels we conveyed to King County, check the website at King County Parcel Viewer, at: http://gismaps.kingcounty.gov/parcelviewer2/. Enter parcel numbers: 292507-9003, 292507-9004, and 202507-9062. When we conveyed title of our portion of Carnation Marsh to King County on December 30, 2010, we retained ownership of 10.19 acres on the east side of the Snoqualmie River across from Carnation Marsh. It is a landlocked property accessible only by boat. We still own it.

94. There are many online sources for coffee statistics. These were culled from: "11 Incredible Facts About The Global Coffee Industry" in *Business Insider,* online at: http://www.businessinsider.com/. [Downloaded July 5, 2016.]

95. For more information about eco-friendly coffee, including details about fair trade coffee, see Helen Ross et al., "Coffee, Birds and Trade Policy: making the connection," a white

paper published by Seattle Audubon Society in partnership with Equal Exchange West (October 1999). Available online.

96. Shade coffee is not the only eco-friendly product Seattle Audubon has promoted. For many years and through hundreds of hours of effort, we have encouraged local private and public owners of forests to become FSC certified. FSC (Forest Stewardship Council) certification means that wood products, including paper, are harvested and produced under strict ecological, sustainable, and socially responsible standards. We committed to use FSC paper in all our business and publishing endeavors. Under the leadership of Conservation Director Alex Morgan and the Conservation Committee, Seattle Audubon also lobbied Washington's Department of Natural Resources to pursue certification for the state trust forests they manage. In 2001, DNR announced that 172,000 acres in its South Puget Habitat Conservation Plan Planning Unit (located in King, Pierce, Thurston, Lewis, Kitsap, and Mason Counties) were now FSC certified. It was a significant victory, but more work remains to be done.

SECTION 2: EDUCATION

1. Seattle Audubon Society report to *Bird-Lore,* Vol. XVIII (1916), p. 475; a copy of this report can be found in University of Washington Libraries, Special Collections, Seattle Audubon Society Records, Accession #1171-001, Box 1, Folder 2. See also "Miss Kate Thompson Receives Supplies," in *The Seattle Wren* 4:1 (October 1936), p. 4. A copy of this issue can be found in University of Washington Libraries, Special Collections, Seattle Audubon Society Records, Accession #1171-001, Box 12, Folder 17.

2. "The Audubon Society," a typewritten report, p. 4. A copy of this report can be found in University of Washington Libraries, Special Collections, Seattle Audubon Society Records, Accession #1171-001, Box 1, Folder 2.

3. *SAS History,* Vol. 1, pp. 3 ff. This is one of two looseleaf binders currently in the Seattle Audubon archives.

4. Edna Daw, "Audubons Form New Junior Group," *Seattle Post-Intelligencer* (October 9, 1955).

5. "Audubon Adventures," found online at National Audubon's website, https://www.audubon.org/. [Downloaded May 16, 2016.] Total enrollment nationally in Junior Audubon Clubs from 1911 to 1930 was 4,478,437 ("The Audubon Society," Circular #22, National Association of Audubon Societies, p. 4, found in University of Washington Libraries, Special Collections, Seattle Audubon Society Records, Accession #1171-001, Box 1, Folder 2.)

6. In Spring 2016, Seattle Audubon launched a new club for

kids, based on a suggestion from a third-grade FUN participant. The new club is called The Rookery, for all youths up to age eighteen. The club provides benefits such as in-home birding and conservation challenges and special invitations to membership activities such as bird walks. See "Introducing The Rookery—A Membership Program for Youth," *Earthcare Northwest* (Spring 2016), p. 4.

7. "Seattle Girl Scouts," a typewritten paper found in University of Washington Libraries, Special Collections, Seattle Audubon Society Records, Accession #1171-001, Box 19, Folder 28, circa 1934-1935.

8. "Biographical/History Information," National Audubon Society records 1883-1990s, in New York Public Library Archives & Manuscripts. The New York Public Library Archives are available online. This particular manuscript was accessed at: http://archives.nypl.org/mss/2099. [Downloaded June 2, 2016.]

9. Karen Hollweg, "Dissemination of Denver Audubon Society's Urban Education Project." National Science Foundation Award Number 9155423 (May 14, 1992), AISL Program Reference Code: 9177; Program Element Code: 7259. Grant available online at NSF's website: www.nsf.gov/. [Downloaded July 10, 2016.]

10. Karen S. Hollweg, "Ecology Education for City Children," in *The Ecological City: Preserving and Restoring Urban Biodiversity*, ed. by Rutherford H. Platt, Rowan A. Rowntree, and Pamela C. Muick (University of Massachusetts Press, 1994), pp. 268 ff.

11. Board minutes, August 10, 1989, in *SAS History*, Vol. 2, a looseleaf binder currently in Seattle Audubon archives.

12. Soon after the Board made its decision, Seattle Audubon realized it would have to have someone on staff committed at least part-time to this project. There were too many volunteers to find and train, too many supplies to ready into kits, too much administrative detail to work through. JoAnn Riecke spearheaded a phonathon to raise money to hire a Coordinator. Seventeen volunteers raised more than $800 in one day, which was enough to hire the first Coordinator, Keith Geller (Board minutes, October 12, 1989, and December 14, 1989, found in *SAS History*, Vol. 2). In later years, Anita Lagerberg took over as Coordinator and—with the help of volunteer Martha Nester—expanded the program into many schools, serving hundreds of children each year. After her came Kintea Bryant, who, as Education Director, expanded the program even further. Now Christine Scheele, Education Manager, is about to launch a new phase of FUN, in which volunteer docents from Seattle Audubon train hands-on volunteers, enabling FUN to reach even more schools.

13. Kelly Grobecker, "Audubon class teaches kids about nature's way," *University Herald/North Central Outlook* (August 18, 1982), p. 8. See also: "SAS Summer Youth Program," *Earthcare Northwest* 22:9 (June 1982), p. 9. (Copies of this and other *Earthcare Northwest* newsletters are in Seattle Audubon Society archives.) Other early contributors to Nature Camp included Board members Lexie Borrie-Bakewell, Dorothy Erbstoesser, and Dyanne Sheldon.

The Board decided in the first year of Nature Camp to support a scholarship fund to make it possible for families to send their children to camp regardless of family income. Donations were solicited, and members responded generously, as they continue to do today. Three of the most generous donors were Della Patch and Eleanor and Bob Grant, who left bequests to Seattle Audubon to provide scholarships for kids, not only to attend Nature Camp but also to participate in BirdWatch, banding camp, and other classes. Their bequests also supported education for other programs, including FUN and education in general.

Della Patch taught science in Seattle schools for 47 years. She was an active member of Seattle Audubon for decades, serving in many capacities, but she always had a special place in her heart for children. After she retired, she volunteered to mentor kids in shelters to help keep them from dropping out of school. Della was an enthusiastic hiker and birder who led countless bird walks for adults and kids. Her special place was Green Lake, which she used to orbit every day, beginning in the 1920s. She died in 1999 at age 100.

Bob and Eleanor Grant were also actively involved in Seattle Audubon for decades, serving in many capacities. Bob was President of Seattle Audubon from 1984 to 1986. Eleanor was Chair of the Membership Committee from 1980 to 1998—almost 20 years—and had great success attracting new members. They both believed strongly in the power of education to change hearts and minds and always sought to help kids connect with nature. They remained active at Seattle Audubon into their final years, sharing their unique style of firmly principled yet also warm and caring activism. On their 50th wedding anniversary, they established the Eleanor and Bob Grant Education Fund, a perpetual source of scholarship funds for kids to go to Nature Camp.

Another important source of scholarships and education funding is the Hazel Wolf "Kids for the Environment Endowment Fund," a Seattle Audubon fund established in Hazel's honor after she died.

14. Michael Donahue, "Summer Camp Opens Up New World for Kids," *Earthcare Northwest* 23:1 (September 1982), p. 10.

15. Jan Auman, "Audubon Camp Has a Successful Summer,"

Earthcare Northwest 24:1 (September 1983), p. 7.

16. Jan Auman, "SAS Nature Camp Offers Fun, Exploration," *Earthcare Northwest* 23:8 (May 1983), p. 1.

17. "2016 Session Descriptions," online at Seattle Audubon's website: http://www.seattleaudubon.org/. [Downloaded June 4, 2016.]

18. Photograph originally published in *Earthcare Northwest* 23:1 (September 1982), p. 1.

19. Among the early supporters who served on the Steering Committee, helped mentor kids, and served on staff were: Izzy and Kendrick Wong, Martha Taylor, Dan Suiter, Lyanda Lynn Haupt, Michael Donahue, Kristen Ragain, Emily Sprong, Arden Thomas, and Shirley Sekarajasingham. For more details about the formation of BirdWatch, see papers in Seattle Audubon's archives, "BirdWatch Past Years" folder.

20. Recently, the program has been expanded to include middle school kids as well. Seattle Audubon Education Manager Christine Scheele believes this will help fulfill a long-term goal of our organization: to provide lifelong learning for every age group from toddlers to elders. The revamped teen program is called Young Birders. See: "Young Birders," on Seattle Audubon Society's website at: http://www.seattleaudubon.org/. [Downloaded June 6, 2016.]

21. "Audubon Society Will Take Another Journey," *Seattle Daily Times* (June 2, 1916), p. 19.

22. "New Audubon Society Starts with Good List," *Seattle Daily Times* (May 9, 1916), p. 15.

23. "Seattle Audubon Society," in the Women's Clubs section of *Seattle Daily Times* (July 8, 1916), p. 4.

24. "Audubon Society To Study Birds In Systematic Way This Winter," *Seattle Daily Times* (October 14, 1917), p. 67. See also: a Seattle Audubon announcement describing the class, which was sent to members. A copy of this announcement can be found in University of Washington Libraries, Special Collections, Seattle Audubon Society Records, Accession #1171-001, Box 1, Folder 12.

25. Reference found in *SAS History*, Vol. 1, section titled "Summary 1916-1952," in the tab "SAS History Pre-Org-1929." This looseleaf binder can be found in Seattle Audubon archives.

26. Although Master Birders are required to give community service hours to Seattle Audubon as part of their commitment to the program, the ways they choose to serve are as individualistic as the Master Birders are. Many have volunteered to work in the Nature Shop, where they are on call to answer people's questions about birds. They lead field trips, teach classes, serve on committees, become Directors on the Board,

are elected as officers of Seattle Audubon, and represent us regionally and nationally. Some who have special expertise give back to Audubon professionally, as book editors, print production experts, artists, legal or financial advisors, and scientists. One of the most important ways many Master Birders give back is to help with other Master Birder classes. Most of all, wherever they go, Master Birders share their knowledge of birds, following Dennis Paulson's example.

27. Master Birders sometimes go on to help institutions other than Seattle Audubon. Martin Muller, for example, co-authored the species account for Pied-billed Grebes in *The Birds of North America,* a comprehensive reference covering the natural history of all of North America's breeding birds. The print version, updated in 2002, is eighteen volumes and 18,000 pages long. It was a joint project of the American Ornithologists' Union, Cornell Lab of Ornithology, and the Academy of Natural Sciences. See: Muller, M. J. and R. W. Storer, "Pied-billed Grebe (*Podilymbus podiceps*)" in *The Birds of North America, No. 410,* A. Poole and F. Gill, eds. (The Birds of North America, Inc. Philadelphia, PA, 1999). There is also an online version retrieved from the Birds of North America Online: http://bna.birds.cornell.edu/bna/. [Accessed June 17, 2016.] Muller also volunteers with the Falcon Research Group, a nonprofit organization dedicated to research, conservation, and public education about raptors. For more information about FRG, consult their website: http://www.frg.org. [Accessed June 17, 2016.]

SECTION 3: SCIENCE

1. Most of the historical data from past Christmas Bird Counts (CBCs) are available online at the National Audubon website: http://audubon.org. For data on Washington State's counts, navigate to the CBC page, enter a year range, and locate the count circle (country = US, state = WA, count circle = WASE). Seattle Audubon is also working on posting our CBC data on the Science page of our website. The page does not yet include the older records, which are stored on paper at University of Washington Libraries, Special Collections, Seattle Audubon Society Records, Accession #1171-001, in various boxes and folders.

2. Personal email from Hal Opperman, April 9, 2016: "Seattle Audubon Society had a Bird Records Committee for many years. It ran the statewide telephone hotline; published a bird sightings column in *Earthcare Northwest,* Seattle Audubon's newsletter; maintained a 'Checklist of Washington Birds'; sponsored the Washington Breeding Bird Atlas; and ran the Seattle Christmas Bird Count. It never had a mission of systematically compiling and reviewing all the

rarities records, the way standard bird records committees do in other states.

"In 1988, the Washington Ornithological Society (WOS) was formed. One of the first things it did was set up a formal committee for reviewing records and maintaining an 'official' state bird list. The new Washington Bird Records Committee (WBRC) is still operating today. Seattle Audubon gave its state checklist to the WBRC; WOS has published it ever since.

"Seattle Audubon's Bird Records Committee continued in existence, but with a more limited and local mission. The sightings columns continued, and so did the telephone hotline. Before long, WOS implemented its Washington bird sightings database, from which quarterly reports of the most noteworthy information were published regularly in *WOSNews,* and also started the BirdBox, a voicemail-based hotline that no longer required someone to summarize the sightings into a weekly tape, the way the Seattle Audubon hotline did. All of these developments—WBRC, Washington sightings database, and BirdBox—pushed Seattle Audubon to the margins of the central position it once held in the state record-keeping community. The hotline shut down; news of bird sightings thinned out, and the *Earthcare Northwest* column was discontinued.

"By then I was chair of Audubon's Bird Records Committee, having succeeded Gene Hunn in 1996. We still had the CBC to look after, as well as some county breeding bird atlases we had started (which eventually were published online as Sound to Sage). We concentrated on these, and before long began to understand that our place in the Washington State birding picture was one of citizen science, where we had superior resources in the form of skilled volunteers for fieldwork and data management. After much discussion, the Bird Records Committee developed a revised mission statement and recommended to the Board that its name be changed to the Science Committee. The recommendation was accepted in 2000 as part of a major reorganization Seattle Audubon went through. The old Board position of Science Advisor, occupied for years by Estella Leopold and filled by Herb Curl after she retired, was discontinued and its responsibilities were folded into the newly created Science Committee, along with those of the former Bird Records Committee."

3. Science Committee, "Seattle Audubon Scientific Committee Summary of Activities and Plans," a report prepared for Mark Buckley, Executive Director (January 10, 2005). This report is currently in the Seattle Audubon archives.

4. Eugene S. Hunn, *Birding in Seattle and King County* (Seattle Audubon Society, 2012), pp. 128-129.

5. Other parks and sites were added—and sometimes dropped—as well. Currently, eight sites are covered in the

Neighborhood Bird Project: Carkeek, Genesee, Magnuson, Discovery, Golden Gardens, and Seward Parks, the Arboretum, and an open space in Lake Forest Park. For a more complete description of the Neighborhood Bird Project, see "Our Parks, Our Place; Janice Bragg: The Neighborhood Bird Project," pp. 96–100 in text above.

6. See "It All Adds Up; Eugene S. Hunn: Christmas Bird Count," pp. 91–95 in text above.

7. See "Sound Vision; Toby Ross: Puget Sound Seabird Survey," pp. 106–111 in text above.

8. See "Birds on the Wire, Science Online; Tom Aversa: BirdWeb & Sound to Sage," pp. 101–105 in text above.

9. Important Bird Areas are worldwide sites of critical habitat for birds, as identified by the application of internationally agreed-upon criteria. Audubon Washington began identifying state IBAs in 1998. In 2001, Audubon Washington published a list of 53 IBAs. It was thought that the worldwide criteria could be scaled so they better fit statewide conditions, and in 2004, these new criteria were applied. There are now 75 IBAs in the state. For more information online, see Audubon Washington's website at: http://wa.audubon.org. [Downloaded March 25, 2016.]

10. Frank M. Chapman, "A Christmas Bird-Census," *Bird-Lore,* Vol. II (1900), p. 192. *Bird-Lore* was the first official organ of the National Association of Audubon Societies. It billed itself as "an illustrated bi-monthly magazine devoted to the study and protection of birds." It evolved into *Audubon* magazine, which is still published today.

11. *Op. cit.,* Endnote 1 above.

12. C. John Ralph, Thomas E. Martin, Geoffrey R. Geupel, David F. DeSante, and Peter Pyle, *Handbook of Field Methods for Monitoring Landbirds, General Technical Report PSW-GTR-144-www* (Pacific Southwest Research Station, U.S. Forest Service, U.S. Department of Agriculture, Albany, CA, 1993). Available online at many sources.

13. Personal email from Toby Ross (June 3, 2016): "In 2015 there were on average 73 volunteers attending the surveys each month. Over the course of the year (2015), they spent approximately 2,190 hours surveying."

14. Matthew Mega, "Urban Trees: Help Needed," *Earthcare Northwest* 52:1 (Autumn 2010), p. 5. Past issues of Seattle Audubon's newsletters are currently in Seattle Audubon's archives.

15. To access the City of Seattle's tree map, go to http://web6.seattle.gov/SDOT/StreetTrees/. [Accessed May 18, 2016.]

16. C. J. Battey and T. Ross, *Impacts of Habitat Restoration and*

the *Status of Avian Communities in Seattle City Parks* (Seattle Audubon Society, 2014).

17. For a history of how the Washington Ornithological Society's Washington Bird Records Committee began and how Seattle Audubon's own Bird Records Committee evolved into the Science Committee, see Endnote 2 above.

18. For a list of BirdWeb volunteers, see "Seattle Audubon Launches Online Guide to the Birds of Washington State," *Earthcare Northwest* 44:3 (November 2002), p. 18. Our newsletters are currently in Seattle Audubon archives.

19. Personal email from Seattle Audubon Development Director Claire Catania, April 6, 2016: "Seattle Audubon launched BirdWeb in 2002 to be a definitive online guide to the birds of Washington State. The site was redesigned in 2006 and included new features such as sounds for most species and information about the birding sites and eco-regions of our state. It gradually grew in popularity to be Seattle Audubon's most popular website, drawing 1,500 to 2,500 daily visits. In 2010, Seattle Audubon launched the most recent version of BirdWeb to improve user experience, expand the image selection, and provide users with more compelling opportunities to also visit Seattle Audubon's website. Since the launch of this version, the number of people visiting www.seattleaudubon.org via BirdWeb has more than tripled."

Personal email from Science Manager Toby Ross, June 1, 2016: "The latest numbers for BirdWeb from 2015 are: 499,053 users; 1,794,912 page views; 601,633 sessions/hits. Greatest number of sessions/hits in one day in 2015 = 3,188."

20. The report was called "Washington State GAP Analysis Final Report" and was published by Seattle Audubon in a book titled *Breeding Birds of Washington State—Location Data and Predicted Distributions Including: Breeding Bird Atlas & Habitat Associations*, by Michael R. Smith, Philip W. Mattocks, Jr., and Kelly M. Cassidy, 1997.

21. For a history of Sound to Sage and a list of all the volunteers who helped launch it, see the Sound to Sage website at: http://soundtosage.org/. [Downloaded April 10, 2016.]

22. For more information on the Puget Sound Seabird Survey, visit http://seabirdsurvey.org. [Downloaded June 20, 2016.] To get involved, contact Seattle Audubon Society.

23. A good source for further information on Distance Sampling can be found at the Distance Project website: http://distancesampling.org/. [Downloaded June 20, 2016.] The Distance Project is currently sponsored by several organizations, including the U.S. Office of Naval Research, Marine Life Sciences program, the National Marine Mammal Laboratory, and the U.K. Biotechnology and Biological Sciences Research Council, among others.

24. The scientific paper, "Using citizen-science data to identify local hotspots of seabird occurrence" can be accessed online at https://peerj.com/articles/704/. [Downloaded June 20, 2016.]

25. One of the most influential of all Publications Chairs was David Hutchinson (owner of Flora & Fauna Books), who headed up the Committee for nearly ten years, beginning in 1988, and who also served on Seattle Audubon's Board during that time.

Off and on before his tenure, the Board would set aside special monies in the budget for publishing, though never very much and never for very long. The reason for the set-asides most probably had to do with the fact that book publishing requires that all production costs be paid upfront and recouped slowly as each book is sold. Nearly every book Seattle Audubon has ever published made a profit by the time the book sold out. But that could take many years and was hard to keep track of in the general budget, which operated from one fiscal year to the next.

Hutchinson was able to stabilize and grow the Publications Fund considerably and describes his experience thus in a personal note:

"The fund really started to grow with the earnings from *Washington Wildflowers*, a manuscript donated by the authors. The thought was that Seattle Audubon could use the fund to publish new books of high commercial quality which might not otherwise get published but were important to our members. With the growth of the Nature Shop, Seattle Audubon was able to receive income from retail sales, which were recorded back into the Publications Fund to recover its wholesale costs. We always recovered our costs before releasing another book. The following field guides centered on the Pacific Northwest passed through our hands at this time: shorebirds, amphibians, reptiles, wetland plants, and butterflies, plus we published the Washington Breeding Bird Atlas. Though many of these books are now out of print, they served their purpose well and still have good value as used books."

Eventually, the Publications Fund was folded back into the general budget at a time when Seattle Audubon ran a deficit and needed to balance the budget.

26. A copy of the checklist can be found in University of Washington Libraries, Special Collections, Seattle Audubon Society Records, Accession #1171-001, Box 15, Folder 20. A copy of the April 1935 issue of *The Seattle Wren* can be found in Box 12, folder 16.

27. Stephen Jay Gould, "Unenchanted Evening" in *Eight Little Piggies: Reflections in Natural History* (New York: W.W. Norton & Company, 1993), p. 40.

SECTION 4: PARTICIPATION

1. David Garcia is now the Shop Manager, having taken over from Russ Steele.

2. George Johnson wrote several short histories about himself and his involvement with Seattle Audubon sales. These are currently filed in looseleaf binders labeled "History" in Seattle Audubon archives.

3. "New Audubon Society," *Seattle Daily Times* (April 18, 1916), p. 12. See also, "Seattle Bird-Lovers to Organize Monday," *Seattle Daily Times* (May 6, 1916), p. 2; "New Audubon Society Starts with Good List," *Seattle Daily Times* (May 9, 1916), p. 15; and "Audubon Society," *Seattle Daily Times* (June 11, 1916), p. 5. The Chamber of Commerce rented space in the Central Building—located at 810 Third and Cherry—before its move to the Arctic Building [see *New Seattle Chamber of Commerce Record,* Vol. IV, #6 (June 1, 1916), p. 13]. The records of the Chamber of Commerce are archived in University of Washington Libraries, Special Collections.

4. George Johnson papers, currently in Seattle Audubon archives.

5. Seattle Audubon Board minutes, December 14, 1989, currently in Seattle Audubon archives.

6. Sources for this list include Hazel Wolf herself, as quoted in Susan Starbuck's book, *Hazel Wolf: Fighting the Establishment* (University of Washington Press, 2002). Other sources include minutes from Seattle Audubon Society's Board meetings, which are currently stored in three places: University of Washington Libraries, Special Collections, Seattle Audubon Society Records, Accession #1171-001 (various boxes and folders); Seattle Audubon archives; and University of Washington Libraries, Special Collections, Emily Haig Papers, Accession #1898-001 (various boxes and folders). Finally, sources include personal emails from various Audubon chapters.

7. Personal email from Grace Hubbard, April 23, 2016.

8. *Earthcare Northwest* newsletters are currently in Seattle Audubon archives.

9. "New Audubon Society Starts with Good List," *Op. cit.,* Endnote 3 above.

10. *Gardening for Life—An Inspirational Guide to Creating Healthy Habitat*, published jointly by Seattle Audubon Society, National Audubon Society, and U.S. Environmental Protection Agency (EPA), 2003. Available in Seattle Audubon Society's library.

11. Frank Graham, Jr., "Audubon Chapters: A History," available online at National Audubon Society's website: http://audubon.org/. [Downloaded March 2, 2016.]

12. "Audubon Club Will Exhibit Colored Films," *Seattle Daily Times* (November 4, 1945), p. 42.

13. Minutes of the Board, February 12, 1956, archived in University of Washington Libraries, Special Collections, Seattle Audubon Society Records, Accession #1171-001, Box 11, Folder 12. After a long discussion, the minutes state the Board decided Screen Tours was worth the financial risk. Emily Haig "then asked the Board to put aside any personal feelings in this matter, and requested that all stand together and work hard towards making next year's Screen Tours a success."

She wasn't joking about the amount of hard work the Screen Tours took. Aside from the tasks already mentioned, there were seemingly an infinite number of jobs that needed attention, many of which don't necessarily come readily to mind. For example, somebody had to arrange to get the brochures from National that advertised each show and then make sure they were overprinted with Seattle Audubon's name. When the brochures came back from the printer, someone had to address envelopes to mail them to members. There had to be enough stamps on hand and mailbags to put the outgoing brochures in for the Post Office, and on and on. The Chair in the early years of the Screen Tours Committee, Miss Eugenia Lane, had resigned by the time the 1956 Board vote was taken—she was apparently burned out from all the work—but she offered to break in the new Chair. Then, according to the minutes, "she also pointed out that the Chairman should not have to do all the work, and stressed the need for a big committee and an all-out effort of all committee members to insure a successful year."

14. Screen Tour promotional flyers can be found in University of Washington Libraries, Special Collections, Seattle Audubon Society Records, Accession #1171-001, Box 19, Folder 24. More such promotional brochures can also be found in University of Washington Libraries, Special Collections, Emily Haig Papers, Accession #1898-001, Box 19, Folders 6 and 7.

15. *The Seattle Wren* 1:1 (1933) can be found in University of Washington Libraries, Special Collections, Seattle Audubon Society Records, Accession #1171-001, Box 1, Folder 2. The newsletter was published quarterly in January, April, July, and October. It had a press run of 250 copies, far in excess of the number of members. Subscriptions were free to members, 50 cents per year to non-members.

16. Earl J. Larrison, "Pronouncing Bird Names," *The Seattle Wren* 9:1 (April 1940), p. 4. This issue can be found in University of Washington Libraries, Special Collections, Seattle Audubon Society Records, Accession #1171-001, Box 12, Folder 20.

17. Funding was always a problem for the newsletter, and in 1937, *The Seattle Wren* was folded into *The Puget Sounder,* a newspaper printed in Bellingham. Subscriptions were $1 a year, and the newspaper's revenue was augmented with ads for every kind of business, from hair salons to funeral parlors. The Publishing Committee hoped this partnership would bring in new members and shared revenue, but after a year of no growth, the experiment ended and *The Seattle Wren* was reinstated in January 1938. The first issue of the revived newsletter included a plea to readers to let the Committee know its efforts were appreciated. L. Roy Hastings, the editor, wrote an impassioned defense of the value of newsletters. He couched it in the form of a welcome to Portland Audubon's newsletter, the *Audubon Warbler,* noting that there was now a complete chain of Audubon Society publications stretching throughout the Far Western states.

Alas, even with this paean to publication, *The Seattle Wren* managed to hang on only until April 1941. For nineteen years after it folded, Seattle Audubon's members were served with somewhat sporadic mimeographed bulletins announcing activities and issues. In 1960, the Committee held a contest to give these bulletins a name and regularize their publication. *Audubon Warblings* was born, though it continued to be a simple set of mimeographed pages. It served members until 1967. At that time, a contest was held among members to choose a new name, and *Seattle Audubon Society Notes* was created. (See *SAS History,* Vol. 1; this looseleaf binder is currently in Seattle Audubon archives.) *Seattle Audubon Society Notes* continued to be mimeographed until July 1972, when the Committee reported that at 2,500 copies, the newsletter could no longer be mimeographed. A printer was chosen but the homemade look remained.

In April 1979, *Seattle Audubon Society Notes* was redesigned into an eight-page newspaper because an ad hoc committee had discovered we could print eight pages on newsprint more cheaply than four pages on higher-quality paper. In September 1981, *Notes* became *Earthcare Northwest,* which it remains to this day.

Copies of all these newsletters printed prior to 1980 can be found in University of Washington Libraries, Special Collections, Seattle Audubon Society Records, Accession #1171-001 (various folders), . Copies of newsletters printed after 1980 can currently be found in Seattle Audubon archives.

18. For more on the Label Ladies, see "The *Earthcare Northwest* Mailing Team" by Lorraine Hartmann, *Earthcare Northwest* 17:2 (October 1995), p. 4. A copy of this issue can currently be found in Seattle Audubon archives.

19. "Ducks Unlimited," by Ellsworth D. Lumley, *The Seattle Wren* 7:1 (January 1939), pp. 1-4. A copy of this issue can be found in University of Washington Libraries, Special Collections, Seattle Audubon Society Records, Accession #1171-001, Box 12, Folder 19.

20. The popularity of Lumley's diatribe against Ducks Unlimited was reported in a subsequent issue of *The Wren* in an article titled, "'Ducks Unlimited' Written by Mr. Lumley Making *Wren* History." [*The Seattle Wren* 7:3 (September 1939), p. 4.] Lumley's article was read in practically every state in the West, said *The Wren,* and many in the East. Many publications quoted it, increasing the demand for copies. An unprecedented reprint was ordered. Then a national publication, *Nature Magazine,* mentioned the article, and demand went up so much that the editors of *The Wren* feared they would have to do a third printing. (A copy of the September 1939 issue of *The Wren* can be found in University of Washington Libraries, Special Collections, Seattle Audubon Society Records, Accession #1171-001, Box 12, Folder 19.)

21. "Seattle Bird-Lovers to Organize Monday: Audubon Society Will Be Formed at Chamber of Commerce—First Walk Planned," *Seattle Daily Times* (May 6, 1916), p. 2.

22. To prepare participants for a field trip to a ranch owned by one of Seattle Audubon's members, the following notice was mailed: "The closing event for this season will be the overnight trip to Hidden Ranch, the home of Mr. E. S. Paschall, to take place next Saturday, June 18th [1927]. Take your own provisions for supper Saturday night, and for breakfast and lunch on Sunday. Bring your own plate, cup, spoon, etc. Coffee will be provided for the party. Bring your own blankets. Women are to use the hay mound in the barn for sleeping quarters. The men are to have the use of the house-porch or the outdoors if they prefer." (Notice found in University of Washington Libraries, Special Collections, Seattle Audubon Society Records, Accession #1171-001, Box 1, Folder 12.)

23. Faraway birding hotspots became popular destinations of Seattle Audubon field trips during the 1970s and '80s. A sample of such destinations includes trips to Costa Rica organized in April 1973 [*Seattle Audubon Society Notes* 13:8 (April 1973)] and May 1983 [*Earthcare Northwest* 23:8 (May 1983)]; to the Pribilof Islands in June 1973 [*Seattle Audubon Society Notes* 13:8 (April 1973)]; to the Northwest Territories in July 1977 [*Seattle Audubon Society Notes* 17:7 (March 1977)]; to Florida in May 1983 [*Earthcare Northwest* 23:8 (May 1983)]; to Hawaii in October 1983 [*Earthcare Northwest* 23:8 (May 1983)]; and to the Yucatán Peninsula in spring 1989 [*Earthcare Northwest* 30:6 (April 1989)]. (Note: Descriptions of all these trips can be found in the newsletters cited, currently located in Seattle Audubon archives.)

24. It wasn't really that simple, as Phyllis Moss recalls:

"Neighborhood Bird Walks were the brainchild of Don Ostrow back in 2001. I stepped in as Coordinator in 2012 when Don retired. Don thought a more informal approach to Audubon-led bird walks might engage people who perhaps weren't very familiar with Seattle Audubon, or weren't sure they liked bird-watching enough to join the Society right away. Neighborhood Bird Walks can be just the thing to invite people to get more involved. In addition to coordinating Neighborhood Bird Walks, I serve on the Field Trip Committee with a lot of other dedicated people. Together, we have scheduled hundreds of walks and trips.

There's a lot of work that goes into planning Neighborhood Bird Walks and field trips. Successful walks and trips depend on an unseen flock of volunteers who work very hard to make everything go smoothly. Some of them take information over the phone when people call to sign up. Others post trip descriptions on the website, prepare trip lists for the leaders, receive the trip leaders' reports after the trip, and process them. To schedule field trips, our Committee has to find and support new leaders, develop new trips, and implement Seattle Audubon policy as it applies to field trips and walks. Then there are the trip leaders themselves. Many put in hours of effort ahead of time, scouting the route. During the trip, they keep everyone together and safe. They try to make sure everyone on the trip gets what they want out of the experience. It sounds so simple to read an account of a walk or field trip. 'So-and-so led a group of bird-watchers out to Kirkland on a spring day to find birds.' Yes, and all Hamlet had to do was stand on a stage and recite a few words!"

25. Beginning in 1924, Seattle Audubon began to lobby City government to make Green Lake a bird sanctuary, or at least Duck Island. "The marshes were now being made a dumping ground and the area filled," reports one member in a summary of the Society's activities from May 1923 to May 1924. "A protest and appeal to the City of Seattle to have this work stopped was sought to back a proposal to create a bird reservation at Green Lake." (See annual summary, 1916-1952, in *SAS History*, Vol. 1, pp. 9-10. This looseleaf binder is currently archived at Seattle Audubon.) Later in that same summary is a report that states: "The Seattle Audubon Society's proposal to have a feeding station for birds at Green Lake did not meet with success. Dr. Hanley of City Health Department was not in favor of the idea—plans for Green Lake did not include a bird feeding station but a bathing beach and beauty spot." (*ibid.*, p. 11.)

26. A special kind of bird walk happens once a year every spring: the annual Seattle Audubon Birdathon. Birdathons were a kind of spinoff from all the "thons" that were raising money for organizations in the 1960s, '70s, and '80s, beginning with marathons for charity and soon morphing into walkathons, jogathons, phonathons, bike-athons, and any other kind of "thon" people could think of. They were popular because they were fun. They often had an element of contest in them, as participants vied to see who could go the farthest or last the longest. And it was all for a good cause.

Seattle Audubon's first Birdathon was launched in April 1980, involved 255 birders, and raised $2,400. The event grew rapidly in subsequent years, with prizes awarded for the most birds seen, the most money raised, the most money per species seen, the youngest Birdathoner, the most unusual bird seen, etc. Mystery celebrities sometimes joined the teams out in the field. One year former Governor Dan Evans was the celebrity; another year it was beloved Seattle actor Clayton Corzatte. Specialty events added to the fun: Gene Hunn's Big Foot Day took participants all over King County using only public transportation and bipedal locomotion. Master Birder teams from different years would often challenge each other. The Board and the staff also competed. Field trips would also be scheduled for Birdathon, in which participants would donate a fee to Seattle Audubon (field trips are usually free to members).

It was and is a big scheduling challenge for staff and the Field Trip Committee, but the effort is worth it. In the 2016 Birdathon, participants raised more than ten times as much as we did in our first year. Altogether, the total raised since our first Birdathon is approaching seven figures—all for the purpose of helping birds and habitat. A special kind of bird walk indeed.

27. Ann Mahnke, "Birders' Class Leads to Eruption Adventure," *Seattle Audubon Notes* 20:9 (June 1980), p. 8. (This issue is currently in Seattle Audubon's archives.)

28. The first officers of Seattle Audubon Society were: Mrs. Charles Crickmore, President; Mrs. Harry D. Moore, First Vice President; Professor Trevor Kincaid, Second Vice President; Miss Kate Thompson, Secretary-Treasurer; Mrs. Ralph Krows, Corresponding Secretary. L. H. Gray, Ralph Krows, and Miss Ida Culver were elected to the Board, as reported in the *Seattle Daily Times* (April 18, 1916), p. 12; also recorded in *SAS History*, Vol. 1. (This looseleaf binder is currently in the Seattle Audubon archives.) In fact, for the first eleven years of its existence, Seattle Audubon elected only women to be President of the Society. It wasn't until 1927 that a man became President: Cecil M. Baskett, who served for two years. (See Appendix I: "Seattle Audubon Presidents," p. 168 above.)

29. "Audubon Society to Study Birds in Systematic Way This Winter," *Seattle Daily Times* (October 14, 1917), p. 67.

30. One result of our sometimes fraught relationship with National has to do with how people can join Audubon. There are two ways. One way is to join Seattle Audubon directly, in which case, you have no connection with National. The other way is to join National. If you join National Audubon, you will be assigned to a chapter based on your zip code and your member information (as well as some "dues share") will be shared with the chapter. Some chapters automatically say, "If you join our chapter, you join National." But others—Seattle Audubon being one—say that membership in the chapter is distinct from membership with National. That feature at Seattle Audubon is a legacy of times when we were less connected to National.

One of the most heated of our "family" arguments with National Audubon occurred in 1987. As described in National Audubon's own historical record: "The most controversial measure of budgetary retrenchment was taken in 1987 when Audubon's Board of Directors, in a major organizational 'restructuring,' voted, without consulting with its chapters, to eliminate the regional office system. This provoked a grassroots rebellion of chapter leaders throughout the country and a proxy fight to 'democratize' the board led by Audubon's former Executive Vice President, Charles H. Callison. The quarrel was quelled when the Board reinstated most of the regional offices and agreed to accept a quota of Board Directors nominated by the chapters." (The bulk of National Audubon's records have been archived by the New York Public Library, available online at: http://archives.nypl.org/mss/2099.) [Downloaded June 1, 2016.]

Among the chapter leaders who fought hard to retain the regional Audubon centers and ensure that local chapters were represented on the Board was Seattle Auduboner Bob Grant, who had been elected by the Washington chapters to serve on National's Board. Partly due to his efforts, and the efforts of many others over the years, National Audubon now fully acknowledges the importance of local chapters, under the paradigm: "Twenty-two state programs, 41 Audubon centers, and nearly 500 local chapters. All working together as One Audubon." (See National's website, http://audubon.org.) [Downloaded June 3, 2016.]

The spirit of cooperation is growing in another way, too. Seattle Audubon is currently working with National to better coordinate membership efforts and bring our family closer together than ever.

31. "Audubon Society Meets," *Seattle Daily Times* (March 10, 1918), p. 7.

32. "How Many Great Blue Herons Do We Have in Puget Sound?" by Don Norman, announced in *Earthcare Northwest* 30:5 (March 1989). (All newsletters referenced here can currently be found in the Seattle Audubon archives.)

Perhaps the most popular talk given in the early days of the Society was a slideshow by Asahel Curtis on October 16, 1924 (from *SAS History*, Vol. 1; this looseleaf binder is currently in Seattle Audubon archives). Reportedly, there was standing room only at that meeting, as the locally famous photographer showed slides of the Olympic Mountains.

33. For a description of Carsten Lien's talk, see the annual summary of events of Seattle Audubon, May 1960 to May 1961, *SAS History*, Vol. 1. (This looseleaf binder can currently be found in Seattle Audubon archives.) Also see Lien's book, *Olympic Battleground: The Power Politics of Timber Preservation* (The Mountaineers Books, 2000).

34. "An Accidental Big Year," *Earthcare Northwest* (Fall 2014), p. 5.

35. "The Mountain Gorillas of Rwanda," by Dr. James W. Foster, *Earthcare Northwest* 30:3 (November 1988). "Ecology of Tropical Coral Reefs," by Dr. Douglas Fenner, *Earthcare Northwest* 30:4 (December 1989).

36. "Wooden Leg Helps Crane Acting as Watchdog," *Seattle Daily Times* (March 18, 1917), p. 38.

37. "Birds of Bikini and the Effects of the Atom Bomb," by Frank G. Lowman (loose bulletin sent to members, dated January 18, 1951, found in University of Washington Libraries, Special Collections, Seattle Audubon Society Records, Accession #1171-001, Box 1, Folder 8.)

38. The fact that Seattle Audubon has kept a certain distance from Audubon Washington (National Audubon's regional arm) doesn't mean we haven't fully participated. In fact, over the years, many Seattle Audubon members have served on Audubon Washington's board, including Charlie Kahle, Chuck Lennox, Cathy Jaramillo, Rob Faucett, Jane Hedberg, Trish Booth, Dee Arntz, and Marina Skumanich. Seattle Audubon members' leadership extends to National Audubon's Board itself; NAS board members from Seattle Audubon include H. W. Higman, Bob Grant, Charlie Kahle, Tom Wimmer, Estella Leopold, and Marina Skumanich.

39. *Seattle Audubon Society Notes*, University of Washington Libraries, Special Collections, Seattle Audubon Society Records, Accession #1171-001, Box 13, Folder 4. See also annual summary of events of Seattle Audubon, May 1968 to May 1969, *SAS History*, Vol. 1.

40. See RCW 79.90.120 and 130. The Department of Natural Resources manages the IBA information through its Natural Areas Preserve program. Audubon chapters can add new data about birds by working with DNR. Local chapters are also active in monitoring IBAs in their areas.

Local chapters (including Seattle Audubon), Audubon Washington, and WSACC also partnered to get the Evergreen Communities Act passed into State law, changing RCW 76.15 to give incentives to cities to plant and restore urban forests.

41. A copy of this issue may be found in Seattle Audubon archives. A loose original of this article can be found in the back pocket of the looseleaf binder, *SAS History*, Vol. 1, currently in Seattle Audubon archives.

42. The Nisqually National Wildlife Refuge (officially renamed on July 19, 2016, as the Billy Frank Jr. Nisqually National Wildlife Refuge) was established on the site of the old Brown farm at the delta of the Nisqually River in 1974. It had taken a lot of political pressure by local supporters and environmentalists, including Seattle Audubon, to save the delta from development. Olympia resident Margaret McKenny, together with another local environmentalist, Flo Brodie, organized the Nisqually Delta Association (NDA) in the mid-1960s to stave off a move by the City of Seattle to put a solid-waste disposal site near the mouth of the river. The Port of Tacoma tried to get permission to expand with a deep-water port on the Pierce County side of the river. This too was defeated. NDA found willing sponsors who submitted bills to the State Legislature every session for ten years to get funding to purchase the delta for the Washington Department of Game (now named Washington Department of Fish and Wildlife). Seattle Audubon and other environmental groups lobbied heavily for the passage of the Shoreline Management Act [1971 Wash. Sess. Laws 1st Ex. Sess. Ch. 286], which did provide some protection for the Nisqually estuary.

The "muddy little lot" Hazel mentions is a small piece of property lying within the boundaries of the Nisqually National Wildlife Refuge. It was purchased so that Audubon would have legal standing in case something were to go wrong in the refuge. There is considerable acreage on the delta that still belongs to the Washington Department of Fish and Wildlife. Seattle Audubon's thinking was that if there should be disagreements about how the refuge was managed, Audubon would have a voice. It looks like a happy arrangement after all these years—there have been no arguments, and the only complaints are from nonhunters who don't like the regime of closure of certain places for hunting. Nevertheless, Ducks Unlimited worked as hard as Audubon did to get the delta designated as a refuge; both groups share a commitment to duck species preservation.

43. Another important milestone for Seattle Audubon was our sponsorship of the first statewide conference to bring together environmental groups and Native American Tribes to find common ground on issues that we could all work together to solve. The Indian Conservationist Conference was held at Daybreak Star Cultural Center in 1979. The conference was the brainchild of Hazel Wolf, who describes it all in Susan Starbuck's biography, *Hazel Wolf: Fighting the Establishment* (University of Washington Press, 2002). Also see "Earthcare Groups Meet with Tribal Leaders" in *Seattle Audubon Notes* 20:3 (November 1979), p. 3.

Holding this conference was a bold move, coming at the height of bad feelings between many whites and Native Americans over the Boldt decision of 1974, granting the Tribes the right to half the total salmon catch. Hazel's drive to form coalitions whenever possible created a long-lasting bridge between Seattle Audubon and the Tribes.

44. Lyanda Lynn Haupt, *Rare Encounters with Ordinary Birds* (Seattle: Sasquatch Books, 2001).

45. Adelaide Lowry Pollock, "The Western Martin Calls," in *The Seattle Wren* 2:4 (July 1935), p. 3. A copy of this issue can be found in University of Washington Libraries, Special Collections, Seattle Audubon Society Records, Accession #1171-001, Box 12, Folder 16.

46. Earl Larrison and E.N. Francq, *Field Guide to the Birds of Washington State* (Seattle Audubon Society,1962). Earl Larrison and Klaus Sonnenberg, *Washington Birds—Their Location and Identification* (Seattle Audubon,1968).

47. Zella M. Schultz, "The Growth in the Glaucous-Winged Gull: Part I," in *The Murrelet* 32:3 (Sept.-Dec., 1951), pp. 35-42; and "Part II," in *The Murrelet* 33:1 (Jan.-April 1952), pp. 2-8. A popularized description of Schultz's work with gulls can be found in her book *On the Wings of the Wild Wind—Occasional Paper #21*, Center for Pacific Northwest Studies (Western Washington University, 1986).

48. Protection Island is a 365-acre triangle of land in the Strait of Juan de Fuca nine miles west of Port Townsend. For a more detailed history of the island, see Rob Carson, "Island of Broken Dreams," *Pacific Northwest Magazine* (January/February 1983), pp. 34-42.

49. Seattle Audubon became involved with saving injured birds through SAS member Della Schumacher, who ran a rehabilitation clinic for birds, supported financially by us. When Schumacher died in 1964, volunteers continued her work informally until 1966, when the Board established the Seattle Audubon Bird Clinic. It was run by Zella Schultz and Eleanor Stopps out of Zella's home for several years, with the help of Dorothy Ferguson and Dorothy Siewers, and with financial support from Seattle Audubon. Joni Butler took over in March 1969. In 1971, Butler's clinic separated from Seattle Audubon and became the Seattle Wild Bird Clinic. Seattle Audubon continued to contribute financially from time to time. Altogether, it's estimated the clinics helped to save more than 10,000 birds. For a more complete history of these efforts, see *Seattle Audubon Notes* 18:9 (June 1978), p. 4. A copy of this issue can currently be found in Seattle Audubon archives.

INDEX